Justice is Steady Work

Michael Walzer
Astrid von Busekist

Justice is Steady Work
A Conversation on Political Theory

polity

Originally published in French as *Penser la Justice: Entretiens avec Astrid von Busekist* ©
Editions Albin Michel – Paris 2020

This English edition first published in 2020 by Polity Press

Polity Press
65 Bridge Street
Cambridge CB2 1UR, UK

Polity Press
101 Station Landing
Suite 300
Medford, MA 02155, USA

ISBN-13: 978-1-5095-4479-0 (hardback)
ISBN-13: 978-1-5095-4480-6 (paperback)

A catalogue record for this book is available from the British Library.

Library of Congress Cataloging-in-Publication Data
Names: Walzer, Michael, author. | Busekist, Astrid von, interviewer.
Title: Justice is steady work : conversations with Astrid von Busekist /
    Michael Walzer, Astrid von Busekist.
Other titles: Penser la justice. English
Description: Cambridge, UK ; Medford, MA : Polity, 2020. | Originally
    published in French under title: Penser la justice : entretiens avec
    Astrid von Busekist. | Includes bibliographical references and index. |
    Summary: "One of the world's most influential political theorists
    reflects on justice, on war and on the key political issues of our
    time"-- Provided by publisher.
Identifiers: LCCN 2020007472 (print) | LCCN 2020007473 (ebook) | ISBN
    9781509544790 (hardback) | ISBN 9781509544806 (paperback) | ISBN
    9781509544813 (epub)
Subjects: LCSH: Justice. | Civil rights. | Political participation. |
    Social justice. | Peace movements. | International cooperation. |
    Political culture. | Judaism and politics.
Classification: LCC JC578 .W35513 2020 (print) | LCC JC578 (ebook) | DDC
    320.01/1--dc23
LC record available at https://lccn.loc.gov/2020007472
LC ebook record available at https://lccn.loc.gov/2020007473

Typeset in 10.5 on 12 pt Sabon by Servis Filmsetting Ltd, Stockport, Cheshire
Printed and bound in Great Britain by TJ International Limited

For further information on Polity, visit our website: politybooks.com

Contents

Acknowledgments

This book is the result of a unique experience. During our conversations, Michael Walzer kindly agreed to respond to all my questions, which were sometimes difficult, and at times critical. He agreed to reflect on the meaning of his work, to comment on the questions his books and articles continue to raise, and on the reception of his ideas, theoretical and political. He also shared some personal joys and political disappointments. Thank you Michael.

I owe special thanks to Amélie Ferey who has transcribed parts of our conversation. Eyal Chovers, Raphael Zagury Orly, Ronit Peleg, and Joseph Cohen were the co-organizers of the Conference on *May 68, Legacies of Resistance* at the University of Tel Aviv in June 2018, where we talked about Michael's political activism during the Civil Rights movement, and the campaign against the Vietnam War (Chapter 2). I am grateful to Tila Rudel and Yael Baruch from the French Institute at Tel Aviv.

At Sciences Po, I am grateful to the co-organizers of our Political Theory Seminar. We welcomed Michael in Paris as guest speaker in March 2018. Gaëlle Durif and Jerôme Guilbert helped us to organize and to screen his talk "Freedom and Equality."

Ariel Colonomos, Azar Gat, and Yoel Mitrani suggested questions, and Tom Theuns translated the Introduction. Ian Shapiro was the messenger between Paris and Princeton.

Thanks to a fellowship from the Israel Institute (israelinstitute. org) I was able to spend a month in Israel. Many thanks to Itamar Rabinovitch, Daniel Skek, and the staff at the Institute.

Judith B. Walzer generously lent me her husband for a while in Tel Aviv; Marc Sadoun has been our first reader; without Hélène

Monsacré, my friend and publisher of the French original, this book wouldn't exist.

Astrid von Busekist

I have only to thank Astrid – who truly made this book. The first (biographical) chapter may read like an interview, but the rest of the book is a conversation, in the course of which I learned a great deal about what I've written and not written, what I think and don't think. We both worked hard but a glance at the endnotes will reveal who worked harder. For this experience of bookmaking, face to face and via email, I will always be grateful.

Michael Walzer

Note on the English Edition

Justice is Steady Work has first been published in French (*Penser la Justice: Entretiens avec Astrid von Busekist*, Paris, Albin Michel, 2019).

Some of Michael Walzer's books, and many of his articles, have not been translated into French, hence the quantity and the length of the endnotes. I have kept most of them for the English edition: it makes it easier to compare passages of our conversation with relevant excerpts from other writings, and to navigate in Walzer's voluminous work.

To prepare our conversation, I had access to some of Michael Walzer's personal archives.

Dissent Magazine has been digitalized; archives from 1954 onwards are retrievable here: https://dissentmagazine.org/.

Astrid von Busekist

Introduction

The insider philosopher

Where should one start a portrait of Michael Walzer? "In the Bronx," he says himself. That is where this grandson of Jewish Galician and Lithuanian immigrants was born. That is where he played as a child on the playground "between the Jewish building and the Irish one." That is where he went to a public primary school, and where he learned elementary Hebrew, first at the Cheder,[1] and then with Mr. Bain.

How did this child, from a modest background in which Judaism and Socialism mixed perfectly (he writes, "when I was young, I thought Judaism and Socialism were the same thing"),[2] come to be one of the most read and commented American philosophers, one of the most actively engaged in the public debate? Between his first article in the 1950s and his most recent book *A Foreign Policy for the Left*,[3] the world has changed many times over. Yet, the 84-year-old man is as firm in his analyses as he was in his early days. Sometimes quiet, often playful, always sharp, he never lost his rigor and never gave up a fight. Many times during our conversations in Paris and Tel Aviv and throughout our frequent correspondence, I was struck by the fact that he is a man of conviction, equally opposed to imprecision and easy surrender. Although his thought evolved in certain aspects, it has remained surprisingly consistent regarding its deepest principles. This is especially true of two aspects that are foundations in the general architecture of his work: his conception of social justice and his thoughts on war. Is Judaism one of the threads that ties Walzer's work together? Probably, but perhaps for sentimental reasons as much as academic ones. As much for his having experienced being

1

a minority as for the relationships that connect him to the state of Israel. The reader will realize this in the coming pages, in which a large part is dedicated to Israel, to Jewish political thought and to the Walzerian understanding of the Hebrew Bible.

Michael Walzer talks the way he writes: in a pure language, unadorned, appropriate and precise – we will return to this. His models here are George Orwell, for his "beautiful English," and Irving Howe,[4] the founder of *Dissent*, who thought any article could be improved by shortening it by ten percent.[5] Howe keeps, says Walzer, "reading over his shoulder."[6] This is not insignificant because the style in *Dissent*, and in the hundreds of papers published by Michael Walzer in its columns – incisive and accessible to all – also corresponds to a political commitment: any democratic argument must be supported by intelligible writing.[7] The philosopher does not have any special status to assert. He is a "pedestrian" whose role, if it is to be effective, is to speak to all, from the inside. To talk, if you like, from the same sidewalk. The transition from committed, critical, and sometimes controversial articles to academic work can thus be harmonious – as long as we "add twenty footnotes" when traveling from one mode to the other. Is this the privilege of a great author or false modesty? I cannot say, but what is sure is that Walzer's work moves seamlessly between the two. They complete and nourish each other. As Michael Walzer often pointed out, he practices political theory as a "license" to defend his ideas and political preferences in the classroom as well as in his writings.[8] The audience changes but the commitment remains the same.

So, who is Michael Walzer? Is he merely a philosopher? He says not. He also claims he is not a "systematic thinker," but I find this hard to believe. Although he rejects the term, he is, rather, a model philosopher. Such philosophers are in the polis. They consider that their role is to search out dialogue with compatriots, and that they owe this to their society, but must equally elevate it. They fight by their fellow citizens' side against injustice and oppression. Committed to democratic dialogue, they do not try to impose a purely theoretical truth that fails to take real life into account. Michael Walzer is a political philosopher. In the following pages, before leaving him the floor, I would like to try to explain why the type of philosophy and social critique performed by Walzer seems to me both unique and vital. For now, given that we discuss them in depth in our conversations that follow, I put on hold reflections on his political activism, his thoughts on war, and on Judaism.

I

A good political philosopher is a person who belongs in the world, or, more precisely, in their world – a world of their fellows. In that sense, they do an "inside job."[9] Social critique, to be relevant, and to be "connected" as Walzer says, must be performed from the inside out. Its object is one's own society. It is made stronger by its ties to the history of shared meanings, the way it exists here and now.[10] The social critic must always be able to assume the standpoint from which they speak. This point is key to understanding Michael Walzer's work. It gives intelligibility to his research, clarifies his contribution to public debates, and characterizes the man.

How he understands social critique emerges in distinctive ways through various and renewed readings:[11] his work on "thin" and "thick" morality,[12] (formulated as a response to critics of *Spheres of Justice*),[13] his thoughts on reiterative universalism, on the sense of community and the place of the nation in the international system,[14] his contextualized reading of tolerance,[15] his writings on war – albeit in an oblique way – and his interpretation of the Hebrew Bible. For a thread connects his first notes from the 1960s on the role of the prophets in *The Revolution of the Saints* (the topic of his senior honors essay at Brandeis and his dissertation, published later)[16] and his last books (*In God's Shadow*[17] and the edited volume, of which the third volume came out in 2018).[18]

A good social critic is therefore a distant descendant of the biblical prophet: "social criticism is less the practical offspring of scientific knowledge than the educated cousin of common complaint,"[19] says Walzer. The critic is a specialist of protest.[20] Like the prophet, their critique is immanent – they deliver an inner-world message expressed to the public in simple terms.[21] Ahad Ha'Am, Ghandi, and Orwell are such characters – they belong to us.[22] Their message relies on their daily experience of a shared moral life. Workers rather than revolutionaries, they must have "courage," "compassion," and "a good eye."[23] They are animated by benevolence; whether their criticism is correct matters as much as their personal morality.[24] The identity of the critic, member of "the Ancient and Honorable Company of Social Critics,"[25] is a mix of proximity to the society they address and critical distance toward their peers. They are at a distance far from authority and social domination,[26] and quick to protest oppressive and unfair social practices. Like Socrates, in this sense, they stand "a little to the side, but not outside: critical distance is measured in inches."[27]

Many texts illustrate this accurate if uncomfortable position. Walzer exposed himself to criticism in two respects: from his peers, because he was not part of dominant philosophical streams of his time, and from his readers, especially left-wing ones, whom he reminds of the virtues of moderation and patience. He is accused of conservatism and statism in the debate between liberals and communitarians, and when he defends the legitimacy of state borders; yet, when he criticizes the hubris and authoritarianism of a part of the left, he is accused of helping his enemies' projects; and when he defends a decentralized and pluralist version of justice, as in *Spheres*, he becomes an apostate. In his writings as well as in our conversations, however, he insisted that the core virtue of his engagement is his practical instinct: if individuals are contextualized, critique must be also.

II

Philosophical practice, social critique relies on *interpretation*. The specificity of interpretation comes out once we contrast it with two other modes of social critique: *discovery* and *invention*, which are both either unsatisfactory or incomplete (too "heroic," says Walzer) to access a shared moral law. Discovery, according to Walzer, corresponds in the first instance to the transmission of a revelation. Someone must give an account of divine commands. Thus, coming back from the mountain or the desert, the prophet emerges as the discoverer of moral law. In a secular world, however, moral law is figured by doctrines: Utilitarianism, for example, or Marxism. The secular philosopher takes a step back by giving up on their specific identity, to proclaim their objectivity, to speak from "no particular point of view."[28] This is also their main weakness. Compared to the powerful novelty of divine revelation-discovery (which Michael Walzer trusts more), the philosophical translation of discovery is a retreat. Yet, both types of discovery, religious and philosophical, are actually *re-discoveries*: they give shape to universal principles that were buried, though known and experienced by members of a society. Modes of critique premised on "discovery" thus owe their authority to God or to a so-called objective truth. By analogy, discovery corresponds to the work of the executive in the classical distinction between the three branches of power: it must pronounce and then enforce the law. We will return later to the specific place of the Law of Moses in Walzer's texts, in particular in the chapter on the politics of the Hebrew Bible and Jewish political thought.

The mode of invention, like that of discovery is also linked to the philosopher's supposed detachment. Yet here, it is the philosopher-

4

as-builder who takes charge. Inventing a new morality of justice and virtue à la Descartes, the philosopher-as-builder creates a moral system that looks completely independent from their world. To build such a system, they need a plan, a procedure or a "method" in Descartes' words. In contemporary philosophy, John Rawls or Jürgen Habermas incarnate this second category rather well: their reasoning, which replaces divine authority or the authority revealing His Word, is comparable to the magisterium of universal representation. Internal and analytical, it relies end-to-end on the respect for argumentative procedure. Whereas all should be able to identify themselves as co-authors of invention, and agree on the political and moral rules resulting from deliberation – as is the case with Rawls' original position of "Justice as Fairness" – participants are idealized, hypothetical actors specifically designed to reach a consensus. Real world democratic debates on the contrary are messy: the participants, real actors – ordinary people, democratic citizens – are invited to the table, but they cannot be coerced to agree.[29]

In its maximalist version, it is the invention of a new universal moral code that creates "what God would have created if there had been a God," or corrects what God or nature could not deliver.[30] This philosophical act is, properly speaking, authoritarian.[31] It overrides the constraints of democratic deliberation. In a more nuanced version, invention is *particular*, adapted to a society and to its specific practices. Needless to say, Walzer prefers the minimalist position: "Why should newly invented principles govern individuals who already share a moral culture?"[32] This is where the plot thickens: social morality pre-exists, discovery is always rediscovery. Philosophers can shape and invent ideal types but, as reporters of the divine Word, they will always be mediators, reinventors. Hence, the critical strength of invention does not lie with the *ex nihilo* creation of a new moral world but in the corrective character it brings to our already existing moral institutions.[33] This is an important lesson of modesty for philosophers and social critics. It also tells us about the place Walzer gives to the critic: limited, closer to a poet than to Plato.[34]

Properly speaking, the philosopher or the social critic is not an inventor: on the one hand, they always work (rework) a social morality, something that is already there; on the other hand, they do not smooth out the sharp edges of social or political reality (dispute, negotiation, compromise, manipulation, but also the socialization of individuals and the empirical realities of deliberation). The outcome of philosophical conversation, as "inventors" understand it, entirely depends on the rules by which it is conducted. The shape of reasoning prevails on the content: "once one has a conversational design, it is hardly necessary to have a conversation,"[35] says Walzer, because true conversations are unstable and turbulent, necessarily "more radical than ideal speech."[36]

Simply put, inventors hold that one can think about justice by glossing over the real conditions in which debate takes place. Excluding *a priori* any relation of power or domination, civilizing our speech, orienting it toward the goal desired by the philosopher, cannot account for real disagreements between citizens. This is what Walzer intended to depict in *Spheres of Justice*, but also in his critique of participative democracy, another testimony of his sensitivity toward citizens' real lives. Of course, it would be wonderful if we were all permanently politically engaged, he says, but this overlooks citizens' other obligations and desires: to play with their children, to make love . . .[37] It underestimates the virtue and legitimacy of representation. It is not necessary to be on a permanent state of political alert, it is enough to be heard when one has something to say. A democracy must take its *Kibbitzers* into account.[38]

Sensitivity to turmoil and attention to historical reality probably explain Michael Walzer's unique place among the philosophers of his generation. In contrast, invention (of which he shows the limits) looks very much like analytical philosophy as it was practiced by most of his Harvard colleagues in the 1970s. While Walzer examined hundreds of soldiers' memoirs and thousands of pages of military history to write *Just and Unjust Wars*, his colleagues made "weird" (these are his words) thought experiments. While he tried to make a distinction between "spheres of justice" corresponding to different places and different distributive criteria, his colleague Rawls built his *Theory of Justice* on the basis of the veil of ignorance – precisely a form of thought experiment – which led to a unique model. Indeed, *Spheres of Justice* rebuts two ideas: the idea of a Rawlsian "overlapping consensus" (to which Walzer opposes the horizontal pluralism of autonomous spheres of "complex equality"), and the idea of a single metric of distributive justice (he writes: "I argue that to search for unity is to misunderstand the subject matter of distributive justice").[39] Our social worlds are, in real rather than hypothetical situations, simply incommensurable.

Societies differ with regard to the spheres they invest with meaning. These spheres can be defined by the goods that are being distributed within that particular sphere; and each one uses its own criteria of allocation. Social goods must be distributed for different reasons, by different agents, to different individuals, so that no sphere exercises undue domination over another. Principles of justice are relative and "pluralistic in form," "the inevitable product of historical and cultural particularism."[40] If each sphere has its own distributive criteria, the meaning of goods themselves is contingent and relies on social convention. Distributive justice, like liberalism itself,[41] is thus understood as an "art of differentiation."[42]

This is what distinguishes Walzer from his colleagues and from justice "builders": we cannot appreciate what we owe each other as long as we don't know how people are related to each other and to the goods they make and distribute among themselves.[43] In other words, the singularity of individuals and societies does not only rely on the things and goods they make, or on the meaning they attach to these things and goods, but is mostly found in the progressive and socially unique objectification of the meanings of these things and goods.[44]

III

If the goal of discovery and invention is to find an external metric or universal standard to allow us to appreciate our own morality, or to design ideal scenarios unavoidably detached from real life, interpretation acknowledges moral life as it is, as a moral world already lived in and in which the interpreter fully takes part. It takes political relations seriously. It corresponds to the Judiciary in the metaphor of the branches of government. Choosing interpretation, the "most familiar form of moral argument,"[45] is decisive for the work of a critic, for the understanding of our moral universe and for a certain type of particularism associated with communitarianism. The interpreter does not have the same ambition as the philosopher-as-discoverer or the philosopher-as-builder.[46] This is true even if the interpreter shares with the best of them their rejection of domination, injustice, or tyranny, and even if he believes, like them, in universal prohibitions (not to kill, not to exploit, not to harm). Indeed, he knows that these are only framing-values (a "minimal code")[47] of which the shape and meaning, unique to each society, need to be specified. And since "shared social meanings" (social actions and their justifications in a given society) are a result of common histories and continuous debates, they are necessarily plural.

The interpreter does not feel the need to have the final say. He prefers the "more or less" and the infinite variety of readings that preserve ongoing adaptations and changes.[48] Scribes of the Hebrew Bible did not try to erase the Book's internal contradictions. They attempted neither to gather in a single text all three legal codes,[49] nor to reconcile the meaning of the two covenants (Mosaic and Abrahamic), because, as Walzer says following the rabbis, "a dissenting opinion may turn out to be true." Supporters of the Grand Soir will probably find such an indetermination frustrating, but they will have to admit that all the revolutions that radically turned their backs on the past failed. Walzer shows this in *The Paradox of Liberation: Secular Revolutions and Religious Counterrevolutions*: states born from secular revolutions of independence (Algeria, India, and Israel) that did not take idiosyncratic social values – especially religious ones – into account, were later confronted with "religious revival."[50]

This is why Michael Walzer prefers the slow pace of social democracy (dialogue and incremental change) to the rapid and often brutal movements of revolutionaries.[51] And this is why the claim of philosophical truth makes him suspicious: it claims universality whereas opinions are plural. Seemingly common and familiar, such opposition between truth and opinion nonetheless has significant political consequences. When the truth formulated by the philosopher is, for example, picked up by the judge (when judicialization of politics replaces democratic debate);[52] or, conversely, when democratic debate takes the form of philosophical argument (when "deliberative democracy" is posited as the philosophical ideal of political participation).[53]

The interpreter is a poet looking forward. A democrat or a sophist addressing their compatriots: there would be no critique possible without hope.[54] Fundamentally hostile to the final adjudication of meaning,[55] the interpreter is able to change their mind, to dive back in the books, and to revisit their work. In a literal sense, the interpreter's social morality is debatable: if it were not for the constant discussion and justification it triggers,[56] it would not deserve to be called a morality at all.[57] Yet, through the creative and argumentative work of social actors, social critique takes the form of an uninterrupted dialogue: with friends, family, our fellow citizens and our adversaries. It is a "pluralizing" activity[58] grounded on – and also producing – social meaning. It is certainly "useful to have a theory," but it is even "better to tell stories [. . .] even though there is no definitive and best story."[59] Hamlet's mirror can enlighten Denmark and show what is rotten only if it succeeds in persuading the Danes themselves to engage in collective reflection.[60] However, the critics' ties with their society bring up the problem of distance. Can one be both a citizen and a partisan?[61] Can one be "inside," while also producing a legitimate critique that requires detachment and universal concepts? Walzer answers this objection in two ways:

by making a distinction between good and bad critics, and between thick and thin morality.

IV

There are good and bad prophets. The good ones? Amos, Socrates, Locke, Montesquieu, Camus, Gramsci. The bad ones? They rather resemble Jonah, Plato, Sartre, Marx's acolytes, and sometimes Foucault. (Simone de Beauvoir has a strange intermediate place as the only woman among the eleven portraits composing *The Company of Critics*.) They have in common that they turn their detachment from society, their hostility or even treason, into an epistemic virtue.[62] The main difference between the two types of critics is one of moral distance. Indeed, there is no virtue in giving up (mentally or physically) one's identity in order to be a good critic. In principle, critique rests on debates internal to a society.[63] Yet, the notorious critical distance must also be ensured. This is somehow covered by, firstly, the fact that there is *debate*, i.e., an engagement with other ordinary interlocutors who have replaced God in this role in secular centuries.[64] Second, it is specified by the relevant forum for this debate: inside society, with all the concurrent tensions that permeate a given dominant culture and formal universalism. To illustrate these contradictions, Michael Walzer relies on Marx and Gramsci. All dominant classes – Marx's capitalist bourgeoisie, Gramsci's hegemonic culture – whose class interests are presented as "universal" values are, in the end, hoisted with their own petard by the masses' experience of concrete inequality and the unveiling of bourgeois or hegemonic ideology. Formal equality guarantees to all men and women an equal right to sleep under the bridges of Paris, mocked Anatole France, but such injunctions open the eyes of those who suffer. Ideology puts on the suit of universality but clashes with the vigilance of the social critic.[65]

Here Walzer does not define a theoretical position or a philosophical critique detached from reality. His work rather echoes the program and commitment of *Dissent*'s founders, to which he dedicated a great deal of time and labor. To show its proximity to real politics and to its readers, *Dissent* explicitly defines itself as a magazine rather than an academic journal and thereby stands out from the sectarianism and theoretical purity of the ivory tower. *Dissent* expresses pluralist commitments. It is political, "connected" with social problems, and with the difficult battles internal to the American left; it sets a stage for debate and takes into account its authors' engagement to shaping a democratic culture. Created by two young ex-Trotskyists in the

9

1950s, the magazine met a remarkably long-lasting success, partly due to the fact that its contributors took the lessons of social critique seriously. Always among the closest to events, *Dissent* managed to grasp the American Zeitgeist, while providing citizens with a critical mirror wherein to reflect. With hindsight, Michael Walzer has his own interpretation of the events that marked the life of this unique publication in the American intellectual landscape. Social critique "from the inside" must lean on a shared moral culture; it is not immediately universalizable. This is as true regarding experience and interpretation, as it is regarding tolerance, to which Michael Walzer dedicated a book.

V

Walzer's approach to tolerance is indeed characteristic of the attention he gives to the history of values of an indigenous vocabulary. As a core liberal value at the basis of pluralism (legal, moral and religious), a full understanding of tolerance is necessarily contextual. Writing the history of its expressions enables one to underline two important things: the cultural context in which tolerance is expressed, and the difficulty of abstract reasoning.[66] Locke, for example, assumes a particular place in this history: he was intelligible to his contemporaries because he argued in the language of faith, but he became, through the never-ending reading mentioned earlier, the very symbol of the secular normative discourse on tolerance. Why was Locke received in this way? Although he was far from England when he wrote his *Letter Concerning Toleration*, his exile in the Netherlands did not prevent him from writing what Walzer calls a "Whig manifesto." Yet, the *Letter* is not a political text properly speaking; the tolerance recommended by Locke is formulated in the language of classical English Protestantism.[67] Before it became, by successive iterations, a general credo, Lockean tolerance appears as an idiosyncratic message addressed to English Protestants: salvation as we understand it is not compatible with persecution, it is contrary to our "moral being."[68] Ideas can only be successful when they are embodied by, and lean on, a constellation of social meanings and practices.

However, it is not certain that an author's "emotional" belonging to their society,[69] their proximity to or their empathy with its values, are immediately intelligible either theoretically or practically. The contrast between Camus and Sartre illustrates this. Camus defended, as he says in his *Notebooks*, "common values." He was connected to his home country, attached to a code of honor (and justice), and driven by his "primary loyalties." Neither universalist nor ideological, his position was sensitive, "intimate," "familiar."[70] An advocate of the Kabyle people, he was critical of the indifference shown by the colonial regime toward them, and spared no efforts in exposing their repression in the Sétif Province in Algeria. In his own way, Camus sought a solution to the Algerian war that would respect all identities, Algerian as well as Pied Noir, whose differences should be, according to him, suitably negotiated.[71] In Sartre's eyes, this partisanship was a sin of love – the expression of a sensitive person, a local, trapped in his own condition: "the life of a critic has to start with the rejection of his own socialization, the refusal of his own society."[72] Merciless self-criticism, "unconditioned alignment with the actions of the under-privileged,"[73] and his role as a "guardian of fundamental ends,"[74] make Sartre a man without roots.

To be heroic, such detachment, says Walzer, has a price: by removing themselves from their own people, intellectuals such as Sartre forget the "texture of moral life."[75] Radically "desocialized,"[76] running away even from comradeship "for the ties of history and sentiment corrupt his thinking,"[77] they lose their bearings and miss their target. Social criticism from those who describe themselves as enemies and traitors is corrupted.[78] Walzer cannot forgive Sartre for his preface to Frantz Fanon's *The Wretched of the Earth*.[79] Amos and Jonah are, in a way, Camus and Sartre's biblical twins. Prophets, the faces of collective protestation, are the original representatives of social critique. Amos incarnates the internal perspective and Jonah – who has nothing to say about the substantive morality of the people of Nineveh – the external one. Prophecy is indeed, in Max Weber's words,[80] the first form of a political pamphlet.

VI

Michael Walzer often quotes these early representatives of social critique. Some of their messages seemed to him still "painfully obscure" in 1985,[81] yet he came back to them regularly and, progressively, his knowledge of biblical texts reached great depths. From then on, Walzer no longer reduced the prophets' role to the mere illustration of a particular type of social critique – that which confronts governments and condemns the hypocrisy of the mighty, who may observe one day, merely to exploit the powerless the next.[82] Henceforth, Walzer takes them on their own terms. He still sees in their exhortations a sort of foreshadowing of modern critique, but he also finds in biblical texts the ingredients of proto-democratic thought. Amos,

Walzer's favorite prophet, does not transmit an esoteric message. He uses common language and so seeks to accomplish what the modern critic too must try to achieve.[83] Prophets may have no "philosophical imagination," but they live among their own people, and, therefore, can channel an unrivaled power of social transformation. Can one talk about a "social-democratic" reading of the Bible? When I asked him, during our conversations, if he did not exaggerate when he turned the text into an early illustration of an "almost democracy," Michael Walzer answered that he did not, and added that today's democrats would do well to draw inspiration from Amos.

Prophets enlighten another aspect of our relationship to the world: depending on whether it is general or particular, our morality is "thick" or "thin." Walzer finds his distinction between thick, universal morality and thin, particular morality in the Bible. The former corresponds to an abstract or absolute universalism (a "covering law" universalism) expressed in the old days by triumphant Christianism and, closer to us, in the Universal Declaration of Human Rights. The latter corresponds to a "reiterative" universalism reproducing the particular mores of a given society beyond its frontiers by successive iterations. This type of morality takes the form of a bottom-up universalism, minimal and plural, that originates in the pragmatic cohabitation or partnership between nations.

The "concrete lives" of individuals in their societies give birth to a certain number of universal essentials because all moral beings live under commands and all are able to repeat (reiterate) their liberation from Egyptian yoke. Particular traditions – always following the same idea of shared meanings – are the best guarantee of the recognition of the Other. God may know those who are His, but, as Amos, Isaiah, and Jeremiah tell the Israelites,[84] He also recognizes members of other nations and blesses each one of them according to their specificities. Walzer tries to integrate this wisdom in his own writing: "[One comes] to pluralism only through an act of empathy and identification [. . .] the value of universal truth is as uncertain when seen from inside a particular community as is the value of pluralism when seen from outside every particular community."[85] Taking the Hebrew tradition backwards by considering that it cannot align with pluralism or modernity would thus be to betray the prophets' pluralistic wisdom.

This view may be difficult to reconcile with the constraints of the contemporary political reality Walzer analyses, following the prophet's footsteps. The most hotly debated issues in Israel should in his view marry biblical wisdom and the teachings of the state's founding fathers as the requirements of Israeli national sovereignty are not always in harmony with Jewish traditions. Michael Walzer knows this, but he considers it necessary to conciliate and reconcile, as he says in our conversations, find a common tongue between religious tradition and secular modernity. Partisans of the former should renounce the *Galut* mentality that may befit a dispersed people obeying an important rabbinic teaching: "the law of the Kingdom is the law" – a diasporic international law of sorts; the latter should be open to the treasures of the Hebrew Bible.

VII

The ramification of the particular/universal dialectic also enlightens Walzer's analysis of tolerance and mutual respect. Indeed, in contrast to an explanation grounded in conservative or relativist communitarianism, this dialectic offers a more convincing explanation for Walzer's commitment to political belonging and to societies' self-government and self-determination. It grounds the importance he gives to the nation and the state. Values such as loyalty, friendship, or patriotism have a universal meaning, yet to experiment with their blessings is always a singular experience.[86] The art of difference mentioned above is the program of reiterative universalism. Its goal is peace. It is by starting from particular experience that we can hope to mutually rise to the recognition of universal principles through repetition, successive additions, debates and discussions about our "specialized" morality, and that we can hope to identify as creative agents of that morality, as "moral makers." Such identification implies, however, that no universal code is "correct,"[87] and that no one code has the last say regarding morality or justice. It is through reiterative universalism that one can, as Walzer says, defend nation-states' autonomy and independence. The issue often came back during our discussions which, I think, clarifies Walzer's ideas on borders and on socially conscious multilateralism.

A universal law to govern states or nations would mean, practically, the institution of a global state and, theoretically, giving up value pluralism: no teleological thought (whether it preaches the victory of the working class or the arrival of the messiah),[88] is compatible with individual or collective freedom, as shown by Isaiah Berlin.[89] The defense of states' independence, of their territorial borders, and of the specific type of political communities that nations are, expresses more than some arbitrary nationalism, acquiescence of pluralism, and a hostility to domination. The ideologue's program is of unification, forced assimilation, and repression in the name of a unique version of what a political nation ought to be. Humanists should instead privilege reform, cultural pluralism, and inclusion. There are many versions of this recipe (from empires to voluntary partnerships, through to federations),[90] but one first needs to acknowledge the cultural creativity of each community and the equal value of them all.

Walzer's justification of territorial borders must be read in this light. Their legitimacy lies in their role in defending common goods: a fair and redistributive democracy cannot exist without the limitations that demarcate the primacy of solidarity between compatriots and allow for the regular functioning of the welfare state. Walzer is not insensitive to the fate of those who do not belong to the inner circle – migrants in particular – toward whom states have special duties. Membership is a precious good that should be distributed fairly, he argues in *Spheres of Justice*, and this also implies that the vulnerability of individuals must be taken into account. Walzer's reflections on reiteration are hence faithful to the interpretative approach (reiteration is a kind of continuous interpretation). They correspond, in the international context, to a scaled-up version of the "spheres" of justice, where each particular community has its own sphere. Finally, they enlighten, at the domestic level, Walzer's attachment to the kind of multiculturalism advocated for in the columns of *Dissent*.

It is also through the lenses of reiterative universalism that one can better understand the meaning of the "connected social critique" that Walzer endorses. They outline the singular identity of his engagement, both liberal and social-democratic. The community and the nation need shared meanings. These meanings, which have such a prominent place in *Spheres of Justice*, are not, as some critics say, a mark of conservatism.[91] They are, on the contrary, the result of a continuous and dynamic process which is subjected to continuous revision. In this way they constitute a "moral legislation" and acquire their particular objectivity precisely because they were "socially constructed and agreed upon."[92] This construction and this objectivity are quite far from those of the advocates of "the construction of social reality," like Searle.[93] What Walzer has in mind is simple and deep: we assign norms and values to things and goods that govern our relationship with them and with other individuals. Things, or (material and immaterial) goods, are therefore intermediaries of social relations, and must be understood as something more than goods *simpliciter*. They become, through their circulation and through the complex process of determining their meaning, liaison officers between individuals. They literally create the social world.

Individuals are caught in a web of social meanings that they themselves contributed to create over time. These meanings have normative consequences on our behavior (what Walzer calls "moral legislation"). Shared meanings are not objectively right or wrong, true or false; our behavior however is objectively right or wrong in terms of the shared meaning we give to the good.[94] Rather than emanating from an authority, reiterated social construction is the best way to explain the "appearance of identical or similar used and valued objects in different societies."[95] All societies build their own social meanings – this is where the universal part lies – but each of them follows different imperatives. While individuals are the agents in this collective enterprise of the social construction of values, they are also its main critics and interpreters. What is objective here is not the specific content of their respective imperatives, but the fact social meanings are constructed in this way in every society.

The philosophy defended by Walzer is tied to the preservation of particulars, to the respect of local values, and to the defense of pluralism. The liberalism he promotes strongly associates the virtue of separation with the virtue of sharing. It is an art both of difference and of conversation. Of difference because it insists on the autonomy of spheres[96] and "complex equality" that ensures respect for all; of sharing because it insists on contextualized individuals who, beyond their particular affiliations, can get along. The critic must encourage political commitment, prompt debate, and solicit that which is noble in each of us. The individual advocated by Walzer is a free being, who nevertheless acknowledges his debt to his own people. A contextualized individual is involved in an endless conversation with his peers – all his peers. Would this characterize him even as a child growing up in his neighborhood of the Bronx? I did not ask, but I am certain that even today, after so many books, papers, and conferences about individuals and communities, justice and war, Judaism and universalism, democracy, liberalism, and socialism, he would not disown any of his early writings.

Our conversation has been long, rich, amicable, and personal. We disagreed here and there, but what motivated our discussions was a keen sense of humor and a profound solidarity on what really matters.

1

Who Are You Michael Walzer?

Astrid von Busekist: Michael Walzer, the long conversation we are about to begin in Tel Aviv will continue in Paris, resume via email or *viva voce* somewhere in between New York and Paris. We will need some time to talk about the many important topics you address in your work. You have written or edited more than forty books, hundreds of articles, you have spoken at countless conferences and seminars, too many to enumerate here: we will have to choose the most relevant contributions. Your curiosity, your commitment to pluralism, your empathy as well, have led you, I believe, to take paths that history, your readings, or simply life have opened up in front of you.

What does the topic of your PhD, *The Revolution of the Saints* – the Protestant saints – and your latest writings on Jewish political thought and the Hebrew Bible have in common? What is the relationship between your texts on war and your reflections on justice and equality? How much do your analyses of political doctrines and practices owe to your activism on the ground or within *Dissent*? I believe there is a natural coherence in your way of thinking about social and political issues. You have built some new walls, broken down old ones, but your house stands firmly on its foundations. You do not repeat yourself, you do not contradict yourself, but you modify sometimes, and you enrich always.

I suggest we talk first about some pertinent moments in your biography and move on to the following topics from your long bibliography: your political activism, your editorial work for *Dissent*, your reflections on war, political theory, social justice, Israel–Palestine, and your reading of the Hebrew Bible. We will probably spend less time on other aspects of your career – they will not be entirely absent from our conversation but, as you have written much, we have to make choices, with the firm ambition to hold onto the thick thread of your thought.

When did you begin thinking about the topics that would shape your writings? How has your childhood and your early education influenced and nourished your adult life as an American, Jewish, and public intellectual? This is where I think we should start. But where exactly?

Michael Walzer: We should start in the Bronx – or just a little before. My father was born in the United States, in New York, on the lower East side. His family was from Austrian Galicia, the part of Poland that had been incorporated into the Austrian empire. Moses Walzer, my paternal grandfather, renounced his allegiance to the Emperor of Austria when he became a citizen, in the 1880s, in Chicago. I have no idea how he got to Chicago. My father grew up in New York. My mother was born on a farm in Connecticut in 1906. Both my parents were born in 1906. Her father had come over sometime around 1900, leaving the family behind. He worked in New York in the garment industry. And then, with the help of the Baron de-Hirsch Foundation, he bought a farm in Connecticut and brought his family over. My mother was the child of the reunion. All her siblings were born in Europe. She was the American. I visited the site of the farm many years later, on the way back from my graduation at Brandeis, with my parents. The farm was now a summer camp. My mother knocked on the door of her primary school teacher, who opened the door, looked at her and said: "Hello Sadie Hochman." So, she had made an impression!

My mother went to elementary school in Wallingford, and then the family sent her to live with a Jewish couple – relatives I suppose – in New Haven, because the nearby high school in Wallingford had its graduation ceremony in a church, and my grandfather insisted that she go to a high school where she wouldn't have to graduate in a church. She lived in New Haven for four years with this family, going back on weekends to her parent's home. She started college in New York, but her father died shortly afterwards, and the farm had to be sold and she had to go to work, so she spent only one year in college, nothing more. My father did not go to college; he went into the fur business, which was the family business. My parents met in the late 1920s. I remember my mother describing how they argued over the 1928 presidential election.[1] It was the first time a Catholic had run for president. My mother was in favor, my father against – or maybe the other way around, I can't remember.

17

Busekist: Both your parents came from religious families?

Walzer: My mother came from a religious family, my father not. My mother's family was certainly religious – as the high-school story tells. After my grandfather died, my grandmother moved to New York and lived with my mother and then with both my parents after they were married. She died in 1943 or early 1944, when I was eight. My mother worked for a law firm as a secretary, a firm where John Foster Dulles was a senior partner. She was the first Jew employed by that firm. She doesn't know exactly why they took her, but they did. She worked for one of the junior partners. I was born in 1935 in the Bronx. We were living on the Grand Concourse in a huge apartment building with a large courtyard, almost entirely Jewish. Next to our building was another big apartment building, which was almost entirely Irish, and there was a playground in between the two, where we sometimes played together, or sometimes fought or "challenged" each other without fighting. I was the first child; my sister was born five years later.

My father went bankrupt in the fur business during the downturn of 1937, and then he went to work in a factory that became a defense factory during the war, making some kind of precision tools for the army; he worked there through the war. He was exempt from the draft because he was the father of two children. My mother was not working at that time. With two children she didn't work – that was the way things were then; there was no day care. I remember her sitting in the courtyard with other women, watching the kids. I went to an elementary public school nearby, PS 64, and to a Cheder in the afternoon. When my grandmother died, my parents took me out of the Cheder and hired a private Hebrew tutor who came to the house. Mister Bain. I remember his name. He taught me the prayers, the alphabet; we read simple stories. I was eight.

In 1944, the war was obviously growing to a close, and the defense factory where my father worked was beginning to shut down or slow down. My mother had an uncle in Johnstown, Pennsylvania, who offered my father a job as the manager of a jewelry store. Fur and jewelry are similar businesses – the luxury trade. We moved to Johnstown in November 1944. I was nine. My mother pushed me up one grade. I should have been in 4th grade but I went into the 5th grade. We lived in Westmont, a small suburb of Johnstown, built on a hill after the big flood of 1889. At first the Bethlehem Steel executives and managers lived up there, but Jews were moving in during the 1940s. That became easier when the Supreme Court declared restrictive covenants (written into the deed, forbidding sale to Negroes or Jews) unconstitutional. Johnstown had a Jewish community of about 2,000 people, and three congregations, naturally. A small orthodox congregation, and two pretty big conservative and reform congregations. My parents joined the reform congregation, whose rabbi was Haim Perlmutter, a student of Stephen Samuel Wise,[2] who was one of those people pushing classical Reform toward something closer to a traditional service; Wise and Perlmutter were also strongly Zionist.

Johnstown had an interesting Jewish community. There is a book about the Jews in Johnstown[3] by Ewa Morawska, a Polish sociologist who left Poland when the Polish army repressed Solidarity and came to the University of Pittsburgh. I met her when she was a fellow at the Institute many years later. Looking for a place to do fieldwork, she decided on Johnstown, a steel-town, seventy miles east from Pittsburgh. She first wrote a book about the Slavs in Johnstown,[4] and then about the Jews, with some interesting findings. First of all, the Slavs in Johnstown were traditional antisemites, they knew all the Christian antisemitic language and recited it to her, but they nevertheless preferred to deal with Jewish shopkeepers, Jewish doctors, and Jewish lawyers. These people the Slavs were familiar with; the Yankees were unfamiliar . . .

The "little steel strike" directed against the smaller companies, including Johnstown's Bethlehem Steel[5] had been broken in Johnstown in 1937. A Senate investigation had shown that the mayor and half of the city-council were actually on the payroll of the steel company and had broken the strike with hired vigilantes. But after the investigation and the scandal that confirmed the involvement of the mayor, the NLRB (National Labor Relations Board) organized a vote and in 1941 the Steel Workers Organizing Committee won a 4 to 1 victory and the union came to Johnstown. By 1944, when we arrived, the town was booming. The steel industry was doing very well, and because of the new union contract, the workers had more money than they ever had before. So they could come to my father's jewelry store and buy a sixteen-year-old daughter her first necklace or bracelet. The jewelry store was called Rothstein's, and it too was prospering.

Busekist: You said Johnstown had an interesting Jewish community. I suppose you joined a synagogue?

Walzer: We joined the (reform) Beth Zion Temple. My parents immediately became active in it, and were close friends of the rabbi and his wife. I was Bar Mitzvah'd in 1948 with "Ki Tisa" as my parasha,

19

the story of the golden calf. I remember, I had to stand on a box to look over the bima [the podium], because I was very short! Ki Tisa includes the line when Moses comes down from the Mountain and says: "Thus says the God of Israel: take every man, his sword, go through the camp and kill every man, his brother, and his neighbor." I told the rabbi that I didn't want to read those lines. He was a very smart man, so he didn't tell me I had to read them. We just argued for a couple of weeks and eventually I read the whole passage – which maybe shows that I was going to grow up a Menshevik and not a Bolshevik. Bar Mitzvah ceremonies in those days were very simple events, there was a luncheon right after the service and that was it. There was nothing more.

Busekist: But the parasha is an important part of your biography: you say somewhere that it has been a fundamental reading for your future work, the beginning of a longstanding interest on the meaning of Exodus.[6] You didn't know what a Menshevik was at that time did you?

Walzer: No, I didn't. But here is another part of the Johnstown story. My parents were kind of Popular Front leftists. In New York, the daily newspaper we read was *PM* – a Popular Front newspaper.[7] Max Lerner and I. F. Stone wrote columns.[8] I learned to read reading *PM*. When we moved to Johnstown, *PM* had failed. It was replaced by another newspaper called *The Compass*, which we subscribed to for a while, before that disappeared too. And then we subscribed to *I. F. Stone's Weekly*, which was a critical left-wing magazine or, better, newsletter. I. F Stone was a very fine journalist and in the early days, an ardent Zionist who published a book in 1946 with pictures by Frank Capra and a text about the immigrants coming to Israel.[9] I grew up reading things like that. I met him many years later. Our first apartment in Cambridge was owned by Izzy Stone's daughter and he used to visit her; so we would see him then. So, at the age of ten in Johnstown, after several years of reading *PM*, I wrote a ten-page history of the Second World War, which ended with the line (copied from somewhere) "Russia fights not for the lust of conquest but to end conquest!" That was my politics in 1945.

1948, the year of my Bar Mitzvah, was a very emotional year. I should tell my UJA story.[10] My parents decided that I was now a Jewish adult and took me to the annual UJA dinner, which was the main fundraising event of the Johnstown Jewish year. There was one big hotel in Johnstown, owned by a Jewish family, and the dinner was held there. We listened to a very moving speech by a man from New York, who talked about the independence war, the refugees, and the new state. And then pledge cards were passed around. You filled in the pledge card at the table, you put it in a little envelope and passed it to the head of the table where Sam Rappaport sat. He owned the biggest furniture store in town, he knew everybody's business: who had a kid in college, who had a sick parent, who was in trouble, who was doing well . . . He would open the envelopes, look at the pledge and if he thought it wasn't enough he would tear the card in half and pass it back down the table. I remember how relieved I was that our card didn't come back! That was the way Jews raised money, supposedly without coercive power. I was very impressed by that event, and I've written about it since in an article in *Foreign Affairs*. They asked me to write about humanitarianism and I talked about the paradoxical character of *Tzedakah*, which is a voluntary gift that you have to give. I tried to compare foreign aid and *Tzedakah*.[11] Foreign aid should be something like that.

In 1948, I also begun publishing on a hectograph – do you know what a hectograph is? – a little newsletter, in imitation of Izzy Stone, called *Between the Lines*; I wrote about politics and I was thirteen . . . In 1948, the issue among Jews was: should they vote for Wallace or Truman?[12] We may have known one Jewish Republican in Johnstown, but basically it was a Democratic community. I should have been, given everything I had learned growing up, a supporter of Henry Wallace, but I was angry, even at thirteen years old, when Wallace refused to defend the airlift to Berlin. I published a special issue of *Between the Lines*, which circulated to my relatives and a couple of friends at school, announcing that I supported Harry Truman.[13] My mother sent a copy of the newsletter to the White House, and I received a letter from Harry Truman. My mother, my agent before I knew what an agent was, called the *Johnstown Tribune*, and they published the story. There is a picture of me with the letter, with my little sister looking on.

Busekist: In other words, you already had a real political consciousness at that age. Did you talk about politics at home, with your parents? This is what you said during the celebration of the 125th anniversary of Jewish life in Johnstown: "I do remember one interesting political moment: in 1949 or 1950, the Pennsylvania state legislature passed a bill to promote driver education in high schools across the state – a response, I assume, to the growing number of people who could afford to own a car. The state would provide a training car to any high school

21

that organized a course. Our school board decided to refuse the offer and not to organize a course because, I was told, the state-provided car constituted 'creeping socialism.' (I can imagine a similar response from the Tea Party today.) My parents didn't have a car yet, and I very much wanted to learn to drive, even with the help of the state of Pennsylvania, so I circulated a petition asking the school board to relent and establish a drivers' education course. One of my teachers, the world history teacher, actually called me in to ask me, looking very worried, where my parents were born. She must have thought the petition was a Soviet plot. My parents, I told her, were born in New York and Connecticut. I kept circulating the petition and got a lot of signatures, but we didn't get the course. (The teacher didn't really take me for a Communist spy; she gave me an 'A' in world history that year.)"[14]

Walzer: Yes, certainly we talked about politics and they encouraged me. Johnstown was a pretty safe place. When Ewa Morawska wrote her book and talked to some of the people who came to Johnstown before my parents did, they described the strikes of the steel workers. The organizers who came to Johnstown were mostly Jewish, and so they turned to the local Jews, because they needed a place to stay. The local Jews, who were shopkeepers in a town then controlled by Bethlehem Steel, were sympathetic, they supported the union but not out loud. "Sha!" – Be quiet – that was the way Jews lived in the old days. My parents were the beginning of the next generation. Still, when we were in Brandeis and the Rosenberg trial came up four or five years later, we, some of the students of Brandeis University, organized a petition opposing the death penalty. My parents were nervous about that, but we were not nervous. So that was when the real generational change occurred.

So, I went to high school: Westmont Upper Yoder Junior–Senior Joint Consolidated High School! Most crucially, it was a "consolidated" school, which meant it incorporated Westmont, a middle and upper-class suburb established after the flood of 1889, and a nearby working-class suburb called Upper Yoder. At my high school working-class kids and upper-middle-class kids studied together but did not share the same fate: in 1952, when I graduated, half the boys in my class went to college and the other half went to fight in Korea. If you knew their address, you knew which way they were going. That was an education in the American class system. But Westmont must have been a little unusual for the following reason. There were about seventy-five kids in my class: five Jews: two boys, three girls. And among the two boys, Gordon P. was elected president of the class and I was elected president of the student council, which couldn't have happened in many places in 1951. Almost all my friends were non-Jews; my closest friend was Pat Gleason, who was the nephew of the local Republican party boss. But we were close even though we disagreed about many things. The Republican party was radically different in those years. Pat and I went to hear Joe McCarthy[15] speak at a fairground outside Johnstown – that must have been in the early 1950s. He was less frightened or appalled than I was, but McCarthy wasn't his kind of Republican.

Busekist: Why do you believe that this couldn't have happened elsewhere?

Walzer: Two Jewish boys elected to the two most prestigious positions! I ran against the captain of the football team. But I was supported by the girls . . . We had to make speeches at the school assembly. When Steve Carney, who was the captain of the team spoke, the whole team stood up, and most of the girls didn't like that. The three Jewish girls in my class were so much more sophisticated than I was. I dated girls who were one or two years younger. My first girlfriend was non-Jewish, I had to assure my parents I was not going to marry her. She was fourteen! Her name was Irene Adcott. "Good night Irene" was a popular song in those years, and my friends would start humming it when I walked into the room. She must have been of English stock. Her father managed the local Woolworth's. I did not know that some years later I would be picketing that chain![16]

Busekist: So then came graduation. Apparently, you only have fond memories of your high-school years.

Walzer: Yes, they were good years. I had two close friends: Pat, whom I just mentioned, went to Georgetown when I went to Brandeis. He then ran for the State assembly, probably from Westmont. He was elected, but he died of cancer quite young. The other one was Jim ("Doc") Quest and I continued to see him, he lived in New York for a time, I would run into him on Fifth Avenue. He went to Cornell. So, middle-class kids from Westmont got into good schools.

Busekist: Was Brandeis the obvious choice because it was an almost all-Jewish university?

23

Walzer: When I applied to Brandeis, it was a brand new Jewish university. It was established in 1948. The first class graduated in June 1952 and I came in the Fall of that year. But I also applied to Penn State University and I got in. I was given an American Legion scholarship if I went to college in Pennsylvania. At Brandeis, I also got in, but I didn't get a scholarship. My parents were not earning a lot of money; Brandeis would have been hard; but the rabbi called the President of Brandeis and I got a full tuition scholarship. So, I went to Brandeis and not to Penn State. My parents were very happy about the scholarship. They had heard of some of the teachers there, and at Brandeis I would meet only Jewish girls (*laughs*). I worked in the campus store. I think I worked every year that I was there and made some money. The scholarship paid only for tuition.

Brandeis had a lefty faculty, and a lot of students who were what we called "red diaper babies." Sachar, the first president, who was himself a good New Deal liberal, needed to put a faculty together quickly. He hired people who couldn't get jobs elsewhere in the McCarthy era. He hired Jewish leftists who didn't have a PhD because the Jewish left in those days was a kind of college substitute. Just being there was a good education, chiefly a Marxist education, but not only that. Irving Howe who had never been to a graduate school taught English, and I studied with him. Brandeis had "general education" courses, in imitation of the Harvard curriculum. Humanities 1 ran from the Bible to Shakespeare. That course was taught by Marie Syrkin, whom I adored. She was the daughter of Nachman Syrkin, and the biographer of Golda Meir;[17] she had written a book called *Blessed is the Match*, which was the story of Hannah Senesh, which I had read as a teenager.[18] Irving Howe taught the second half of the Humanities class, from Shakespeare to . . . I don't remember where he stopped. Maybe with the Russians.

The teacher I spent the most time with at Brandeis was Frank E. Manuel.[19] In fact, I took a course with him every year. He was one of those Jewish radicals who went to work in the New Deal and then with the OSS (Office of Strategic Services) and came to Brandeis from there. I was a history major in Brandeis, and the specialty there was the history of ideas. So I took Lewis Coser's class on Marxism, and a course on the Enlightenment, among others, with Manuel. He was the one who told me to apply to Harvard in political science, because "political science is not a discipline" he said; "you can do whatever you want."

Busekist: You worked on a newspaper at Brandeis: the *Justice*. You must have brought your expertise from *Between the Lines* to the

Justice? After all you were a veteran of journalism by then . . . And the *Justice* was engaged on the left I presume?

Walzer: Yes, because the whole campus was, but the *Justice* was mostly concerned with local issues. Once again, I ran for student council president and won, though President Sachar didn't approve of me. Have you been to Brandeis? Well, one of the issues in my time there centered on the three chapels. Abe Sachar[20] decided that Brandeis was the Jewish contribution to American higher education. It was a secular university, though Jewish sponsored, and he wanted to prove its secularism by raising the money to build three chapels, Jewish, Catholic, and Protestant. I think the school had 95 percent Jewish students, although they were telling people it was only 75 percent of the student body. We thought three chapels was ridiculous. This became a campus issue.

Busekist: Were you against the chapels because of the fundraising to build them or because of the symbol?

Walzer: We thought Brandeis should be like any university sponsored by a religious group. It should be like Harvard, which had a Protestant chapel, and then the Catholics built their own Aquinas Center and the Jews built their Hillel House. That's what we thought Jewish self-respect required. You shouldn't be bending over backwards as if to prove that you are Jewish but not too Jewish. The other big campus issue was the movie *Birth of a Nation*,[21] which had both racist and antisemitic themes . . . Some students proposed to bring the movie to campus, and there were arguments about whether it should be shown or not, and . . . this became an issue in the student council election. I was in favor of showing it, but only with a discussion about the movie afterwards. My opponent was against showing it, so he was supposedly more Jewish than me . . . I guess, I don't know. But anyway, I won the election. My second presidency!

Busekist: Did you experience antisemitism in these years?

Walzer: What seems so strange is that in Johnstown I had no sense of it at all . . . I mean, some of the working-class kids in high school would use expressions like "don't Jew me down" when bargaining about money, but I don't think they associated the phrase with any actual Jews. They would have been fourteen, fifteen . . . This is in high school. But otherwise, I had no sense of antisemitism. Well, the country club in Westmont did not admit Jews.

Busekist: That was the explicit rule?

Walzer: Yes, it was explicit, no Jews or Blacks. Bethlehem Steel did not hire Jews or Blacks either. So I must have had some awareness at least ... The country club was mostly a golf course, but also sponsored a dancing class for high-school kids. I refused to go. The class was open to everybody, but I refused to go, since Jews were not allowed to be members. A lot of kids went with me downtown, to the Kelly Dancing Studio, which was run by Gene Kelly's mother and sister. So, I was taught to dance by Gene Kelly's sister along with my friends![22] Having said this, I really did not experience antisemitism as a threat then.

Busekist: You said you had an awareness. Being denied access to the country club is quite violent, and so is explicitly not hiring Jews or Blacks. Did that seem normal to you back then? You seem quite calm about this.

Walzer: First of all, not many Jews were going to become steel workers. In those days, the Jewish merchants, because of the Union, were doing really well. The first generation of lawyers and doctors were also doing well. My parents never set foot in a home of a non-Jew. All their friends were Jewish ... it was an entirely enclosed adult community. But we, their children, lived comfortably among the others. When we moved to Westmont, we bought a house on a street where we were the first Jews. On one side, we were very warmly welcomed. My mother, who grew up on a farm, planted what was called in those days a victory garden, with the enthusiastic help of one neighbor. The people on the other side never talked to us.

Busekist: Because you were Jewish? I am sensing, that it did not really shock you beyond measure. But it would today.

Walzer: Yes, of course.

Busekist: Your parents were born in America. But they probably lived with the memory of the Holocaust, as did all Jews of that generation? Were they afraid that something like this could happen again?

Walzer: Yes, I am sure they were more sensitive than I was. They were certainly aware of how enclosed their own life was. But the Jewish community was a good place to be in Johnstown in those years. When I was elected president of the Westmont High student council, I went to see the school principal and told him that Westmont had to stop playing basketball games on Friday nights – because of the Jewish Sabbath. I am grateful today that he smiled, and listened, and pretended at least to take me seriously. Tiny minorities can't shape the general calendar and commonly are afraid even to try to do that. The games continued on Friday nights, and I went more often than not. I will let that story sum up my Johnstown experience: I felt safe enough as a Jew, and assertive enough, to go in and make a request like that; and the principal responded in the best possible way. This was a place that was tolerant of trouble-makers, and we all have to make trouble, sometimes." [23]

Busekist: How did your parents react to the topic you chose for your senior thesis at Brandeis? Did they think it was a strange thing to do to work on the English Puritans?

Walzer: No, they did not. They followed my career closely, my mother especially. But I went to a Jewish university, I married a Jewish girl. We went to Israel. They were not worried. I could write about the English Puritans . . .

Busekist: What about you? With hindsight it doesn't seem so, but at the time it may have been an awkward choice. How come you got involved with English Puritanism and the Reformed Church?

Walzer: Well, I think it had a lot to do with my monolingual world. I was a lefty who wanted to write about revolutions. My French was terrible, my Russian was non-existent, so I was left with the English revolution. I started on the Puritans at Brandeis, actually . . . After my second year at Brandeis, after studying with Irving Howe, I told my parents that I wanted to be an intellectual. They said: "Can you make a living from this?" But the academic world was expanding in those days and taking in many freelance intellectuals (like Howe), so there was a way to make a living. My mother knew that I couldn't be a rabbi, although she would have been happy with that, because, she told me, I would never be able to handle the hospital visits. She was very smart. The common alternative was to become a lawyer. I am sure that at some point, my parents expected me to go to a law school.

Busekist: After graduating from Brandeis, you got a Fulbright scholarship and you travelled to Britain to go to Cambridge University, with your wife, Judy.

Walzer: Yes, I met Judy in my sophomore year. She came from Music and Art high school in New York. I had put myself on the orientation committee for the freshmen so that I could meet younger girls, since the girls in my own class somehow had more sophistication, as usual. But Judy was my age, since my parents had pushed me one year up. Anyway, I was on the orientation committee and that actually meant that I carried her suitcase to her room. She had a boyfriend at that time who was at Harvard. But she also had a good friend who picked me out as the person she should be with and eventually brought us together. One of those classic stories. There was some kind of folk-dance event, and she came to Judy and said that she should go because I wanted to meet her, and she came to me and told me that I should go because Judy wanted to meet me. Anyway, it worked. We decided, well, we had to get married because I got a Fulbright, and in those days, you couldn't go to Europe together without being married. It was a different world. Both of our families would have been very upset. We were married in New York in a synagogue on Long Island where Judy's mother's sister lived. With six rabbis in attendance, one of them Rabbi Perlmutter, who came from Johnstown with my parents.

Busekist: Judy grew up in the Bronx also?

Walzer: She grew up in the Bronx, but went to middle school and high school in Manhattan. These were public schools, but not local public schools; they were schools where you had to take a test to get in. At the High School of Music and Art, she joined haShomer haTzair.[24] At Brandeis she was a History major – and she also studied with Irving Howe. She wrote occasionally for *Dissent*.[25] But that was much later on.

Busekist: Cambridge was a milestone in your education.

Walzer: Yes. My tutor at Cambridge was Geoffrey Elton who was a sixteenth-century historian.[26] He wrote about Thomas Cromwell. He was the scholar who made Thomas Cromwell into a major figure – the founder of the British civil service. Geoffrey was hostile to intellectual history, he was an institutional historian, but he was amazingly sweet and helpful to me. He was our model English Empire Tory. For us he was the classic Englishman. Our friends in Cambridge were not English: a South African Jewish Communist couple, a Welsh kid, and an Indian. Those were our closest friends in Cambridge.

When we went back to the States, I started at Harvard while Judy was finishing her last year at Brandeis. One day she got a note from Victor Ehrenberg, a visiting professor, inviting her to tea, inviting us to tea. And we went to have tea with Ehrenberg[27] and his wife, and the first thing he said to us was: "You know my son." We had absolutely no idea that Geoffrey was Jewish! He had been in the army, in intelligence, and the army changed his name. Perhaps he took the change very seriously; in any case he married a non-Jewish woman, a lovely woman named Sheila, according to the rites of the First Book of Common Prayer of the Anglican church. He never told us about his father, which was very embarrassing at the moment when we met his father. But I think that he was so kind to me because I was a Jewish kid.

We were in England during the 1956 Suez war, and we attended one of the anti-war rallies. I was very confused by this war. At the time we didn't fully understand the collusion between Israel, France, and the UK. It seemed like a neo-colonial war on Britain's part. I do remember being impressed with the British police. After the last speech at the anti-war rally, the bobbies started moving through the crowd, saying: "It's all over now; please go home." I was amazed! And people indeed went home. During our stay in England, Judy went to lectures by F. R. Leavis, the leader of the *Scrutiny* group [*Scrutiny* was a literary magazine, thought to be of the right]. And we made one trip to Oxford that year to hear Isaac Deutscher[28] do his imitation of Lenin (or was it Trotsky?) We attended a meeting of the *Universities and Left Review*, founded that year, which later became the *New Left Review*; we met Charles Taylor and Stuart Hall[29] – though we didn't get to know them until some years later.

Busekist: Yes, I was wondering why you often quote Stuart Hall. You like Stuart Hall.

Walzer: Yes, on our second visit to England in 1964 we became close friends with Margaret and Michael Rustin.[30] Margaret was the sister of the woman Stuart Hall married.[31] Anyway, we were there in 1956 but not really participants, watching when the British New Left made its first appearance. Obviously, I had disagreements with Hall, but also some important agreements. Politically, I suppose, I was closer to Charles Taylor,[32] who also became a friend.

When we left Cambridge at the end of the academic year, in 1957, we met a couple of Brandeis friends in France and drove together across Europe. We stopped in Dachau. And then we drove across Yugoslavia to Piraeus and got on a ship to Haifa. It was a very special boat, I think we were the only paying passengers. There were two sets of Jewish refugees on this boat: Polish Communist Jews who had taken their kids out of the State's schools when Gomulka brought the priests back in 1956 and Egyptian Jews who came via Italy after the 1956 Suez war. Those two groups were on the same boat: the Egyptian Jews were bourgeois, traditional, and the Polish Jews were secular and leftist. We became friendly with one of the Poles, a translator, who knew English very well; he had a nine-year-old son.

One day, we were with his father and he came running up; he had seen the Egyptian Jews praying in the morning and he said to his father: "I thought that Jews were people who didn't pray." The piece I wrote about this is one of my most sentimental ones ... I remember the Jewish Agency people helping both groups prepare for life in Israel and teaching them Hatikvah. It was quite extraordinary when Haifa loomed into view, and one of the Polish Jews started to sing. And I thought about how these two very different kinds of Jews, none of them Zionists to start with, have no other place to go. My emotional account of the voyage was published in a German book called *Mein Israel* and then in English in a compilation of essays on the experience of first coming to Israel.[33]

We stayed in Israel for about six or seven weeks. We had no money so we hitchhiked around the country. We went first to kibbutz Nahshon.[34] I've written about that too. Nahshon, the person, is the invention of some Midrashic rabbi, who was disturbed by the passivity of the Jews in the story of the Exodus from Egypt. He appears in one biblical genealogy, nowhere else, but in the Midrash, he is the one who, without waiting, plunges into the Red Sea because he has faith in God's deliverance. The Kibbutzniks thought he was planning to swim across; he was an early activist![35] We stayed in Nahshon for a while. Some of Judy's friends were there, some of whom stayed in Israel, and some came back. They had come expecting a different life, where you farm, you work hard all day, and then gather in the evening to listen to Mozart. It wasn't like that!

We then went to the North, where we visited a large refugee camp, I guess it was that; it was not yet a settlement, in the Galilee somewhere ... Kiryat Shmona or near there.[36] We went to a kibbutz at the bottom of the Dead Sea, Ein Gedi, where they were just celebrating the birth of the first child born in the kibbutz. We were all over the country. I had a pen-pal in Jerusalem, from Johnstown days, and we also went there and met his family. They were very "Yekadish" (as Russian Jews say about German Jews) and we were not.

We had come on an Italian ship, but we want back on an Israeli ship to Genoa. I think it was either in Genoa or in Israel that we got a letter from my mother telling me that they were leaving Johnstown and moving to Chicago because Rabbi Perlmutter had gotten an appointment in Chicago and he wanted my mother to be the executive secretary of this congregation. It was the biggest reformed congregation in Chicago. Judy and I came back to Cambridge and then visited my parents in Chicago. I didn't go back to Johnstown until my 25th high-school reunion, and then a couple of years ago on the 125th anniversary of Jewish life in Johnstown. The 125th anniversary of Jewish life, which begins with the first Jewish funeral – that's the way they dated it! They had a celebration – it wasn't much of a celebration. The 2,000 Jews had dwindled to about 200. Bethlehem Steel was dead, closed, and most of the Jews had left, but they still had this celebration. I gave the keynote about growing up Jewish in Johnstown.[37]

When we came back to the US, we rented an apartment on the wrong side of Beacon Hill, the cheap side of Beacon Hill, in Boston. Judy had to go to Brandeis every day and there was a convenient train. I had an easy subway ride to Harvard. Judy was a senior and I was a first-year graduate student. I think that the first year of graduate study is the worst year of an academic life. I was very unhappy. The purpose of graduate school is to turn a bright young person into a professional political scientist, but I wanted to be an intellectual, I didn't want to be a professional political scientist! I thought my fellow graduate students were prematurely middle aged, but I did find a couple of protectors on the faculty, which is very important in graduate school.[38]

Busekist: Louis Hartz and Sam Beer at Harvard whom you worked with?

Walzer: Yes, Louis Hartz was a historian of American political thought. He had written *The Liberal Tradition in America*, where he made a very influential argument about American exceptionalism,[39] and Sam Beer was a political scientist, an expert on the UK,[40] and a good example of an American social democrat. In those days, the Harvard faculty consisted of people who had almost all done their dissertation and their first book on political theory, whatever else

31

they did afterwards. Sam Beer was in comparative politics, but his first book was on Kant. I wrote my dissertation with him. He and Hartz were my protectors. As I had to study American politics I did so with V. O. Key;[41] and I studied Eastern Europe with Zbigniew Brzezinski,[42] whom I would later meet when he was in the White House.

Busekist: What did he teach? International relations?

Walzer: He taught East European politics – critically. I also took a course with Rupert Emerson[43] on imperialism and wrote an essay for his class on the Indian Communist Party (which I used again, years later, when I wrote about the religious revival in India in *The Paradox of Liberation*). One thing I remember learning from Louis Hartz, who told us in the first meeting of his class, "when you write papers, never define your terms. As you write, you should make clear to the reader what you are talking about, but never define your terms."

Busekist: That has changed a lot. Did he shape the way you write? You were already a mature scholar when you came to Harvard.

Walzer: I was already a writer, or so I thought, but I wasn't yet a "theorist." At Harvard, political theory was taught as the history of political theory, and that's what I had done at Brandeis, and that's what I did in Cambridge. I was a historian. My dissertation wasn't entirely about the history of ideas, because I also tried to do comparative politics, comparing the Puritans to the Jacobins and the Bolsheviks, but that was a small part of the dissertation. Essentially it was an intellectual history of the English revolution. I read hundreds of Puritan sermons, and that's where I first encountered repetitions and citations of the Exodus story, but I didn't yet write about that. And I definitely wasn't yet trying to write what was called "normative" political theory.

Busekist: The Exodus indeed comes up often as we said earlier, in *The Paradox of Liberation* and in other books: you see the Exodus story as a pattern for many revolutions.

Walzer: Yes, it has been a constant reference point in my writing. So we spent one year in Boston and then we moved to an apartment in Cambridge. Judy became a graduate student at Brandeis, still taking the train but not every day, and I was now in my second year at graduate school. I began to find some graduate student friends and fellow leftists; we created a New Left club in Cambridge in 1958–1959, and I was now writing pretty regularly for *Dissent*. From Cambridge, England, I had written a piece on the Hungarian revolution and a critique of the British left's response. Quite a few leftists argued that the Soviet repression was, as we used to say, "historically necessary." I was already a fierce anti-Stalinist – I didn't think that the Soviet Union represented the march of history. In Cambridge Massachusetts, I found some friends who agreed with me.

Busekist: We are in 1961 in Cambridge . . .

Walzer: Yes, we founded the New Left Club in Cambridge.[44] We wrote some kind of statement criticizing the invasion of Cuba and went around collecting signatures. It was published in the *New York Times*.[45] I remember asking faculty members to sign. A lot of them did. My friends in the New Left Club included Stephan and Abigail Thernstrom.[46] She, and Steve too, later became a kind of neocon. Gabriel Kolko[47] was also one of the new leftists, who later wrote books about and against American foreign policy. I remember him best because he came to me one day and asked where I was keeping my thesis notes, my early drafts. Wasn't I worried about fire? He had just bought a fireproof box for his notes! I still have a metal box, probably not fireproof, in which I keep passports and important papers now. Kolko was a worrier, he worried about nuclear war and talked about moving to Australia to be safe. I think he never got further than Canada. The Thernstroms were the people we were closest to until we left Cambridge for Princeton, when we drifted apart.

Busekist: After Harvard, you went to Princeton, right? And then you went back to Harvard and, years later, back again to Princeton?

Walzer: Yes, we came to Princeton the first time in 1962. I had some title, the James Madison Preceptor, which gave me one year off during my first four years in Princeton. That's when we went again to England. Judy had finished grad school classes at Brandeis and was working on her dissertation, on the English novelist George Gissing, in Princeton and then in London. She worked at the British Library, and I was writing. I had already rewritten my doctoral dissertation into a book. So that was done. It was submitted first to Oxford, which didn't take it, I don't really know why; an American writing on English Puritans should have interested them. Maybe because I wasn't a professional historian. But Harvard took it, and if I did any revisions at that point it would have been in England that year. That was *The Revolution of the Saints*.[48] There was a review in one of the historical journals, which said in substance, "This is not a bad book considering that the author's not a historian."

Busekist: How was the British New Left different from the New Left in America?

Walzer: The New Left in Britain had the advantage of a Labour party with which they had, naturally, a very complicated relationship. The important thing for me about Stuart [Hall] and Michael Rustin was that they left the editorial board of *New Left Review* the year I was in England (1964) and founded a new magazine, *Views*, which was less rigidly Marxist than NLR, closer to social democracy.[49] It was funded by the son of a wealthy family who was also the editor, but Stuart and Michael were the intellectual leaders. I wrote several pieces that year and went to editorial meetings. Clancy Sigal,[50] the novelist, wrote for the magazine; he was then living in England. I remember him because he wanted to write a critique to be published with every article we accepted!

Busekist: An interesting way of doing editorial work . . . Why did Rustin and Hall leave the *New Left Review*? Because they thought it was too internationalist, too Marxist, too Trotskyist?

Walzer: It was too rigid for them. They had a different sensibility, more, how do you say it, relational? They were still Marxists of a sort, but (something like the founders of *Dissent*), they were hostile to anything that smacked of sectarianism; they wanted to live in the "real world" . . . I didn't like the *New Left Review* because the editors were so hostile to Israel.

Busekist: That was my next question.

Walzer: But that wasn't their reason for leaving; I am sure it wasn't – and it was never an issue for them as it was for me. At some point, I think, they went back to NLR, and then they left again and started yet another magazine: *Soundings*.[51] There was a troubled relationship with Perry Anderson,[52] who was the editor and leading light of NLR.

Busekist: Is this similar to the troubled relationship between Irving Howe's *Dissent* and the New Left or the SDS?

Walzer: There might be some similarities. The *New Left Review* wouldn't have been Stalinist, but it might have had something like Isaac Deutscher's view of the Soviet Union as a "deformed socialist, but still a socialist society." *Dissent* was different, and Howe, you are right, was a Trotskyist when he was younger but, like Stanley Plastrik[53] and Manny Geltman,[54] Howe and the entire group became disillusioned with the internal life of the Trotskyist sects. One of the first pieces in *Dissent* was about sectarianism and why it was a bad politics.[55] They wanted to speak to a larger audience. And a similar motivation must have figured in the founding of *Views*. The *New Left Review* became an international, very successful magazine, but Stuart and Michael [Rustin] may have been more sympathetic to E. P Thompson's version of English radicalism.[56]

Busekist: That is interesting for someone who had the career of Stuart Hall, Jamaican-born, sensitive to different expressions of culture, to be English-oriented rather than an internationalist . . .

Walzer: Yes, Stuart was a Euro-Marxist, but he wrote almost entirely about English politics and culture. He wrote for a magazine called *Marxism Today*. A series of a quite brilliant analyses of Thatcherism was published there and republished after his death.[57] Stuart was well known as a sympathetic student of popular culture and an early defender of "hybridity." I don't think that was a central part of Michael and Margaret [Rustin's] politics, although they were certainly sympathetic, and very close to Stuart and Catherine and their children. Michael is a good social democrat – actually one of the best.

Busekist: We are now in the middle of your second long stay in Britain.

Walzer: That's it and in the middle of my four years in Princeton. During this stay, I was asked to write a book. An American publisher – this was a very bad idea, but we were all enthusiastic about it – proposed a twelve-volume history of political thought: six volumes of historical narratives, and six volumes of documents, extracts from all the big books. I signed a contract to cover the period from Machiavelli to Marx, but only on the continent because someone else was doing British political thought from Hobbes and Locke to John

Stuart Mill. I was not supposed to write about any of the British. So, I sat in England and I wrote this rather peculiar book. I still have my handwritten text of the whole book!

The enterprise failed. I didn't have to return the advance, but I was left with this unpublishable manuscript; Machiavelli but not Hobbes, Rousseau but not Hume. The British volume is the only one that was published; I doubt that it sold many copies. I used the material in a course that I gave at Harvard on continental political theory. But I never typed it up or tried to make a different kind of book out of it. I have it all. All handwritten. It was my last production in the history of political thought because, back in Princeton, I became friends with a group of philosophers and I began to write, tried to write, what was then called "normative political theory."

Busekist: We will talk about that peculiar group later. Let's stay in Princeton. You didn't give up your activism once you were back in the US?

Walzer: Indeed. Before going back to Harvard and before SELF, we organized one of the first teach-ins about Vietnam; that would have been 1965. The university was not really in solidarity with us, we were a small group who organized the teach-in . . . some faculty members came and spoke. It was soon after teach-ins in other places. The first teach-in was in Michigan, I think, and this was probably the third or fourth. Very soon after. John Schrecker,[58] a friend of mine, was one of the speakers at the teach-in. He and I wrote a piece, one of the first pieces against the war in *Dissent*, based on the talks we had given. I guess that was my first experience of working with a co-author.[59]

Busekist: You haven't co-authored many pieces. I can think of Avishai Margalit and Marty Peretz aside from Schrecker. Are you a solitary writer?

Walzer: I don't know. Political theorists usually don't write together. Have you ever written with other people?

Busekist: Yes, but only once or twice. Once with a former doctoral student and it was a very good experience. Political scientists often write together. It's harder in political theory.

Walzer: Our teach-ins were the beginning of the anti-war movement. One of the early chapters of SDS was founded in Princeton by Jon

Wiener[60] and a few of his fellow undergrads; he became a good friend; he now writes for *The Nation*, and runs *The Nation* podcast. I met him in 1965 when he was an undergraduate and I was the faculty adviser to the Princeton SDS. Jon Wiener did an interview with me on my *Foreign Policy for the Left*, for *The Nation*, a couple of months, maybe two months, ago.[61] So, we've been friends from 1965 to 2018!

Busekist: I have wanted to ask you this question many times. You once said that you are an "American political scientist who happens to be a Jew"; you are a part-time Dissentnik, a part-time academic and you made a "hatzi-alyah" as Shlomo Avineri puts it[62]. . . So who are you exactly Michael Walzer? Could you define yourself in three words?

Walzer: Your question reminds me of what I used to tell my daughters: you will grow up to be a woman, a Jew, and a socialist. Three words. But you will have to give me some more words. I am not fully committed to the academic world, but I was never a sustained militant in the political world either. Nothing like the proverbial "professional revolutionary." I am very much an American citizen,[63] engaged in American politics but I often find it easy to think first about Israel: sometimes, the crucial question for people like me, twentieth-century Jews, should be: what's good for Israel? And yet I am told by people here [in Israel]: "Well, you come but you don't stay." Which is obviously true. So maybe there is a pattern here. Yes. I think of myself as engaged, committed, but maybe not fully engaged anywhere. I am fully engaged with my grandchildren!

Busekist: That is interesting. I have noticed that in many of your books and articles, you mention family life, the importance of family, love, loyalty, and kinship, and you use familial metaphors. You wrote somewhere that one cannot be a full-time militant,[64] among other reasons, because private life counts and is a source of morality.

Walzer: Yes, these are particular obligations. We will have to talk about them.

2

Political Activism, Civil Rights, and the Anti-War Movement

Busekist: Your early political activism has probably influenced your thinking and your writing about the meaning of political commitment and social criticism, but may also have shaped your conception of political theory and planted the seeds for your work on justice and war. Your first articles on the Civil Rights Movement are "The Young: A Cup of Coffee and a Seat" published in February 1960, when Irving Howe and Lewis Coser sent the youngest member of the *Dissent* staff down South, to North Carolina (Greensboro, Durham, Raleigh, and to Shaw, an all-Black university), to report on the lunch counter sit-ins and the picketing; and "Politics of nonviolent resistance" published in the 1960 Fall issue of *Dissent*. It was at Shaw, in October of the same year, that Elia Baker founded the SNCC (Student Nonviolent Coordinating Committee), which played a central role in grassroots politics and had a profound impact on the New Left, in particular the Campus activists, many of whom then joined SDS (Students for a Democratic Society).

Observing what was going on in the South, you were optimistic about the changes grassroots activism would bring about, you believed that it was "proof that it is possible to step outside the realm of conventional politics." In a 1962 piece on the "Young Radicals," you add that "desire for personal encounter, the organizational naiveté of the New Left [. . .] the false sophistication and largely vicarious weariness of the fifties is gone, while the surrender of self to history or party, which so often characterized the men of the thirties, has not reappeared."[1] Would you say something similar to France happened in the US? A "'68 state of mind"? And how would you define it? What would you describe as most typically "'68-ish" in the US?

I ask because the movement in France seems to be quite different from the long period of social and political unrest between the 1950s and the 1970s in America. The Civil Rights Movement on the one hand, starting in the 1950s, but not really ending with the actual Civil Rights and Voting Acts (1964, 1965, 1968), and (the opposition to) the Vietnam War on the other hand. 1968 has many different national and specific histories: Germany, Japan, or Italy have all mobilized differently. The so-called event, "May '68," doesn't really exist, it would be more accurate to describe the "movement" as a series of micro-events that make sense ex post. In France, May 1968 appears to be a typically and specifically "French moment," a prolongment of a cycle inaugurated in 1789 – to the French, Revolutions can only be French and '68 is a revolution). A libertarian movement, leftist without doubt, but neither socialist nor Communist. An impetus given by the students, starting at the universities before spreading to the working class when the students were joined by the workers, ending with the biggest strikes ever in French history.

Walzer: It would be much easier to compare France and the US if the French student movement had started at the height of the Algerian war rather than almost a decade later. 1968 in America begins in the 1960s with the Civil Rights Movement. Activism is dominated by the Civil Rights Movement and then, in a fiercer way, by the anti-war struggle. Those two are very political, very policy-oriented. They really do not have much to do with cultural revolution and even less with sexual revolution. In fact, it is worth mentioning that many of the Baptist preachers who, along with the students, were the leaders of the Civil Rights Movement, were also, if they survived into the 1980s and 1990s, strongly opposed to abortion and gay marriage.

They were focused on liberation, but it was the liberation of civil rights, of Black empowerment. The students may have generalized it and begun to imagine a wider liberation; the preachers probably not. I remember the kids who sat in. I went South in time to see them sitting at the lunch counters, refusing to be moved: they were very well dressed, and they were almost all men.[2] All this is very different, I think, from what happened in France. American feminism is in part a response to the male-led, male-dominated character of both the Civil Rights and Anti-War Movements. Feminism in the United States is largely a 1970s, not a 1960s political movement. The 1960s are first about civil rights for American Blacks. It's quite a story, very complicated, starting with those well-dressed students at lunch counters and ending with Black power and Black nationalism. The

39

students were proud and happy in their newfound pride; you might expect bitterness, given their life experience, but the bitterness only came later, along with the nationalism.

You could tell a somewhat similar story about the anti-war movement, which begins with high-spirited protests against American intervention in Vietnam and ends with the effort to "bring the war home," with the Maoism of Progressive Labor and the bombs of the Weathermen.[3] These are stories of radicalization but only within the scope of civil rights and anti-war, not moving beyond that until later. I think the French story is different. There is one perhaps useful comparison: the most violent left revolutionaries were in Japan, Germany,[4] and Italy. It is interesting that the three countries that had experienced fascist regimes produced the most violent left politics. In this sense, France and the US are similar to each other, and to other lefts, too, including Great Britain, where the left, though not committed in any way to nonviolence, was in fact nonviolent.

Busekist: In a *Dissent* Symposium on 1968,[5] you write that "the opposition to the war has changed American culture for the better in many ways. But it did not produce a sustainable politics; its institutional legacy is virtually nil. In fact, it contributed to forty years of rightward momentum that, only now, is there a prospect of stopping." What about the institutional legacies of the 1960s in France and the US? The Resistance in France had brought about a genuine political legacy, had produced political personnel and achieved institutional change. A great number of French Resistants became French politicians after the war. May '68 has achieved nothing of this kind. But 1968 has a very strong and long-lasting cultural legacy (freedom, anti-conservatism, anti-establishment, libertarianism, a complete change in the university system). What about the political and the cultural legacy of the 1960s in the US?

I ask for two reasons. You quote, firstly, the visionary remark of one of the young Black students: "we don't want brotherhood [. . .] we just want a cup of coffee and sit down [. . .] if we negotiate, my grandchildren will still be worrying about that cup of coffee"; and you note, secondly, that political engagement or political curiosity of the Black students who initiated the sit-ins was also "virtually nil": they were well behaved, and not interested at all in presidential campaigns for instance.[6] They were not politicized beyond what they were doing there at the sit-ins, but they were strongly influenced by the "Black reverends," and religion played an important role.

Walzer: Right. The Civil Rights Movement very quickly produced two organizations: the Southern Christian Leadership Conference (SCLC), which was made up of the Baptist preachers, and the Student Nonviolent Coordinating Committee (SNCC), which was the kids. There was cooperation between these two but also tensions. In fact, one of the interesting features of the 1960s politics is the interaction of young and old, which was sometimes contentious but sometimes not. In the Civil Rights Movement, the Baptist preachers played a very important role in helping the students – providing adult support (and probably calming the parents of the students). They helped without trying to pre-empt what the students were doing or to replace the student leaders. This is an issue that comes up again now, in 2018, when high-school students are protesting against the American gun culture. These students also need adult support, but too many adults are eager to replace them – or to treat them as cheerleaders rather than as activists in their own right. The Black preachers didn't do that, they did not try to speak on behalf of the students. The student movement was sustained alongside the preachers, but it was an independent movement. In fact, the 1960s was a great time to be young; youthfulness was in the air, and this accounts not only for the politics, but also for the cultural transformations of that decade.

Busekist: Was this "the young's" entry into politics? Maybe that was what made them so happy: for the first time in their life they did something meaningful for them and for the community. What also struck me in the February 2008 piece (but you say so in other articles) is that you insist a lot on the kind of solidarity that the Blacks displayed at that point. They were "anti-individualistic" and "anti-heroic"; they were united by a desire for action, a sense of solidarity, and a spirit of collectiveness.

Walzer: Yes, yes, yes. I never fully figured out their relationship to the Baptist preachers, however. They were churchgoers. And certainly, their parents were. It was an important part of their identity. But there were also tensions between the kids and the preachers, which I never fully understood. On my second visit to the South, I went to church services, and listened to the sermons – the Black Baptist sermon is a work of art and an exercise in participation: the audience joins in and echoes what the preacher says. These are very, very skillful speakers. King, whom we all got to hear, may not have been the best of them. Abernathy[7] was very powerful. My sense of the students I met is that they were indeed proud of themselves and happy. At this stage, they

41

weren't bitter. I cannot fully explain why, they had all the reasons to be bitter, even if the police violence came only a little later.

The other kind of violence, structural, that threatened all the Blacks, was represented by individual Whites, often in police uniforms, but also only later. In the article you mention, I wrote that when I arrived in Greensboro, the first thing I did was to walk up to a policeman and ask: "How do I get to this Negro church?" There was no sense of danger then; I wasn't afraid, and the students certainly weren't. Now some of them were older – they were Korea war veterans, important participants in the early Civil Rights Movement, but many of them were just kids.

Walzer: Some of my friends at *Dissent* who sent me South expected me to come back with a report about the uprising of Black workers and farmers; I came back instead and told them it was students and Baptists. The combination was very important. And a somewhat similar combination was also visible in the Northern response to the sit-ins. A lot of Northerners went South in those years, most of them young and a high percentage of them Jewish. We, Blacks and Jews, had a couple of years of political cooperation, and then at a certain point, Jews, and other Whites, too, were asked to leave. Telling the Black kids: "Look, we were slaves in Egypt" didn't help convince them that we understood what was going on, or what should be going on, in Mississippi.

Busekist: Despite the surprise of your Northern friends, the support in the North was very strong – the Woolworth lunch-counters and picketing in the Boston area for example – and it was especially strong among the Jews. You went to Brandeis, the only (almost) all-Jewish university where you had been an activist: you wrote for *Justice*, the campus journal and were part of SPEAC (Student Political Educational and Action Committee) and EPIC (Emergency Public Integration Committee); Brandeis even organized a Transitional Year Program in 1968, in part as a response to Martin Luther King Jr.'s assassination.

Isn't it true that the Jews and the Blacks had common objective interests that would have made for alliances? Gaining admission to the Ivy League Universities for example? And didn't they share the same enemy, the Ku Klux Klan in particular, who killed and lynched Blacks in the South, and violently disturbed communal gatherings and desecrated synagogues? Among the deaths during the Freedom Summer in 1964, there were two Jewish civil rights workers, Andrew

Goodman and Michael Schwerner, murdered by the Klan, and there has been a mass arrest of rabbis after a pray-in in Monson.[8]

You noted that among the students going South to support the movement, there was a very large proportion of Jews. There was a large solidarity: half of the White attorneys defending Black people in the South were also Jews; the American Jewish Committee, the American Jewish Congress (and the Anti-Defamation League) actively supported the Civil Rights Movement; Abraham Heschel from the Jewish Theological seminar marched with Martin Luther King Jr., and Martin Luther King Jr. wrote his famous "letter from St. Augustine Jail" to a rabbi, Rabbi Dresner.

However, when the "Black nationalists took over" at one point, "the Jews were invited to leave," and you believe that was right, because "it was their movement."[9] But there was a regular pitting of Blacks against Jews during the civil rights decade, as in the New York City teachers' strike in 1968 for example. Did that come from the inside? How exactly have you been asked to leave?

Walzer: At Brandeis, there were not many Black students in the 1950s, not many non-Jews either. But as leftists we moved into the Civil Rights Movement as soon as the movement appeared; it seemed a natural move. To answer your question: my experience at the end was not one of violent confrontation; I was asked very sweetly to leave. Others were not; the school controversy in New York was very angry on both sides. Looking back, I don't think the Jewish young people who went South tried in any way to take over the movement. I think we were very careful. We knew that the leadership had to come from Southern Blacks. We wanted to be supporters. And the Northern support movement in which I was active was exactly an effort of that kind. We were picketing the chain stores in the North while the students were sitting-in in the same stores in the South. We were following their lead, supporting their political work.

Anyway, I came back from the South to organize, with Harvey Pressman,[10] a friend from Brandeis, the Emergency Public Integration Committee (EPIC), the movement you mentioned, which was one of the groups of the Northern support movement. We were in touch with people in other universities and in other cities. We organized the picketing of Woolworth stores in and around Boston (the Black kids were sitting in in their Southern branches) – where there were a lot of colleges. Harvey was the organizer; that wasn't my talent; I did much of the talking, visiting many campuses to recruit students for the picket lines. At the peak of our activity, we had pickets in front of forty stores, mostly students with some Black people, chiefly from Roxbury in Boston. I spoke once in a Black church in Roxbury and tried to do an imitation of the Baptist sermons I had heard in the South; the audience was responsive, out of kindness, perhaps, but it didn't feel right; I didn't do it again.

I still have a sheet of paper with a list of names, my wife Judy's roster of picketers; she was captain of the picket line in Central Square, Cambridge. I was in downtown Boston. We had to negotiate with the police about all the lines – and we found a lawyer who worked without pay.

Busekist: So the Northern picketing was mostly a White business, and the minority of the Black students involved were college kids. What would you say remains of this common endeavor?

Walzer: Some of the Black students were from Brandeis and Harvard, I think from Northeastern too, but the percentage of Black enrollment was tiny. Maybe two or three percent at the schools where we were trying to recruit picketers. The Black people who were on the downtown Boston picket lines came from Roxbury; they weren't college people. The interaction between us went well, but nothing stuck, it didn't become a working alliance. They must have felt that we were nice people but ultimately not reliable; they didn't trust our staying power. The sense that I got very soon from people in the South was: "It has to be our struggle."

Busekist: In a way, they did it for themselves and you did it for the principle? Is that something they may have sensed?

Walzer: Right, and we were heavily Jewish, with leftish backgrounds – so "principle," or ideology, is the right reading, for we did think that civil rights was part of a larger struggle. The Brandeis contingent and the Harvard Jewish contingent, those were the largest groups on the picket lines.

Busekist: But it still seems that the alliance and the solidarity did go well, at least for a time, given that you were defending common interests.

Walzer: Yes, it did go well. We thought it went well; the Black preachers especially were very welcoming.

Busekist: Toward the Jews in general?

Walzer: Yes, and toward the liberal Reform and Conservative rabbis who came South. That was a very close working alliance. And for me, the break was, I told you, very gentle! The students I met in the South wanted to write a book about their experience and they invited me to write a piece on the Northern support movement. I wrote the piece. I still have it, and I sent it down, and some months later I got this very nice letter saying, "We think it should be an entirely Black book."[11]

Busekist: I guess that is understandable. So, to get back to our chronology, you took one semester off because you were an activist?

Walzer: Yes, we were activists of what you might call the Near Left. We didn't harass people who wanted to go to the Woolworth stores we were picketing; that was the agreement with the police. We had some trouble with the local Trotskyists, who wanted to take over and be more militant, on their terms. But we were much stronger than they were. At a certain point, all that ended; the Trots returned to their sectarian existence, the Black Nationalists took over, and we moved on to the anti-war movement. Somehow the move into anti-war politics from civil rights politics seemed natural.

Busekist: In the early 1960s, the terminology Negro was still the official one, right? How long did it take to make the shift from "Negroes" to African-Americans?

Walzer: Yes, that was the terminology. First, they preferred "Black" to African-American. The Black nationalists. "Black is beautiful." Blackness comes to be central within a few years after 1960, but I can't date it. I don't remember. But I know it wasn't long before, when re-reading my articles, the word Negro jarred.

Busekist: Were there any specific events that led to the drift toward Black nationalism? The roots are probably to be found in the 1950s with the Supreme Court decision in Brown v. Board of Education (1954), the murder of Emmett Till (1955), the Bus boycott in Alabama (1955–1956), the events at Little Rock (1957), etc.

Despite the number of Black organizations in the 1960s, they did not necessarily share the same agenda. Some were in favor of armed retaliation in supremacist areas; SNCC (Student Nonviolent Coordinating Committee) and CORE (Congress of Racial Equality) organized the Freedom Rides in 1960–1961, and marched "against Fear" in 1966; "Black Pride" was gaining momentum with the unforgettable image of the Summer Olympics in 1968; Malcom X and the Black Panthers were in favor of armed self-defense; there was also a strong movement among inmates, the Black Guerrilla Party.

Walzer: I think the drift toward a Black nationalism came in part because success didn't come, it never does, instantaneously. Young people are impatient and perhaps the Black preachers were too assertive about nonviolence and gradualism. So, there was a revolt of activists in their twenties and early thirties who wanted to be more militant than anyone else. This is a common feature of left politics when reform seems too slow; would-be leaders seek to out-do each other in their militancy. You can find a similar phenomenon in religious life, where successive priests or rabbis claim to be more strict, more observant than their predecessors.

We thought at the time that Black nationalism was a political mistake. Understandable under the circumstances of American life, but a mistake nevertheless because minorities must practice coalition politics. The Jews learned that a long time ago. You can't do it yourself if you are ten percent of the population or two percent of the population. You need allies and you need a politics that looks toward making allies. Black nationalism was a rejection of that kind of politics, and it led, I think, to a dead end. Still, if you watched the Black Panthers in California, you could see the pride of these young Black militants who were standing up very straight and on every possible occasion carrying a gun (but the kids sitting-in a few years earlier didn't need a gun to feel proud). That was not a useful politics in the US, but it had its logic inside the Black community.

Busekist: Within the Black movements, but also beyond, the ideological battlefield was about the use of violence. You have written about violence and I would be curious to hear your opinion.

The NAACP Chapter in Monroe (National Association for the Advancement of Colored People), led by Robert F. Williams decided early on, and against the NAACP's commitment to nonviolence, to fight violence with violence. He published a book called *Negroes with Guns* in 1962;[12] he was suspended from the movement but made it to the *New York Times* title page in 1959, and was supported by W. E. B. Dubois. Malcolm X's public speech, "The ballot or the bullet" in 1964 puts an end to nonviolent policies. And by 1968, in

46

Chicago, the National Mobilization Committee to End the war in Vietnam welcomed "all tactics," nonviolent and violent.

On the one hand, there is something to be said in favor of the Black movements' espousing violence; they were often seriously and brutally attacked, institutional racism still existed and the Klan was active: they needed self-defense. On the other hand, there was an actual training in nonviolence: James Bevel, instigator of the Children's Crusade, for example, trained the kids in nonviolent education and nonviolent participation in demonstrations.

You have written many pieces on nonviolent resistance, about Gandhi in particular, but also on "non-cooperation."[13] Resistance as a collective defense of laws and rights is, in your words, "defensive and limited." In the Middle Ages, it required a constituted body of laws and rights, and the existence of groups capable of cooperative and disciplined activity, which you call the "lesser magistrates." Civil collective disobedience in modernity on the other hand is "a politics for amateurs and citizens."[14] In *Just and Unjust Wars* there is a section on nonviolence where you affirm that for nonviolence to be effective, all parties have to previously agree on the value of nonviolence; in other words they must almost already stand on the same side.[15]

What was your reaction to the violence then, and what was the position of the Dissentniks in general?

Walzer: We were not Christian pacifists. We were not pacifists at all! We came from an old left tradition that has always recognized that there was a time and a place for violence in left politics. But in the circumstances of the 1960s, nonviolence made a lot of sense. The politics of nonviolence was an appeal to the American conscience, and it worked – up to a point. It produced the initial successes. The drift toward violence comes in part, as I said, because success is slow and partial, and the vision or the objectives are very big.

Gun control was not a priority of the Black community or Black politics. Most of the Baptist preachers had guns themselves. Many Blacks in the South had guns for self-defense against vigilante mobs, which were often joined by the local police. And I think that even today, many of the Black militants or Black activists are not sympathetic to the gun control movement. They have had a different experience from, say, the high-school kids in Parkland or any of the places where students have been killed. And, of course, you are right: in the 1960s the police response to any form of Black militancy was often brutal – which made nonviolence very difficult to sustain (it required either religious or ideological discipline); carrying guns appeared to

47

be not only brave but realistic. It wasn't, since in any actual encounter the police were sure to win.

The same drift occurred in the anti-war movement, which was nonviolent in the beginning, and yet ended up with both gestural and actual violence – because of impatience, because of escalation in Vietnam, and because of police provocations. So, there was a conflict between the younger and the older political militants and an evolution toward violence. It was justified by quotations from Lenin and later from Mao, and it was the product, again, of youthful impatience. This was even more true in the anti-war movement than in the Civil Rights Movement: the war went on and on, and the American involvement got uglier and uglier.

After My Lai,[16] everyone knew that the war was a moral disaster. And yet it didn't stop. And the young people who joined the Weather people and chose to start making bombs and playing with bombs . . . well, some of them were killed because they really weren't very good at making bombs. What they were doing was not the product of political analysis, it was not the product of a developed ideology, it was rather the consequence of a kind of moral desperation among significant numbers of young people.

Not all of us were desperate, but all of us were really earnest. Here, perhaps, is another difference with France: the political focus on civil rights and war produced a kind of seriousness that we probably thought was a sign of our deep commitment. There was very little wit. In Paris in '68, there was a lot of humor. Not in the US. I don't think there was . . . we were very, very serious people.

Busekist: Did the two movements, the Civil Rights Movement and the anti-war movement come together at one point? Or did the anti-war movement simply take over?

Walzer: Yes, there was a moment when these two movements, the nonviolent Black movement and the nonviolent anti-war movement, did come together, and that was when Martin Luther King Jr. gave his very important speech against the war, "A Time to Break Silence."[17] He briefly came to Cambridge, Massachusetts, to join the local Vietnam Summer project. There were many efforts to mobilize communities against the war. I was the co-chair of the Cambridge Neighborhood Committee on Vietnam. We were knocking on doors and doing SDS style community organizing. We invited King to come to Cambridge and to knock on a door (with cameras recording the event) to help us. He knocked on our door one day, my wife answered, opened the door carrying our one-year-old daughter. So, the two movements came dramatically and very sweetly together. But most of the Baptist preachers did not follow King. Except for him, the movements were mostly distinct.

Busekist: Do you have a picture of Martin Luther King knocking on your door in Cambridge?

Walzer: We took pictures but I don't know where we kept them. I have been collecting material. The Institute for Advanced Studies has built an archive, and I am supposed to leave all my papers there. I have been going through things and I found a lot about EPIC, the Emergency Public Integration Committee, from the 1960s, but not as much as I expected to find from the Cambridge Committee on Vietnam.

Busekist: Activists of all kinds participated in these movements (Jews, Christians, Muslims, Hippies and Yippies, Black Power and Black Panthers, leftist campus organizations, and so on). What do they have in common? Was there any overlap between the *Dissent* crowd and the Hippies or the Yippies for example?[18] Did any of the Dissentniks participate in the Summer of Love?

Walzer: I don't think any of the people involved in the Vietnam Summer were involved in any of the other "summers" . . . We weren't Yippies – and I don't think that we thought of the Yippies as reliable comrades though many of them probably marched in our demonstrations.

Busekist: The events in Chicago and in Paris in 1968 took place approximately at the same time. 1968 has been an important moment for the activists in Chicago. Would you say that all the accumulated frustrations from the Civil Rights and the Anti-War Movement came together in Chicago? Were you in Chicago yourself in 1968?

Walzer: No I wasn't, but Tom Hayden,[19] one of the leaders of SDS was. He had written once for *Dissent*. I have to tell you about community organizing in SDS. Tom Hayden was head of the Newark Community Union Project. This was an SDS, Students for Democratic Society Project in Newark, New Jersey. I was then living in Princeton where Tom would come for rest and recreation. I attended one NCUP meeting.

In an organization like this, it was very important that the leaders be what we called "community people," which meant that Tom Hayden had to sit in the back of the meeting that was supposedly being run by people from the community. The difficulty was that everybody got crooked necks, looking back to get signals from Tom about what to do. I tried to argue with Tom: "If you are leading, you have to sit up front and take responsibility, you cannot sit in the back and pretend you are not leading," but that was the style! We were all convinced of the importance of community people. My co-chair of the Cambridge Neighborhood Committee was a community person, the late Carolyn Carr Grace. She was a film editor but not an academic, which was crucial, and a new mother, which was even better. She later went to law school and became a very strong civil liberties lawyer as a result of the Cambridge Neighborhood Committee experience. But she was originally our community person – and far better at working in the community than I was.

Tom stopped in Cambridge on his way to Chicago to ask for support, he knew two or three of us in Cambridge. We sat with him. He described the planned demonstration and the tactics that, he hoped, would provoke a police response. We said no. We wouldn't join in that effort. Tom Hayden chose one form of anti-war activity. My friends and I chose another.

So, no, I was not in Chicago. But I did travel with Eugene McCarthy. I thought that he was the most promising candidate if we actually wanted to stop the war, not to bring it home but actually to stop it. And then McCarthy was undercut by Robert Kennedy, and Robert Kennedy was assassinated, and we got Richard Nixon. If Kennedy hadn't been assassinated, I think either McCarthy or Kennedy could have won the 1968 election – which Humphrey lost in part because so many people on the farther left did not vote for him – which was crazy.[20]

Busekist: Some facts are noteworthy during that same time. In Chicago in 1968, during the convention, and during the riots, while the Illinois Institute for Technology bought land around the campus at the expense of the poor Black neighborhoods, the Black students from Northwestern wanted to segregate their dorm, which was a new, albeit understandable thing to do at that time. They also requested a specifically Black curriculum, Black staff, and Black professors. The number of Black students at the Universities of Illinois and Chicago at that time was around five percent.

Walzer: The demand for Black studies, for the creation of a department focused on the history, sociology, and politics of American Black communities, was indeed one form of campus activism; the other crucial form was opposition to any academic involvement in military studies or training – as in ROTC (the Reserve Officers Training Corps). We tried to shut down any form of contractual work for the Pentagon. Those were the chief forms of campus politics. And again, there were radical disagreements about each one. Many of us opposed the creation of departments of Black Studies because we thought it would let all the other departments off the hook. The historians, the sociologists, the political scientists, would not have to create specific courses because those courses would be taught in Black Studies – and so Black students would be confined to a ghetto within the university. But the Black militants wanted just that, and they were paradoxically supported by many conservative professors who wanted just that: the creation of an academic ghetto, which would minimize pressure for change in their own departments and disciplines.

Busekist: Interestingly, there were no interracial movements in the Civil Rights Movement. Despite some attempts by the Black students, that has never worked out.

Walzer: No. It didn't work out then, although the Civil Rights Movement in the beginning was an interracial movement or, at least, we thought it was; over the years White liberals and leftists have supported Black empowerment and often voted for Black politicians. But what is called "identity politics" has been more prominent in our political life, with separate movements for Blacks, Hispanics, women, and gay people, and definitely not enough mutual engagement. "Black lives matter," for example, is a very important expression of legitimate Black anger at police behavior, but Hispanics are not treated much better and there is no "Hispanic lives matter," and there is no effort to create a coalition of groups that might work together for the reform of the police. That is a feature of American political life, and it is one of the signs of our weakness.

Busekist: With hindsight, what would you say today about the article you wrote with Irving Howe, "Were we Wrong about Vietnam?"[21] Although the war had "damaged the magazine" because "*Dissent* seemed to care more about somebody flying a Vietcong flag at a mass anti-war demonstration than about what American guns and bombs were actually doing to Vietnam,"[22] you insist that "Vietnam was not the best place to oppose Communism" because the Communists had won the battle for hearts and minds and had become the authentic representatives of Vietnamese nationalism. Vietnam was a colonial war, a civil war, and a cold-war battlefield. Did *Dissent* miss the opportunity to speak to the greater number?

Walzer: We weren't really visible in the larger movement. The visible people were the ones carrying the Vietcong flags in all the big demonstrations. Our politics, opposing the war and also the Vietcong, didn't exactly attract a lot of people. But we all went to the same demonstrations. There was a time when my political life consisted in getting on the bus, going to Washington, getting off the bus, being handed a placard, marching around the Pentagon, getting back on the bus, and going home. But I was writing on the side.

Busekist: What is your hope for political activism today?

Walzer: The cultural revolution that we haven't talked about and that later produced real changes in American life is part of the post-1968 achievements. I think the feminist movement is, for all its incompleteness, the most successful American revolutionary movement of the twentieth century. Furthermore, the Civil Rights Movement produced Black mayors in a number of cities, most of them unhappy cities in economic decline, whose taxes don't give the Black mayors much of an opportunity to do the things they would like to do. There are more Blacks in the professions and in managerial, mostly governmental, positions, but for the Black poor, little has changed. The anti-war movement and the SDS didn't produce any lasting change. They weren't run by organizational men or women – much like Occupy. The Occupy movement of 2011 did not produce any ongoing politics, in part because its leaders refused to play the role of leaders. They insisted that there were no leaders. There was a telling moment in one of the meetings in New York of what the movement activists called the "general assembly." Somebody stood up and said: "We've got to begin to recruit more people." And somebody else jumped up and said: "Recruitment? That's a fascist idea."

With that kind of politics, you don't have much chance of survival and even less of sustaining a movement, so we are not in a good situation right now, but there are signs of hope: the two women's marches, and the march for gun control were impressive events, and there are signs of electoral mobilization in the wake of the Midterms.[23]

Busekist: You just mentioned feminism (a subject which we will get back to): you marched in the women's march as "Grandfather of nasty woman."[24]

Walzer: I did march alongside my granddaughter. Trump had called Hillary a "nasty woman." My granddaughter carried a sign saying "nasty woman," and I carried a sign saying "grandfather of nasty woman." Some photographers took our picture. Yes, the marches were a good sign, but whether the people marching, especially the young people marching, are going to register and vote is still an open question. The 18- to 29-year-old cohort of Americans vote in smaller numbers than any other age cohort. Much smaller numbers. That was one of the problems for Bernie Sanders who got those extraordinary turn-outs in his meetings, but many people never registered, never voted. That has to change and one of the things I have been telling my grandchildren, who are in high school, is that they have to make sure that the seniors in their school, the 18-year-olds, register and vote in November 2018.

Busekist: Is the contemporary challenge for democratic politics in America registration above all?

Walzer: Yes, and especially because of the Republican effort to push down the size of the electorate and to prevent many people, especially poor people, from voting. The Democrats also have to choose attractive candidates; there are a lot of attractive candidates, perhaps too many in some districts where they are competing against one another. The danger is that the losers aren't going to rally their supporters for the winner. This is an old problem on the left and the party has to make some smart choices. There are "red" (strongly Republican) districts that can only be won by a fairly right-wing Democrat; and you have districts where it's important to go with someone who is more like Bernie Sanders.

Busekist: You didn't use the term "participatory democracy" which is usually thought to be part of the New Left's vocabulary in America. Do you still think that it is a valuable ideal that has its place in the American left today?

Walzer: I once wrote an article called "Two cheers for participatory democracy."[25] I am committed to maximizing the engagement of citizens in democratic politics, but participatory democracy can also be the ideology of the activists. My experience in the Cambridge Neighborhood Committee on Vietnam is that some of the student militants who were willing to spend 24 hours a day in political activity just tended to take over, because the people whom we wanted to be participants had families and jobs and children and couldn't devote the same amount of time to politics. So participatory democracy has to be given a structure that permits the participation of people who have other things to do. We were not sufficiently aware of that in the 1960s.

Busekist: What is your opinion on the dividing line between the "identity-politics" left and the "traditional" socialist left? Do you agree with the idea that the former, who cared about immigration, multiculturalism, and sexuality in its various forms, is the left that has lost the working classes?

Walzer: We are all confused about that, whether the major effort of the Democratic party and people on the left within the Democratic party should be to win back the working class, the Reagan Democrats, and the White ethnic workers. We are talking about men mostly because at least some significant number of women will vote Democratic. But we cannot give up the necessary leftist position on immigration, nor on various feminist and gay rights issues. I would not do that. I would attempt a very strong economic appeal to workers in distress, but I would maintain left positions on civil liberty and civil rights. The Clinton strategy was based on the premise that with a strong turnout among Blacks, Hispanics, and Asians, and the professional class, the upper middle class (which is now the social base of the American left) the Democrats can win. That may be right, but it doesn't mean that we shouldn't also present a strong economic program – indeed the left is obligated to do that.

As for the new social base of the Democratic party, consider the fact that Princeton, New Jersey, which is one of the richest towns in the US, voted 8 to 1 for Hillary. By contrast, Johnstown, Pennsylvania, the steel town in Pennsylvania where I grew up and where the mills have long since closed, voted 2 to 1 for Trump. The kind of people who live in Princeton are now, amazingly, strong supporters of the Democrats (though not yet leftists), and if you add the Blacks, the Hispanics, the Asians, and militant women, you get a majority. With these people, if they turn out and vote, you can win an election. But I think it is still very important to make the economic appeal as best we can in places like Johnstown.

Busekist: What would you say about the influence of the intellectuals in the 1960s in America?

Walzer: Any left movement will have an intellectual aspect, there will be ideological debates, there will be quotations from great theorists, but neither civil rights nor anti-war was primarily an intellectual movement.

Busekist: À propos patriotism. It seems that there is a way for the leftists to be genuinely patriotic in America, more so than in the Europe, maybe because of the role the Constitution plays in the American national imaginary. Isn't it possible to argue that equality is American and inequality is un-American, and being in favor of immigration in a country made of immigrants would be a typically American stance?

Walzer: I think you are right. During the Popular Front of the 1930s, the Communist Party did focus on that theme. Between the 1930s and the Hitler/Stalin pact, Communism was a very patriotic, even a fiercely patriotic movement. I remember Paul Robeson singing *The Ballad for Americans* – it is a wonderful cantata, all about themes from American history. Culturally, the Popular Front was a success and very smart, although some of the Communists were quite cynical about it. The phrase "useful idiots" comes from that time: people joining the front organizations without knowing who was running them. Politically, the impact of the CP was short lived (as the Wallace campaign in 1948 demonstrated), but culturally, it had an impact. We did not produce anything like that in 1968. There were the beginnings of many social and cultural changes – in sexual mores and pop music, for example, but not in political culture.

Busekist: Did the American intellectuals, the anti-war activists among the Dissentniks, comment on the Algerian war? I know that you are very familiar with that war, you wrote about it, and you wrote about the position of some French intellectuals, Sartre, Camus, Beauvoir in *The Company of Critics*.[26]

Walzer: The American left was obviously sympathetic to the FLN. The *Dissent* people were not. Mainly because of the terrorist attacks but also because there was another movement called the Algerian National Movement (MNA in French), lead by Messali Hadj – I think he came out of one of the Trotskyite sects; the *Dissent* people knew him, and he wrote once or twice for the magazine.[27] Hadj opposed

FLN terrorism. The MNA was strongest among Algerian workers in France, less strong in Algeria itself. *Dissent* was sympathetic to Algerian independence but critical of the FLN.[28] In Algeria, the FLN murdered every member of the MNA that they could find, which I guess explains *Dissent*'s position. We defended a similar position during the anti-Vietnam movement later on.

All of this was a part of my political education . . . It was easy for me to sympathize with Camus against Sartre and to condemn, as I did in *Just and Unjust Wars*, what Sartre wrote in his introduction to Fanon's essay.[29] There were certainly leftists in the US who supported the FLN and apologized in one or another way for the bombs in the cafés and all the rest, but we didn't. We had a different position, which meant that we weren't close to the people at *Les Temps Modernes*. And there was no anti-war movement among students in France, at least nothing we knew of, so there were no people we were in touch with, except for the last MNAers . . .

Busekist: You sympathized with Camus, not only for theoretical reasons, not only because he was committed to social critique but because you believed he had something to say about friendship and loyalty. You ask an interesting question about Camus: how come Camus never came up with a two-state solution? That wasn't really on the agenda, despite some minor proposals at the time. Isn't this a very Israeli kind of thinking?

Walzer: (*laughs*) Yes. Yes, there was never a proposal for partition, and I guess the populations were too mixed for anything like that to . . .

Busekist: They were territorially mixed, yes. The return of more than a million people to France in the early 1960s was a terrible challenge for the French state, and a terrible loss for most of the Jews in particular who had lived in Algeria for centuries. Some had Arabic as their mother tongue.

Walzer: Right. Yes, I was sympathetic even or especially to Camus' statement about his mother.[30]

Busekist: Which is probably apocryphal, we don't know whether he really said that . . . but if he did, it says something about Camus' personality and the way he thought about priorities and justice.

Walzer: It introduced a kind of humanity into the left discourse which sometimes is too rigidly correct. The "correct" ideological position is something to which I have never been sympathetic.

3

Dissent

Busekist: In the early 1950s, not that long after the Second World War, the Republicans controlled the House and the Senate, and McCarthy was hunting Communists. By then, the members of the Communist Party had dwindled, the Socialist League was in bad shape, and the anti-Stalinist left was ill organized. What are the reasons that may have led two young intellectuals, Irving Howe and Lewis Coser, who wanted to "reassert the libertarian values of the socialist ideal,"[1] to start a magazine – instead of going into politics?

Walzer: I have to travel back a few years in order to answer your questions. Irving Howe, who was my mentor at Brandeis, invited me to write for *Dissent* (no one was paid). I don't remember how I got so close to him. He invited me to a party at his house that celebrated the first issue of *Dissent Magazine*, the Winter issue 1954. I was a Popular Front leftist, and I was immediately converted to anti-Stalinism. Irving Howe founded *Dissent* with Lewis Coser, who also taught at Brandeis. I took a seminar on Marxism with Coser, studied literature with Howe, and I was very taken with their views, with Irving's especially. I think that I've already told you that I went home at the end of my second year and told my parents that when I grew up, I wanted to be an intellectual. I meant, a left intellectual. At Brandeis, the 1960s began in the 1950s. We had our political organizations, one of them anticipating SDS; we were active in supporting the Supreme Court decision that desegregated schools.[2] *Dissent Magazine* was founded in 1954, and a few of us, students of Howe and Coser, very quickly became "Dissentniks": fiercely anti-Stalinist leftists. That politics, which is still my own, made for problems when Vietnam came.

58

But I have to take another step back. Just after Judy and I got married in June 1956, and before leaving for England in September, I spent the summer doing research for Howe and Coser for their history of the American Communist Party. On their behalf, I read every issue of *The Daily Worker*[3] from sometime in the 1920s through the Popular Front period and into the 1940s. I read every issue, taking notes, including on the comic strips, and it was that summer that I wrote my first piece for *Dissent*. It was the summer of the Khrushchev speech,[4] which led to a great crisis in the American CP, and which I followed closely because I was reading *The Daily Worker*. So, I wrote about what happened in the American Communist Party: the beginning of its disintegration.

Once in England, we read the novels of the "Angry Young Men,"[5] and we went to one of the first of their plays, *Look Back in Anger*.[6] . . . I wrote a piece in *Dissent* about the group and also a piece for an English literary magazine about John Wain.[7] I was doing an imitation of Irving Howe. I wanted to be not only a political but also a literary intellectual . . . But I didn't really have the talent for that, though I did write one last piece of literary criticism, a *Dissent* article on Salinger,[8] which is actually pretty good. I wrote for *Dissent* during my graduate studies, and I think the *Dissent* connection and the New Left Club made graduate school bearable. I felt that I was living with one foot outside of the academic world. And then in February 1960, Irving called me on the phone and said: "something important is happening in North Carolina, I want you to go down there." I was writing my dissertation, I was not going to classes and I was able to just pick up and go.

Busekist: How would you describe the founding fathers? And the intellectual climate in America at that time?

Walzer: Irving and Lew were young when they founded *Dissent*, but they had been politically engaged for a long time, starting in their teens. They were tired of the left sects, and they were looking for a larger audience and a more American engagement – remember that leftist New York in the 1930s and 1940s was something like a suburb of Moscow. The Cold War was an opportunity to stake out a new political position. Hence the double dissent that the magazine represented: first, from the Stalinist left, which was still a political and intellectual presence though, as you say, the CP had dwindled (the Khrushchev speech was still to come); and, second, from a weak and complacent liberalism. Irving called the 1950s "an age of conformity," and that was an accurate description (except for Brandeis University, where we were already in the next age of activism). McCarthyism was frightening, and many liberals chose not to be frightened but rather to seek some sort of safety in an anti-Communism that Irving and Lew thought surrendered too much of the old left's vision. They were looking for a practical left politics that held on to the idea of a radical egalitarianism.[9]

Busekist: *Dissent* was founded by a group of European Jews: Irving Howe (born Irving Horenstein), Lewis Coser (born Ludwig Cohen) most prominently, but with the help of Stanley Plastrik, Manny Geltman, Bernie Rosenberg, and others. You yourself joined the Dissentniks shortly after the founding period, in the late 1950s. Is (was) *Dissent* a Jewish magazine? One may say that the identity of the founders is either anecdotal or on the contrary a central element of the magazine's editorial line. If the latter is true, how would you describe the particular Jewish outlook on politics and society?

Walzer: There were a good number of secularizing Jews who simply gave up one orthodoxy and grabbed on to another – looking for salvation in the Communist Party and becoming as certain in their ideological correctness, as dogmatic, as the rabbis they left behind. I don't think of them as being fully emancipated. The men and women who founded *Dissent* were genuinely emancipated – not only from religion but also from all the varieties of Marxist orthodoxy. In what sense were they still Jewish? I would say, in their style; above all, in the way they argued, and in their ability to sustain a skeptical utopianism. Irving loved the old joke about the man hired to sit outside the shtetl to watch for the messiah, so as to give the Jews in the village some advance warning of his coming. "What kind of a job is that?" he was asked. "Well," he said, "it doesn't pay very well, but it's steady work" (*laughs*). That's Jewish irony, and it suffused and sustained *Dissent* for many years, when most of the editors and writers were Jews who welcomed the irony.

But emancipation also had its limits. The crisis and then the war of 1967 was an emotional shock to many of the *Dissent* Jews. Their internationalism had also been anti-nationalist (as mine isn't) and therefore anti-Zionist. But they suddenly realized that they didn't want to see the end of the Zionist experiment – and to their great surprise they also discovered that this "not wanting" was a passionate commitment.[10] Yes, *Dissent* was shaped by Jewish irony and Jewish commitment, and both of these are, these days, in short

60

supply. *Dissent* in the future will be a magazine more like other left magazines.

Busekist: Their attitude is not surprising, Raymond Aron for example, probably the most assimilated Jew among the French intellectuals, had a similar reaction in 1967. How did the board work? Who decided on what? Which articles to publish? When and how to respond to unhappy authors, when to publish a response, etc.?

Walzer: In the early days, every article was sent around through the US mail with a sheet of paper attached on which we each wrote comments, before sending it on to the next editor. Irving would then read all the comments and make the final decision. Later on, with a larger editorial board, he would consult only with some of us. He also dealt with unhappy authors, rejected or severely edited – and was surprisingly diplomatic. But he was such a fine editor that most writers were happy to call the rewritten text their own. I learned how to edit an article from him, though I was never as quick or as good.

Busekist: I found only one nasty letter from you; usually you are rather ironical. You wrote back to Norman Mailer because he wanted to get one of his friends published by *Dissent*; he doubted that you would publish the "White Negro" piece again, and you wrote back simply saying: "try us"!

Walzer: Where did you find that?

Busekist: I can't remember. I did some digging.[11] In the 1950s, speaking about Mailer, *Dissent* published "The White Negro,"[12] which was a great success.

Walzer: That was a big success, and it sold a lot of copies. There were people on the left who condemned Irving [Howe] for publishing it. Because it was somehow not politically correct, I don't remember in what way. He also published Hannah Arendt's essay against school integration.[13] He knew Arendt. He may have worked for her at Shocken. But this piece had been rejected by *Commentary*. So, on free speech grounds, we published it with a paragraph at the top and a response following.

Busekist: Yes, Arendt writes, in the very first paragraph, that she didn't change a line and that she wants the piece to be published as such. It is quite a surprising text; did you agree with the content – the difference between private and public segregation in particular?

Walzer: She was wrong about the public schools. The idea of a category between the private and the political is a good idea. We were thinking about questions of state coercion in the social sphere, but her definition of the "social" is too broad. It shouldn't allow "voluntary" school segregation. Nor should it allow storekeepers on a public street to refuse to serve gay men or women – as in a recent Supreme Court case. Arendt's argument has been revived (though without giving her credit) on the far right.

Busekist: In this contested piece, "Reflections on Little Rock," she claims that marriage laws (authorizing interracial marriages) are far more meaningful than desegregation of schools to achieve political equality: "our political battles [should not be fought] in school yards," and we should not ask our children "to be heroes" she writes. Arendt had carefully distinguished social and political antisemitism in the *Origins of Totalitarianism*, but in this article she writes that "the government should take no steps against social discrimination because government can only act in the name of equality – a principle that does not belong in the social sphere." In her view, "the state has the unchallengeable right to prescribe minimum requirements for future citizenship and beyond to further and support the teaching of subjects and professions which are felt to be desirable and necessary to the nation as a whole. All this involves, however, only the content of the child's education, not the context of association and social life. . . ." Arendt ends on a distinction between the private sphere (exclusiveness), the social sphere (likeness), and the political sphere (equality). In short, schools are social institutions, not political ones. I thought the piece could be read very much as something that Leo Strauss would have said about the cure that can be worse than the disease. When you try to fix "private" discrimination, you destroy the liberal state.[14]

Walzer: But the public schools are not private or "social"; they are the prime place where we train citizens, the people who are going to vote in our elections. Arendt thought that family control over the education of children and over their school friends – the other children that their kids meet in school – was an issue that the state should not interfere with. But children do not belong exclusively to their parents, not if they are going to become politically responsible men and women in a multi-racial and multi-ethnic society. By contrast, there was and is no state enforced desegregation in private and parochial schools. You can segregate private schools if you take no public money, though public money does leak into private schools (to help disabled students, for example) in ways that I am not against. But it is certainly right for the state to require that certain courses, on US history and politics, be taught, and with more than a wink and a nod, in private secular and religious schools.

There's an interesting distinction that can be made between schools and nursing homes. Judy's mother ended her life in a Jewish nursing home. Her daughters tried to keep her at home but couldn't. So we got to know this Jewish nursing home, which I was surprised to learn was funded, about 60 percent, by tax money. I think that was all right, but I would be against tax funded vouchers that could be used in, say, religious schools because I don't want the state involved in the religious formation of children. But old people are already fully formed, and the state should accommodate their religious preferences. So, I have no objection to public funding of Catholic, Protestant, or Jewish nursing homes. But still, I would make a distinction within what Arendt called the social category. I am sure the country club in Johnstown is now integrated. They first accepted very rich Jews, and then they just opened it to everyone, but I would not have favored state coercion for something like that.

Busekist: That is exactly the way she argued: clubs, associations, or country clubs should be allowed to admit selectively, and the state should not interfere. She compared herself – and the Jews in general – with the Blacks, many readers thought that this was not a pertinent comparison; and she said that some things are much more important than having kids fight the battles of the parents. But the state has a duty to form citizens, right? That's what public schools stand for and that, in principle at least, leads to the recognition of diversity and pluralism. This is not about the religious formation of kids, but about tolerance and educating future citizens.

Walzer: Well, yes, there is an argument that putting kids on the line the way we did in those years was wrong. The right place to fight was in housing and issues that involved grown-ups, not children. And yes, I share your thoughts. The state has a duty to form citizens. So, a Jewish parochial school can be required to teach citizenship, the history of democracy, the history of America. And if the students are encouraged not to take secular courses seriously, you can insist on exams.

Busekist: And we should, because if the schools are publicly funded, they should deliver a curriculum that enables equality of opportunities.

Walzer: But also, again, even in privately funded schools, if the kids are going to vote in our elections, we can insist that they be taught what they need to know to vote intelligently.

Busekist: Let's move on to the 1960s. Within *Dissent*, you were the "closest to the campus mood" in the 1960s.[15] The Cambridge Neighborhood Committee and your experience as an anti-war activist in a Northern university town contributes to understanding the social stratification in the mobilization against Vietnam. Maybe you can comment on the outcome of the referendum vote in Cambridge. One of your fellow students at Harvard studied the referendum and analyzed the composition of the 40 percent of the population who voted against the war. By 1968, around Nixon's election, 50 percent of the Americans were against the war, but 35 percent were still supporting it, according to the polls.

Walzer: In France workers and students came together on domestic issues. That did not happen in America because of the war. The Cambridge Neighborhood Committee organized a referendum on the war in the city of Cambridge. Cambridge was supposed to declare itself against the war, the entire city of Cambridge was to sponsor and join in a day of opposition. We got 40 percent of the vote for our referendum proposal. As you said, a graduate student in sociology did a study of the vote in Cambridge. His conclusions were rather hard for some us lefties to accept: the higher the rent you paid, the greater the value of your home, the more likely you were to vote against the war. We lost every working-class neighborhood in the city of Cambridge. We carried Harvard Square and its surroundings. It was clear what was going on. The students doing the canvassing and knocking on doors were exempt from the draft because they were students. They were knocking on the doors of people whose kids were in Vietnam. The class difference was striking; this was the beginning of the alienation of significant numbers of White workers from the left and from the Democratic party. It was a first indication of our failure to convince what was supposed to be our own constituency, to reach them with the right arguments. We were accused of anti-patriotism because we were not supporting the troops. This accusation became a feature of Republican politics – to attack the weakness, the lack of patriotism on the left. It was a theme again in the Trump campaign, but it started back then. To those of us who had been raised on the ideology of class struggle, it was a surprise.

Busekist: Is this because the anti-war movements accepted help from where it came from, and *Dissent* was in an uncomfortable position and internally torn? Among your supporters many didn't want to make enemies on the left, and you ended up making enemies on the left and on the right. You were opposed to intervention and opposed to a Communist victory; but you had "no happy end to offer." This in-between position in the middle of the Cold War was difficult to explain, and your "argument was too complex to be heard"[16] at the time, so you wrote.

Walzer: There were many conflicts inside the anti-war movement. The conflict between the people who wanted to do electoral politics – some of us joined the Eugene McCarthy campaign in 1967–1968 – and the people who wanted to organize draft resistance. There was also a difference between those who wanted to carry Vietcong flags in all the demonstrations, and those of us who were convinced that we shouldn't be doing that. The position of the Dissentniks was very difficult in this period. Less for me than for the older editors who came out of the Trotskyist movement and who knew the names, literally, of every one of the Vietnamese Trotskyists who had been murdered by the Communists. That made it very hard for them to call for an immediate and unilateral American withdrawal.

Busekist: When did they finally do so? After the Tet offensive?[17]

Walzer: Yes, not my friends, who were calling for withdrawal earlier, but some of the others. We tried very hard to sustain a position that eventually became the *Dissent* position. The war had become a greater crime than the Communists were likely to commit in power. We had to oppose the American participation in the war without supporting the Vietcong. It required some subtle explanations. Yes. And there were other subtleties required. I was running around the country in 1967, giving speeches against the Vietnam War, when, all of the sudden, I was also giving speeches in defense of the Israeli attack on Egypt. Some people thought that was inconsistent. I had to explain that wars can be just and unjust. Being anti-war, being anti-*this* war, the Vietnam War, did not require us to oppose every war. That was the beginning of what became my book *Just and Unjust*

Wars. The original unjust war was the American war in Vietnam and the original just war was Israel in Egypt. The rest of the book is an effort to figure out how you can make distinctions of that kind, just and unjust. But on the left, in 1967 and 1968 those were difficult distinctions to make persuasively.

Busekist: What is left of your fellow New York intellectuals of the 1950s and 1960s? Who are your comrades today?

Walzer: Howe and Coser were my mentors, and I still hang out, so to speak, with a few people, left intellectuals, who sustain that kind of politics: Paul Berman, Mark Levinson, Maxine Phillips, Susie Linfield, Mitchell Cohen, Michael Kazin, Jo Ann Mort, Joanne Barkan, and a few others. There is a new generation of New York leftists, without our memories, with whom I talk, sometimes, looking for continuity. But they will make their own way.

Busekist: How different is today's *Dissent* from the *Dissent* of the 1950s and 1960s? Most members are liberals, socialist liberals, or social democrats in the European sense. What led to this evolution? One commentator has argued that "*Dissent*'s goal was not to transcend Marxism or liberalism, but to draw on both traditions while challenging them to live up to their core ideals."[18]

Walzer: The magazine has changed over time – in ways that I may be a little too close to recognize fully. A certain kind of Marxist theorizing was important early on but has pretty much disappeared from our pages. Our commitment to what Michael Harrington called "the left wing of the possible" has produced a closer engagement with American politics – from a standpoint that is probably best called social democratic. But many of our editors would still call themselves democratic socialists, and that name has come back in the last two years because of the Bernie Sanders campaign. It suggests a more radical, more transformative politics, at least in aspiration. We have been pretty consistent in our commitment to cover the labor movement, to mourn its decline and to hope for its renewal. We are also consistently internationalist: we write regularly about politics abroad. While I was co-editor, I insisted on a steady routine of "arguments," where we disagreed among ourselves, especially on foreign policy, sometimes in a tough polemical way. I think that our younger editors don't like that kind of writing; I still do. The consistency that I am most proud of is simply this: we remain strongly critical of every sort of authoritarian politics even when the authoritarian leaders call themselves leftists, as they regularly do in Latin America.

Busekist: Feminism, as well as female board members, came quite late – later than in other publications, maybe even later than in academia?

Walzer: Yes, you are right. The first editors were insensitive to "the woman question" or, maybe, they thought that socialism would automatically, as it were, produce gender equality and no separate struggle was necessary. After Irving's death, when Mitchell Cohen and I became the actual editors, the first thing we did was to bring many more women into the magazine's pages. But we were late, and I am not sure that we ever articulated a feminism of our own – which would have been a good thing to do given some of the academic versions of feminist theory.

Busekist: This poses the question of *Dissent*'s "radicalism." How radical was or is *Dissent*? We have mentioned the relationship between SDS and *Dissent* earlier, when we talked about 1968. *Dissent* was far less "radical" than SDS and was rather reluctant to encourage any revolutionary movement to hasten social change. How do you explain that? Would you say that the generational shift between the founders and the newcomers is one of the reasons? The founders knew the dangers of authoritarianism, sectarianism, and Stalinism of course. They were born before the Second World War. Did they think that the New Left was authoritarian in its own way? That the Third-Worldism of the New Left was renouncing some important principles?[19] Also, when did the real generational change occur? Was it in the 1980s? When intellectuals had become full-time academics, and very different militants (or not militant at all), devoting their time to academia rather than being public intellectuals? According to *Dissent*'s biographer, Isserman, they didn't "master the prose" of political publishing anymore. On the other hand, however, the New Leftists from the 1960s had settled down and came (back) to *Dissent*.

Walzer: The confrontation with SDS and the young radicals of the 1960s was certainly a story of two generations, one whose members had been tested in the Stalinist wars (or, like me, had gone to school with the veterans), and another whose members had no memory of those wars and who proved to be susceptible, as we weren't, to Third World versions of authoritarian politics. Many of that second group came back to us once they were veterans themselves, tired of their own sects and recognizing that they had chosen the wrong comrades abroad. But some version of this disagreement will arise, does arise, with each new generation. The incorporation of old and new leftists into the American academy did change *Dissent* in many small ways. The articles the new professors wrote took a lot more editing, and many of them, anxious about tenure, were less ready to write, or wrote less often for a magazine like *Dissent*. And then they produced a kind of academic radicalism, postmodern and esoteric, fiercely leftist but incomprehensible to any left constituency outside the academy. I don't think that we did enough to criticize that "new style in leftism," but I guess it hasn't had any significant impact on American politics.

Busekist: You have always been a critic of American politics, we have already talked about this. After 9/11, from "Can There Be a Decent Left?" (2002) to *A Foreign Policy for the Left* in 2014 (and the book that followed in 2018), you have been targeting the left continuously. When and why did your worry turn into anger? Because of the new moral authoritarianism of the left? Its anti-Americanism? A certain hypocrisy?

Walzer: Some of our young people have criticized me (and others of my generation) for trying to "police" the left. I mean only to be a "sometime" critic. The left has its own pathologies and we need to talk about them. I am against denial and evasion. And, yes, I am angry sometimes, not only at the moral (and political) authoritarianism of some parts of the left but also at a kind of root and branch anti-Americanism and at a hostility to Israel that often brings with it all the old antisemitic tropes.[20]

Busekist: In its long history, *Dissent* has lived through interesting and stimulating episodes, and some difficult ones. Would you say that *Dissent* has had its "heroic" era and has entered an age of maturity today?

Walzer: Of course, the first years were the golden age, when the magazine worked out a new version of leftism. But all golden ages are mythical even when the name is partly true. I would opt for the 1960s as the heroic time, when we got some things wrong, but kept our heads when so many around us were losing theirs. Later on, in my years as co-editor, we worked hard just to keep going; we thought that it was our job to sustain the tradition of an independent, anti-authoritarian left – until the next period of insurgency. I suspect that there was a kind of doggedness to the magazine during that time, maybe a tired doggedness of the old Dissentniks. But we did recruit a new generation, different from us, who will inherit the magazine.

Busekist: *Dissent* is not only a militant magazine, it is also an "academic" publication by virtue of its content and its contributors. You once said that it is enough to add twenty-five footnotes to a *Dissent* piece to turn it into an academic article. Do you still believe that?

Walzer: *(laughs)* That's a true story about some of my pieces. It's also true, though, that there are articles of mine that were written for an academic audience first.

Busekist: Do you think of *Dissent* as a central or as a parallel activity in your life and career? That *Dissent* has shaped the way you think academically – and how so? In short is writing for *Dissent* and writing for academic journals two professions or vocations or the same kind of work?

Walzer: I don't think that for me political and academic work move along parallel lines; they connect or interact at many points. First of all, *Dissent* forced me to think about and write about current issues, and I then went on to write about some of those issues in a more academic way. For example, the first piece, the foundational piece for *Spheres of Justice* is "In Defense of Equality," published in *Dissent*[21] – a polemical piece that I wouldn't have thought of submitting to an academic journal – without a lot of footnotes and some linguistic repression. I think for me, writing in *Dissent* and writing, say, *Spheres of Justice* were part of one and the same overall enterprise.

Busekist: In other words, you are not only an academic, and you couldn't have been only an academic.

Walzer: No, but I can imagine myself as the editor of the Party's theoretical magazine in a country with a strong Social Democratic party *(laughs)*. My graduate student years were saved by *Dissent*. I succeeded in writing academic papers that got good grades, but I was unhappy in graduate school and very happy with *Dissent*. It was a saving grace to be able to think to myself that "I am politically engaged."

4

Thinking About War

Busekist: *Just and Unjust Wars* (*JUW*) has become a classic, an essential companion for those who work on war. It is at once a history book – you analyze a great number of conflicts in many countries over a long period of time – and a work in moral and political philosophy as you deploy, recalling its origins, the paradigm of just war. Although the term may seem paradoxical, you reflect on the "morality of war," the moral responsibility of states, armies, and combatants. You restate the classical rules of warfare (not to kill civilians, to treat combatants as equals), but you are also interested in situations where the entanglement of violence – ethnic, civil, political – calls for complex decisions. You defend strong theses on the (moral and legal) status of civilians; on the rights and wrongs of humanitarian intervention; on the (il) legitimacy of forced regime change; on the norms of entering war (*jus and bellum*), on the code of conduct during the war (*jus in bello*), and best political practices after the war (*jus post bellum*). But let's start with the beginning. *JUW* becoming such an incredible classic and bestseller came as a surprise to you, right?

Walzer: A complete surprise. Well I had no idea ... The surprise began a couple of months after its publication, when the publishers got a letter from West Point.[1] They wanted to adopt the book; they asked whether Basic Books could provide paperbacks very quickly. Which they did.

Busekist: To be taught as a textbook at West Point?

Walzer: They made it required reading for second-year cadets. This was a total surprise. The surprise continued when I was invited to

70

come and meet the officers who were going to teach the class. The courses were taught in sections of about fifteen to twenty cadets, so there were many young officers teaching. I was invited to come and meet them. The officers who had decided to use the book as a textbook were all veterans of the Vietnam War. You generally come to West Point – if you are not one of the people who are going to join the faculty – as a second or third tour of duty for about three years. These were all people who had been in Vietnam and had obviously been shaken by the war; some of them agreed with what I said about the war, and some of them didn't, but they all thought the cadets should read the book.

While I was talking to them, I realized that the officers of a professional army – I think this may be true in Israel too – are very different from what lefties think they are like. In fact, they are often hostile toward the right-wing politicians who order them into wars that they think shouldn't be fought. This was a great revelation. I have continued talking to them. I have been back to West Point many times. Sometimes just to meet with the officers teaching the course, sometimes to give a lecture to the cadets, sometimes to visit a class, or a couple of classes. It is like and not like a university: when I walk into a class, there is always a student in the front row who jumps up, and says "All present and accounted for, Sir!"

The cadets are more of a political mix. The officers . . . well when I visit West Point, I leave from New York. They send a car, and the car has a driver and an officer who sits with me in the back. And one time, while driving up – this must have been just after the first Iraq war – we got to talking; the officer asked me about the magazines I write for. And then he told me that he had just canceled his subscription to the *New Republic* because it supported the war. This was a professional officer, a lieutenant or captain in the US army.

Busekist: Did your interaction with the officers and cadets from West Point have any bearing on the many different prefaces or postscripts that you wrote for *Just and Unjust Wars* over the years?

Walzer: Well, it influenced the way I thought about the American army, and it gave me additional reasons to try to get the arguments right. There were men and women on whom the arguments might have an impact – not only on their judgments but on their actions.

Busekist: You elaborated what you have called a "legalist paradigm," that can be very generally defined as referring to the norms and rights (a "code of conduct" elaborated in the course of history) that govern the interaction between states in the international society.[2] Allow me to briefly summarize: you present the paradigm in chapter 4 of *JUW* with a domestic analogy: states have rights and duties the same way individuals have rights and duties in the domestic society. Territorial integrity and political sovereignty are such rights, and an act of aggression threatens not only to destroy the international system, but also the rights of states (derived from the rights of individuals). Therefore, only acts of aggression justify war. In chapters 5 and 6 you qualify and revise the legalist paradigm. You do not strictly speaking carve out exceptions, but you relax the legalist paradigm in specific contextual situations: "States may use military force in the face of threats of war, whenever the failure to do so would seriously risk their territorial integrity or political independence. Under such circumstances it can fairly be said that they have been forced to fight and that they are the victims of aggression" (ch. 5);[3] "States can be invaded and wars justly begun [. . .] to rescue peoples threatened with massacre" (ch. 6).[4]

Some of your readers have criticized your successive reevaluations, others find them useful and morally justified, your conceptualization of *ius ad vim*[5] in particular (the use of force short of war). This is an important precision because it limits belligerent velleities and allows to put policies in place where war is not the "continuation of politics by other means" as Clausewitz famously said.

In hindsight do you believe we should change the laws of warfare as they exist today or should we stick to the legalist paradigm but relax it empirically, contextually when needed, as you suggest in *JUW*?

Walzer: Well, I think the basic rules of a society of states, the basic conception of states at war, of state sovereignty, the idea of borders and aggression as I defined it, yes, that still works . . . A special problem, not new but more frequently encountered these days is how to deal with nonstate actors. This is something I tried to write about already in the chapter on guerrilla warfare.[6] It requires a decision on when to treat a nonstate actor as if it were a state. That had already been discussed in nineteenth-century legal texts, but in the age of the Taliban, of ISIS, of Hamas, and Hezbollah, we need to focus again on this question. But mostly I think (defensively, perhaps) that you can deal with all the new questions with the old theory – and that also applies to *jus in bello*, although asymmetrical warfare makes the questions harder . . . but I would still not be inclined to modify the rules. We should talk separately about asymmetric warfare.

The hard fact about asymmetric wars is that even when they are the good guys, which they aren't always, the high-tech army – the US or the Israeli army are the chief examples – doesn't win. Despite all their technology, despite "smart bombs" and drones, and everything else, they don't win. They do most of the killing, and they don't win in part because they do most of the killing. Because these wars are political as well as military events. But, yes, to answer your question, in the prefaces to the book, and in lectures that I've given over the years, I have tried to the hold on to the basic structure of the argument.

Busekist: But you have relaxed some of the rules . . . not the basic structure, and certainly not the analytical difference between *jus ad bellum* and *jus in bello*, but you have amended bits and pieces of your theory against the background of terrorism and asymmetric warfare. My questions pertain to humanitarian interventions, civilians, and noncombatant immunity. Let's start with the civilians. You replied, with Avishai Margalit,[7] to an article published by Asa Kasher and Amos Yadlin[8] in which they claim, crudely put, that in asymmetric warfare, the safety of "our" soldiers takes precedence over the safety of "their" civilians. For you and Margalit, however, soldiers are soldiers, and civilians remain civilians, from whatever side. They need to be protected as if they were our own civilians (or our hostages in your example), and we should rescue every civilian or hostage in every circumstance and treat every civilian wherever he or she comes from the same way we would treat our own hostages.[9] You also contest that "a combatant is a citizen in uniform," and you add: "as a soldier, you are asked to take an extra risk for the sake of limiting the scope of the war."[10] This corresponds to your idea that we should not individualize soldiers. War is a "collective enterprise" where soldiers are members (of states and armies), rather than individuals. They carry no individual responsibility, even if they fight in unjust wars. Soldiers are not supposed to judge the decisions of their leaders, but once engaged – *in bello* – they have to respect the legal and ethical code soldiers versus civilians. However, individual responsibility may be sometimes questioned after the facts, and soldiers have been indicted, as in the Dutch collaborators example.[11]

Walzer: Yes! The army is a collective, but soldiers in the field are not only members but also individuals who are judged by the way they fight, the support they give to comrades, the risks they take to avoid harm to civilians. The crime of the Dutch collaborators was political, not military, but, yes, they were judged as individuals.

Busekist: This is what you wrote in "War Fair": The crucial argument is about the Palestinian use of civilians as shields. Academic philosophers have written at great length about "innocent shields," since these radically exploited (but sometimes, perhaps, compliant) men and women pose a dilemma that tests the philosophers' dialectical skills. Israeli soldiers are not required to have dialectical skills, but, on the one hand, they are expected to do everything they can to prevent civilian deaths, and, on the other hand, they are expected to fight against an enemy that hides behind civilians. So (to quote a famous line from Trotsky), they may not be interested in the dialectic, but the dialectic is interested in them."[12] In the current situation of ongoing war-like unrest between Israel and the Hamas, what should the state do when there is a border storming by civilians who are probably something like semi-combatants? How should the IDF react?

Walzer: Let's begin by looking back. I started in *Just and Unjust Wars* with the siege of Jerusalem and the Peloponnesian wars. But the Second World War is the war I was most often thinking about and using in my examples. So, in the Second World War, allied bombing policy was roughly as follows: in Germany, the Brits flew by night and bombed cities, actually aiming at residential neighborhoods (insofar as they could aim). The Americans flew by day, sometimes at lower altitudes, and tried to hit factories. Much to their credit, I think. But both Americans and Brits were more careful about civilian casualties when they were bombing targets in occupied France. And you can understand why.

There is the famous example of a Norwegian heavy water factory which was located in a town.[13] There was a debate in London about whether to bomb it, and the British decided, in cooperation with, under pressure perhaps, from the Norwegian government in exile, to send commandos in order to avoid civilian casualties. The first commando raid failed with heavy losses to the commando unit, and then they tried a second time and succeeded. But when the Germans rebuilt the factory, they did bomb it and killed some civilians living nearby. But obviously there was a special concern for what they thought of as allied rather than enemy civilians. The Germans were enemy civilians, and the allies were willing to take greater risks for the sake of Norwegian and French civilians. I can understand that, but I think that in principle we have to insist that innocent people are innocent people, and that they should all be treated in the same way as we would treat our own people. I think that's a principle we should assert: soldiers should take risks to minimize the risks they impose on civilians, any civilians. We should try to imagine the appropriate level of risk for all cases. And then, maybe, we can allow soldiers to accept additional risk to avoid injuring their own civilians, a kind of superogatory risk-taking. But equality has to be the general rule.

Busekist: Is this the principle of due care?

Walzer: No, it's beyond due care. Due care is what you should always do.[14] This would be beyond due care – "supererogatory" is the philosophical word. I can understand why soldiers would accept greater risks to prevent harm for their own civilians, but the standards should be the same for everybody. I still believe that. Avishai [Margalit] insisted on that part of the argument, although most of his and my philosopher friends disagreed, but I think that's the right argument. So, the crucial question in asymmetrical warfare is the question of what risk we ask our soldiers to take in order to minimize the risk they impose on civilians who are being used, but who may also be cooperating with the people who are using them. We must minimize the risk we impose on those people – whether they are used willingly or not.[15] Obviously, we can't know whether these particular men and women are or aren't sympathetic, to the people who are using them.

Busekist: Is this a practical norm or a moral norm? I agree with you that we should do whatever we can do, especially regarding interventions against massacre. But whether we should act at all costs for our own soldiers is another question. That was the critique. You would probably agree that there is a difference, to take up a Peter Singer's hypothetical,[16] between saving your own child rather than the child of a stranger. We would all save our own child first, and I believe that is morally defensible. Is there an analogy to be made between the child – our child – and the soldier – our soldier? There is a lot of contextual and empirical reasoning in your work. The norm is clear, but one may depart from the norm, in case, for instance, of supreme emergency?[17] Your evaluation of supreme emergency seems to be an empirical reasoning, whereas the soldier/civilian distinction is a normative argument.

Walzer: I definitely believe that you and I have a right to save our own child first, but we don't have a right to stop there. Maybe it's also possible to save the other child. Similarly, if two groups of civilians, one our own, one foreign, were at risk, we would have a right to turn first to our own, accepting whatever risks were necessary to protect them.

But priority isn't exclusion; the second group of civilians do indeed come second, but when their time comes, we should act in the same way to protect them. The doctrine of supreme emergency is perhaps the most contested part of the book, especially for the Kantian philosophers. I call it an example of utilitarianism in extremity, so, yes, it requires empirical argument to define and describe the extremity. But it is a moral argument nonetheless – about values that have to be defended even at the expense of other values.

Busekist: In an interesting piece about "Moral Absolutes," Jeremy Waldron discusses "threshold deontology," the threshold in fact comprised in your doctrine of supreme emergency, by which he means "treating certain moral rules – such as rules about torture – as a near-absolutes, but indicating a willingness to abandon it when the consequences piling up on the other side pass a certain threshold." He is critical of the ticking bomb hypothetical (I think because we cannot go from an empirical situation to a moral norm without considering the context and the general framework of morality),[18] but he mentions Robert Nozick, Joseph Raz, and yourself, stating: "the threshold deontologist sticks to his principle up to a point, but he is absolved from the charge of utter heartlessness by being willing to switch sides in the stand-off when the stakes get high enough – that is, when they pass the threshold that his version of deontology enshrines."[19] Most critics of trespassing the threshold say that the "ticking bomb scenario" never really exists in the form depicted by supreme emergency situations. But that doesn't seem right, in this country [Israel], these situations do exist.

Walzer: Yes, I have been told that by people who have worked in intelligence. Waldron gave a talk on "Dirty Hands" and the supreme emergency argument at the West Point conference.[20] He identified me, very generously, as someone worrying about things we should worry about.

Busekist: According to Alan Dershowitz we should legislate on torture. He writes that we need new laws, in line with the old laws and principles of just warfare and human rights (the protection of civilians for example), but that we should adapt them to the new threats terrorism poses for civilian victims; and he adds, looking at contemporary American politics that "the hard left insists that the old laws should not be tampered with in the least; the hard right insists that the old laws are entirely inapplicable to the new threats, and that democratic governments should be entirely free to do whatever it takes to combat terrorism, without regard to anachronistic laws. Both extremes are dangerous."[21]

Would you agree with him? That we should legalize torture under given conditions? He affirms that in asymmetric warfare, the lines are blurred between soldiers and combatants, and that terrorism can't be fought with the "old rules" of just and unjust wars; that there is a "Black hole" in the law regarding pre-emptive or preventive inter-rogation, in other words torture.[22] Isn't Dershowitz actually on the side of the "non-pretenders" you seem to value[23] in the sense that he acknowledges the empirical reality of torture, instead of pretending it doesn't exist, or that nothing could be done about it, and concludes that any state action, such as brutal interrogation or torture, should be subject to legal constraints?

Walzer: No, again, I have this position, the position that I take in the "Dirty Hands" essay[24] – which, by the way, is sometimes assigned in first-year philosophy courses as an example of philosophical incoher-ence, since it argues that sometimes (rarely, in fact) it is right to do what is wrong to do (*laughs*). I think torture is – and we should insist on this – torture is always wrong; but if in fact there is a bomb in a school building and this guy knows where it is, then you do what you have to do to find out. But you don't relax the norm and you want the people who torture this guy or authorize the torture, to know that what they are doing is wrong. Sometimes, you have to do something that is always wrong to do. And you want to have people who under-stand that, whose sensibility is of that kind, in political and moral life because that will reduce greatly the use of torture. And then, if torture is used anyway, we need to be clear about its moral meaning and we want some follow up, an acceptance of responsibility. The way Catholics insist on confession for example, and some kind of penance. Or some kind of political follow up, as the Brits did when they established a memorial to the pilots of Fighter Command in Westminster Abbey and didn't do the same for the pilots of Bomber Command, who had carried out the attacks on German cities. Air Marshal Harris,[25] who was the head of Bomber Command, was very embittered, and actually left Britain and went back to South Africa where he originally came from. A year or two ago, I think it was, they built a memorial for Bomber Command, but that's fifty years later.

Busekist: "Dirty Hands" – the title is from Sartre[26] – is a reflection on political morality, about individuals who have to make tough decisions against the background of a shared morality they transgress knowingly.[27] You wrote the piece in 1973, and you have not changed your mind on utilitarianism:[28] "When rules are overridden, we do not talk or act as if they had been set aside, canceled, or annulled. They still stand and have this much effect at least: that we know we have done something wrong even if what we have done was also the best thing to do on the whole in the circumstances. Or at least we feel that way, and this feeling is itself a crucial feature of our moral life."

The moral politician is someone who is capable of making morally questionable decisions for the right reasons; this is probably why the paper is assigned as an example of philosophical incoherence, although the argument is very clear. This is what you wrote about torture in "Dirty Hands": "When he [the newly elected leader] ordered the prisoner tortured, he committed a moral crime and he accepted a moral burden. Now he is a guilty man. His willingness to acknowledge and bear (and perhaps to repent and do penance for) his guilt is evidence, and it is the only evidence he can offer us, both that he is not too good for politics and that he is good enough. Here is the moral politician: it is by his dirty hands that we know him. If he were a moral man and nothing else, his hands would not be dirty; if he were a politician and nothing else, he would pretend that they were clean."[29]

However, one has to be a very optimistic moral person to sustain your argument: the norm should be absolute, but you may relax it provided you know that you are doing harm and act against the rule. Your anthropology is a positive and generous one, you need to trust people to be able to recognize that what they are doing is wrong and not take any pleasure in "preventively interrogating" and torturing other people. I believe that is what Dershowitz is afraid of – his anthropology is negative. He knows that we do torture, despite the legal and moral norm, hence he argues that torture is not permissible in advance but "forgivable" ex-post because this is how the world goes; that is the reason we should have a legal structure to keep brutal interrogation in frame with the law.

Walzer: "Enhanced interrogation." That's the term. I am afraid that if you follow the Dershowitz line, you will have too much torture. And the judges who have to issue the torture warrants will act the way judges act with regard to all kinds of police actions in the States – like "no-knock raids" on private homes, for example – the warrant becomes just something they sign when the police ask for it, while hardly thinking about it. If someone in authority asks for a warrant, they provide it. I can't imagine them saying "no" to a request from one of our national security agencies. I would rather teach people everywhere that this is something we don't do, with the deep understanding that if the ticking bomb case is an actual case, and not a piece of science fiction, we will do what is necessary – as with the doctrine of supreme emergency. You don't want supreme emergency to become an excuse for the continual use of immoral force.

Busekist: I have two questions here. Firstly, is there a recipe for making the right decisions in extreme cases? Secondly, your philosophy has a very clear and identifiable backbone, basic commands not to kill, not to harm, not to exploit. In hard cases, decisions are to be made against a specific context – such as "supreme emergency." But don't you think that we need some kind of a meta-ethical norm, a rule of conduct we can always go back to in order to avoid exceptions? Not a closed or definitive system, but one that would be robust enough to avoid haggling about difficult decisions? For example, you commented on Churchill's bombing of German cities (he allowed Coventry to be bombed too), US decisions to bomb Hiroshima and Nagasaki, because it is more reasonable to save lives today than expect saving lives in the future, which involves too much uncertainty. But these cases are not properly speaking about supreme emergency situations. This leads me to ask you about your dialogue with Jeff McMahan[30] which is in part about these difficult questions.

Walzer: Yes, I think McMahan has actually won the argument among philosophers, and I am pretty sure that I have won it among the Army, Navy, and Air Force officers who read him and who read me.

Busekist: The analytical distinction you maintain between *jus ad bellum* and *jus in bello* – the right to enter war and the rules of conduct during the war – is at the heart of your debate.

Walzer: The crucial debate is over the issue of what I call the moral equality of soldiers on the battlefield,[31] which does depend on keeping *ad bellum* and *in bello* considerations separate. I argue that soldiers on the battlefield have an equal right to fight and are equally bound by the rules of engagement, without regard to the justice or injustice of their war. Which is counterintuitive if you start with the domestic analogy: the bank robber and the bank guard are not moral equals on the bank floor. If the bank robber pulls out a gun, and the guard pulls out a gun, the guard has a greater right to shoot (defending himself or, perhaps, defending the bank) than the robber.[32] I argue that in the

79

circumstances of war, fighting is an activity different from that kind of domestic engagement, and that soldiers fighting wars that we think unjust (they presumably have been told otherwise) have the same rights and the same obligations on the battlefield. They are similars, who probably look like similars to each other: poor guys who would rather be somewhere else.

And indeed, there is evidence in the literature, that this is the common perception, which is why we don't punish ordinary soldiers who fought an unjust war after the war is over. We punish, if there is any punishment, the political leaders or the military leaders who decided on the unjust war. But ordinary soldiers are just sent home and are encouraged to resume their civilian life as if they had done nothing wrong. Even more persuasive, I think, is the fact that the treatment of prisoners of war has nothing to do with just or unjust . . . the rules for prisoners apply to all prisoners. Once they are rendered harmless, they have to be treated "benevolently for the duration of the war." And that's a rule everyone agrees on, including, I think, Jeff McMahan.

So, it is very unclear to me what it means to say that when the Russians invaded Finland in 1939 (wrongly), the Finns had every right to shoot, and any Russian who shot a Finn was a murderer. Well, what does that mean? You're not going to treat them as murderers. I think Jeff believes the doctrine of moral inequality will discourage people from fighting in unjust wars. But you are dealing with 18-year-old kids who are told by their political leaders, and their preachers or ministers or rabbis, and probably by their parents, that this is a war they ought to fight. And when they go to fight it, their engagement just doesn't fit the rules of individual responsibility that apply in domestic society. The rules that hold in a zone of peace simply don't apply in the same way in a zone of war.[33] And that was recognized for a long time, really since the birth of international law, until contemporary philosophers decided that it was wrong.

Busekist: This is the reason why Margalit and you wrote that soldiers are not "citizens in uniforms" in the reply to Kasher and Yadlin we mentioned earlier: soldiers are of a different moral genre from citizens in uniforms.

Walzer: The most famous polemical line that I've ever written was that Jeff McMahan's theory of war would be right if war were a peacetime activity.[34] That has been quoted a lot and Jeff, I've been told, didn't like it.

80

Busekist: However, *jus ad bellum* is part of McMahan's scenario, as combatants of an unjust war are unjust combatants. Soldiers do not decide on wars, they have no say in launching a war, just or unjust. According to you, soldiers should have equal standing and should be equally treated during and after the war, whether it is a just or an unjust war, this is *in bello* and *post bellum*. Soldiers are not responsible for wars, it is political leaders who decide to declare war. In constitutional democracies, leaders are elected, they are accountable for their decisions, and they sometimes make very bad decisions: Vietnam, the second war in Iraq.

Walzer: Well, let's think about the decision to go to war, which may be a commendable decision, to stop a massacre, say, or a criminal decision, an act of aggression. These are issues of *ad bellum*, and they are very important. The responsibility, the credit or the blame, lies with whoever makes the decision, in whatever regime that decision is made. Decisions to go to war are hence indeed imputable to political leaders, or sometimes, in some states, military leaders are responsible – not lesser government officials and certainly not ordinary citizens. There is lot to be said for democratic decision making in those circumstances, although democratic decision making works much less well on issues of foreign affairs, of foreign policy, than it does on issues of domestic policy.[35] And in fact, even in strong democratic regimes, decisions to go to war are essentially decisions of political leaders who often campaign without talking about foreign policy, and who are often elected for purely domestic reasons. People voted for them because they agreed with them on taxes or welfare, and then these leaders, elected for those reasons, have to make a decision on whether to fight or not to fight. It is useful to insist that they should go to Congress to ratify their decisions as Roosevelt did after Pearl Harbor, but Congress is rarely consulted, and I think one of the reasons Congress is rarely consulted is that most congressmen and women don't want to be consulted. They don't want to be the ones responsible for these decisions. That's why, since the Second World War, America has fought many wars and there have been many uses of force short of war, and none of them has been seriously discussed . . . there have never been serious, extended congressional deliberations on any of those decisions. Sometimes you get a chance afterwards to re-elect or defeat these leaders, so they are accountable in a sense, as they should be in a democracy. And I think you could say that Lyndon Johnson lost the second term that he surely expected because of Vietnam.[36] So, there is some accountability.

81

Busekist: Wars are not fought the same way they have been fought in the past, as during the Vietnam War for instance. Technology, for the better or worse, has made huge progress. Whether technology saves lives is yet another question. What is your opinion on the new technologies of warfare, such as drones for example? Aside from the fact that they are available only to rich nations, you seem to think that targeted killings with drones are "politically easier," but that this easiness should make us worry;[37] this is also part of your debate with MacMahan.[38] But you have written elsewhere that in some contexts battles on the ground may be less costly for collateral damages. Given the possibility of using drones, that may now prove too dangerous and too costly. Could you summarize your view on technological warfare in the light of contemporary, asymmetric warfare?

Walzer: I did write a piece on drones, in *Daedelus*.[39] Drones used properly are a way of minimizing civilian injuries and death. There is a kind of aesthetic critique of drone warfare – that it just isn't right, can't be right, for somebody to sit in a hut in Nevada, totally free of any risks, and kill people in Pakistan or Afghanistan. And I can understand that sensitivity, although it's always been a purpose in warfare to minimize the risks to your own soldiers. Drone warfare seems to achieve this in what looks like an extreme way but, in fact, drone warfare, fought properly, is highly risky. The guy in Nevada in the hut isn't at risk. But the precision of the drone attacks depends on having your own people on the ground because information from "native" informants is often unreliable, delivered with their own agenda in mind and not with your purposes in mind. So, you need people on the ground, agents, spies, and that is very dangerous. Drone warfare is not risk free. One of the problems in the way we've been fighting with drones, is that we have relied much of the time on "native" informants. When we kill people at a wedding party, think-ing it's a Taliban meeting, it is probably because we don't have our own people watching from close up.

Busekist: This is an empirical argument: drones may not be reliable simply because individuals themselves may not be reliable.

Walzer: But it's also a moral argument, if you are committed to minimize civilian casualties you have to accept the risks of collect-ing intelligence even if it's dangerous to do that. But if you collect intelligence, if you actually use the drone in the way it can be used, as a weapon of great precision, you can in fact minimize civilian casualties. There are moral and immoral uses of drones. For example, there is a clinic report by a university consortium in the US, Stanford, and NYU[40] that does studies of drone warfare and interviews with the villagers who live under drones and who report that they live in terror, constantly hearing the buzzing in the sky, anticipating the explosion. But that is contradicted by other people who say: if in fact people hear the buzzing, then the drone can't be an effective weapon. The person being targeted, who will know that he is a target, will simply stay inside. So, effective drone warfare requires that the drone fly high enough so people don't hear it. But the drone can also be used for another purpose: to terrorize villagers and encourage them to refuse to harbor potential targets – and this is an immoral use of the weapon.

Busekist: Many articles insist on the traumas drones provoke: not only among the villagers in your example, but also among soldiers who hit the button from Nevada or wherever. They are as traumatized as those who actually fight on the ground, so it is said, which is quite different from the common comparison between drones and a video game.

Walzer: The initial critique is: operating drones is like a video game. But this is not right: apparently people can't run drones for long period of times, it does cause psychic injury, which I take to be a sign of our humanity.

Busekist: What they say indeed about their feeling of guilt resembles what some survivors say, the guilt *vis-à-vis* their family members or fellow citizens who weren't as lucky, the feeling that they haven't done enough to save them, especially in this case, when there are collateral damages hit by drone strikes. The drone operators have a difficult time admitting that they did not fight on the ground, that they contributed to something questionable from a safe distance. So, if I understand you correctly, it is legitimate in principle to argue for targeted killing with drones (the Yemen versus Philadelphia case),[41] but it has to be done "right." Could you explain?[42]

Walzer: It has to be done right. Yes. This is what I wrote about drones in 2016: "Drones make it possible to get at enemies who hide in countries whose governments are probably unwilling and possibly unable to repress or restrain them." This is a war without a front, where the use of ground troops, even commandos, is difficult, sometimes impossible – so drones have been called "the only game in town." But we should think very carefully before relaxing the targeting rules and turning drones into a weapon like all the others. Their moral and political advantage is their precision, which depends on using them only against individuals whose critical importance we have established and about whom we have learned a great deal. Using them like an advanced form of artillery or like "smart" bombs isn't morally right or politically wise.

To put it otherwise: it is useful in asymmetric warfare if you have a weapon of that precision. It turns out that in this kind of war, there are very strong prudential reasons as well as moral reasons for minimizing civilian casualties and even taking risks to do that.[43] Now, when you are fighting the way Americans did in Afghanistan for "hearts and minds," the prudential reasons are stronger, and more obvious. I guess Israel in Lebanon and Gaza is not fighting for the hearts and minds of the people in Lebanon or Gaza, but it is fighting politically for global support or at least to avoid global condemnation, because that does weaken Israel, and so there are prudential reasons, less strong than in Afghanistan, perhaps, but still important reasons for minimizing casualties. I think the IDF knows that[44] just as American officers know it.

Busekist: I believe they do, and they have elaborated very restrictive rules. Targeted killings in Israel have been legalized by a Supreme Court decision in 2004 and are subject to strong constraints. What is your opinion on this ruling by Aharon Barak?

Walzer: If a target is a legitimate target, I don't think there is anything wrong with targeted killing. We can have and we need to have a lot of arguments about what makes someone a legitimate target. But I don't accept the condemnation of targeted killing as "extrajudicial."[45] All killing in war is extrajudicial. But the target has to be defensible, that is, the target has to be a person who can plausibly be described as an active and dangerous enemy. A legitimate enemy.

Can I tell you a story? It might be interesting – about the difference between Israel and America. I was visiting at the United States Army War College in Pennsylvania.[46] I gave a lecture on the first Lebanese war; no not the 1982 war, the 2006 war, the last Lebanese war; there were some colonels just back from Afghanistan, where I think they had been working on the new rules of engagement that General McChrystal[47] announced in 2011. One of them described the following situation: American soldiers draw fire from a small apartment building in an Afghan town. What should they do? This is what the colonel said: in the old days, we would just call in an airstrike on the building. But now we don't want to do that because we don't know who is in the building. We only know that Taliban fighters are on the roof. So what is the captain or the lieutenant on the ground supposed to do? He has to decide: maybe he can get troops onto the roof of an adjoining building who can fire directly at the bad guys, or he can send a scout into the building to see if there are families living there or hiding there. If the building is empty, he might call in an airstrike or the artillery and if it isn't empty, then not. Or, if the lieutenant thinks that those two courses of action are too risky for his men, he should simply withdraw – even though this violates the old American principle "never leave the battlefield to the enemy." He withdraws.

And then the colonel looked at me, because I had just given this lecture on Israel and Lebanon,[48] and he said: "We can get the bad guys at another time, we don't have to worry about a ceasefire." As Israel always does. Which I thought was the expression of an extraordinary sense of sympathy with the Israeli problem. That is something I encountered often: American soldiers think the IDF is fighting the same kind of war they are fighting and encountering the same kinds of problems. And it's true – it's also true that the two armies sometimes act well, sometimes badly, in the same sorts of ways. The Americans in Afghanistan can figure, okay we won't get the bad guys this time, we will get them another time. Israel hasn't always had that option. But there you have some of the dilemmas of asymmetric warfare. The Americans under McChrystal decided that avoiding civilian casualties was more important than winning this encounter at this moment. And the lieutenant on the ground might decide that sending a scout into the building was so risky that he wouldn't do that and would rather withdraw.

I think the Israelis encounter those kinds of dilemmas all the time. I now talk sometimes to the grandchildren of my friends in Israel, or they report to me on their conversations with their grandchildren, who have fought in Gaza or Lebanon. So I learn, for example, about the time when Israeli troops were looking for the entrances to the Gazan tunnels. Hamas obviously knew where the entrances were, so they could set traps. An Israeli unit walks into a trap, and the unit is in trouble. What does the lieutenant do? These kids tell me that sometimes he panics and calls in an artillery strike – maybe before he has to. That serves to rescue his men, but then civilians nearby are killed. Sometimes he figures out how to get out of the trap without doing that – if he's smart and calm. The case is the same with American troops in Afghanistan: sometimes, the unit in trouble behaves well, and sometimes not. And it all depends on a kid, not eighteen but maybe twenty-four years old.

Busekist: In these situations that is a very demanding posture to ask for, regardless of age.

Walzer: Yes, yes. Of course, you can train people for that moment, but even so, what happens at that moment is unpredictable and very hard to judge afterwards.

Busekist: In "Regime Change and Just War" you argue that the 2003 Iraq war was neither a response to aggression, nor a humanitarian intervention, but a *direct attempt at regime change*.[49]

Walzer: My definition of aggression in *Just and Unjust Wars* led me to write an article on Iraq in which I argued that the second Iraq war was unjust, but that it was not an act of aggression. What is aggression and what's wrong with it? I think it was Bismarck (or maybe Clausewitz) who said somewhere: We march into another country proclaiming peace, so we'd be happy if they just accept our terms; they are the ones who decide to fight![50] That line, which I heard or read long ago and have never been able to trace, led me to think that the crime of aggression is to force the citizens of another country to fight in defense of their territory, their sovereignty, and their common life. The invasion of Iraq was welcomed by the Kurds who made up 20 percent of the population and the Shia who made up 60 percent of the population – though this last group did not welcome the occupation.[51] The army just melted away. We did not force the Iraqis to fight, that definition of aggression doesn't work in this case; and yet I thought the war was wrong. In part because we were marching into a country and overthrowing a dictator, changing the regime, with no idea of what was going to come afterwards, with little understanding of the country we were invading and of the social forces at work there. It was a war that wasn't necessary; we didn't stop a massacre – in fact, we had already protected the Kurds from a possible massacre, using force short of war. So, we were putting lives at risk for no good reason. But it wasn't aggression. A number of my friends and people on the left supported the war, because they thought this is one of the most vicious, brutal regimes in the world.

Busekist: Mitchell Cohen among the *Dissent* people for instance.

Walzer: Mitchell Cohen and Paul Berman . . . and even if there is no forgiveness for these people on the left today, I still believe that it wasn't crazy to want to overthrow a regime like that. There were leftist reasons for the war, they just weren't the right reasons, and the war was wrong; we can't go around the world overthrowing regimes we think are brutal and vicious. I remember a debate at NYU a few weeks before the war started with Kanan Makiya. He is an Iraqi exile, ex Trotskyist, I think, who came first to some place in Europe then to America in the 1970s, maybe the 1980s. He teaches now at Brandeis. He wrote a brilliant book called *The Republic of Fear*,[52] a study of Saddam's regime. He supported the war, and I think Mitchell Cohen and Paul [Berman] were very much influenced by him. The NYU debate was a panel discussion with me and him and a few other people. He said that even if there was only a ten percent chance of establishing a democratic regime in Iraq, he would support the invasion; I thought that ten percent was not good enough.[53] If you let loose the dogs of war, knowing that a lot of people are going to get killed, the odds have to be much better than that.

Busekist: The Iraq war was not a crime of aggression according to just-war theory. The occupation on the other hand was unsatisfactory. But I would like to get back to regime change, which is obviously related to occupation in Iraq.[54] In your argument against cultural transformation,[55] in other words a structural and profound transformation of another country, you write that "the classical principle of nonintervention holds that the regime of a country should reflect the history, culture, and politics of that country." You are against forceful regime change, except in the case of post-war Germany where the political reconstruction came with an imposed regime change, the restoration of democracy, necessary to impose peace. But isn't there either a contradiction or, to say the least, a continuum? On the one hand we do not want a dictator to oppress and exploit his people – and surely some cultural traditions are oppressive (against women for example), on the other hand we should resist intervening for direct regime change[56] Could you specify the role of culture and the role of politics in this argument?

Walzer: If you go in to stop a massacre, and if the massacre is conducted by the regime, then, yes, you have to change the regime, but what legitimates the intervention is stopping the massacre.[57] As for more ordinary oppression, like the oppression of women, which is all too ordinary, there are many forms of state opposition short of war, so this is more a question of facts on the ground than a distinction between culture and politics. We can oppose oppression by supporting the people I call "comrades abroad," the international left – dissidents and all the dissident organizations: protest movements, campaigns for freedom of the press, calls for elections, and so on. For all this, we can offer both moral and material assistance. Sending an army across the border promises greater or more immediate effectiveness but rarely delivers on its promise.

Busekist: In the Iraqi case, you recommended measures "short of war" or "force short of war," such as containment: "we can use force, in limited ways, for the sake of producing a new (and if new then also democratic) regime."[58] This is related to another notion you discuss in "World Government and the Politics of Pretending": "politics short of force."[59]

Walzer: The use of force short of war comes, I guess, when politics without force doesn't work. Much too little has been written about it. I meant to get back to that idea, though I haven't done so yet. The classic example for me is the system of sanctions against Saddam's regime after the first Gulf War [1991]. The sanctions included inspections, the no-fly zone, and an embargo – which is usually thought of as an act of war. We enforced the no-fly zone by bombing radar and anti-aircraft installations – acts also commonly taken under international law to be acts of war. We had to be able to fly over Iraq to prevent Iraqi planes from flying and so to maintain the no-fly zone, so we used force. But this was obviously different from what happened in March 2003, and we should think of these acts as acts short of war. They still require some kind of judgment: what is their purpose? In this case, the purpose was to constrain a regime that we had decided not to overthrow in 1991.

It's a way of responding to an act of aggression, afterwards, when you have decided not to conquer the country and put its leaders on trial; you are making peace with the country, but you are enforcing some constraints on its behavior, as a way of preventing future aggression – and those constraints have to be enforced. They are enforced by "the use of force short of war" – which should become a concept in political theory. I thought the Iraq case was a very good example of an internationally imposed regime of this sort. Unfortunately, we didn't know how to run the embargo, or we ran it cruelly so as to impose unnecessary suffering on the civilian population of Iraq. The US Secretary of Defense, Colin Powell, talked about "smart sanctions." Smart sanctions would have targeted only the purchase and import of weapons, or things that could be made into weapons. But the embargo was much more aggressive than that and it affected the civilian population in a way that I think it didn't have to. But the no-fly zone was a great success.

Busekist: Especially for the Kurds of course. Kurdish autonomy was gained via *jus ad vim* as you wrote, which is an "indirect" version of regime change, although force short of war doesn't permit forcible democratization.[60]

Walzer: Yes, it established autonomy for the Kurds, and it protected them from attacks. And I thought that was all very good and made the 2003 war unnecessary. We should think about the use of force short of war in the future, as an international or regional response, of NATO for example, to aggressive regimes. I think this is a topic that political theorists should get to work on, and international lawyers should recognize that there are uses of force that aren't the same as war.

5

Cooperation and Multilateralism: Nations, States, Sovereignty

Busekist: There seems to be an evolution in your work. You have been identified as a strong statist by many of your readers and critics.[1] You have always argued in favor of the legitimacy of states: it is an empirical fact that peoples without states aspire to have a sovereign state of their own. A state is the only entity that is able to protect its citizens, to grant them rights, and to enable an independent existence on the international stage. I would like to ask you about the role you believe states should play today.

In "Politics of Difference" you wrote that "the crucial slogan of this struggle is 'self-determination', which implies the need for a piece of territory or, at least, a set of independent institutions – hence, decentralization, devolution, autonomy, partition, sovereignty. Getting the boundaries right, not only in geographic but also in functional terms, is enormously difficult, but it is necessary if the different groups are to exercise significant control over their own lives and to do so with some security."[2]

The sovereign state remains crucial to protect its citizens, but in your latest writings about multilateralism and international cooperation, you seem to hint at something like post-sovereignty or a diluted sovereignty in order to counterbalance the nationalist aspirations of many political leaders. In short, your recommendations for a foreign policy today are less focused on the state. In *Arguing about War* you even mention "an increasingly dense set of social ties that cut cross state boundaries."[3] Could you specify this articulation between legitimacy of states on the one hand and the necessary loosening of full sovereignty on the other hand?

Walzer: My argument has always been that everybody needs a state[4] – or the functional equivalent of a state. More than this: everybody needs a functioning state, capable of providing physical security, welfare, education – all the things that the state does and that, right now, no other institutions can do effectively. And once everybody has a state, an effective state, then we can begin to talk about transforming state boundaries into less strong lines; we can work for cooperation across the lines; we can hope for political unions like the EU. But I think that the EU was made possible by the definitive determination of boundaries in at least Central and Western Europe after the Second World War. Those lines were not going to be changed again, at least not for the foreseeable future, and that made it possible to start talking about cooperation across them.

My statist views have immediate political implications. I strongly believe, for example, in a Palestinian state alongside Israel – since the Palestinians need a state just as the Jews do, and the Kurds, too, for that matter. But I would hope that once, if it ever comes to pass, there are two states, there will also be lots of ways of crossing the boundary between them. And that might involve, as in the EU, both sides accepting some limitation of sovereignty so as to make cooperation possible. But the construction of a state is the priority, and I am indeed correctly identified as a statist.

I remember there was an Asian economic crisis of some sort back in 1990s. And there was a lot of talk about how a couple of countries, I think Singapore and Malaysia, had responded strongly and effectively and actually saved their people from a lot of economic trouble. This was taken as evidence that state action was still possible even in a globalizing economy. The state can still do a lot. And, as I have argued again and again, it is still the primary agent for providing education, welfare, and some constraints on inequality.

Busekist: But wouldn't you agree with me that the Wilsonian grammar of self-determination – one people, one culture, one state – that is how Wilson envisioned the territorial divisions after the First World War, had very real and undesirable side-effects? We seem to have a taste for neat maps of nation-states, with well-designed borders, but that has been the source of many evils, ethnic cleansing within the states created after the First World War is but one of them. Maybe this explains in part why you said that your Zionism is at once "a universal statism, and a "secular nationalism"?[5]

Walzer: Yes, yes, yes!

Busekist: Is the state really the necessary step? Wouldn't it be possible to imagine other types of units that make people less vulnerable and give them the same kind of rights we want – welfare, education, equality?

Walzer: I agree, it doesn't always have to be the state; the alternative today is some version of autonomy, strong or less strong, and I think if I were living in Scotland or in Catalonia I would argue for autonomy rather than independence, in part for reasons of justice. Catalonia for example is the richest province of Spain, so its secession would leave other Spaniards less well off. That has to be a consideration after many years of cooperation of a sort, at least of economic activities across the provincial lines.

We can think of autonomy as a halfway house between a province and a state, a kind of limited sovereignty. I would also favor experiments in federalism of many different sorts. Take Canada, for example, whose system Charles Taylor calls "asymmetric federalism" because one province, Québec, gets privileges that others don't get for historical reasons. That is another way of accommodating pluralism – maybe Spain needs an asymmetrical system of provincial autonomy. So, the state isn't the only possible political agency . . . But people need institutions that can do what the state does. And the people who don't have those institutions are people in trouble, the way that Palestinians and the Kurds are in trouble.

Busekist: They are very much in trouble. The state may indeed be the first step, but creation of (new) states is also the result of political compromises. This raises two questions: leadership and belonging. Negotiating the creation of a state requires astute leaders (and, to a certain degree, international cooperation and/or approval); a non-contested territory; and consent about the boundaries of belonging. Who are the new members? Who can claim membership? Ideally self-determination should be the result of autonomous decisions on behalf of the people who identify with the state building project. To take up your example, Palestine, there seems to be a threefold problem: a divided leadership, the law of return which is desirable to the Palestinians but almost impossible to reasonably achieve,[6] and the territorial discontinuity.

Walzer: Right. I can only agree; these are hard questions that probably have to be answered differently in each case. Self-determination is usually the project of a political movement, which will begin defining the collective "self" in the course of its struggle. If the movement is divided, the prospects for achieving statehood are dim, as they are right now for the Palestinians (but not only because of their leaders).

Busekist: Nation-states and sovereignty trigger some degree of suspicion in the literature, especially on the left. Some of our colleagues' agenda seems to be dominated by the desire to erase boundaries and to reconsider state sovereignty entirely. In the 1990s there was a lot of talk about "the end of territories," and there is a growing academic literature on the obsolescence of nation-states or the sheer injustice of the classical nation-state, associated with "methodological nationalism," hostility toward migrants, and lack of pluralism (as opposed to some form of cosmopolitanism and open borders).

The authors you respond to in "The Moral Standing of States" in the 1980s are early "cosmopolitans," Charles Beitz in particular.[7] They read *Just and Unjust Wars* as a defense and illustration of statism despite its claim to be grounded in a theory of individual rights. They seem to be puzzled by three features of your work: the role played by communities (they question the legitimacy of the association between states and communities, what you call the "fit" between communities and their political form, the state, or "communal integrity"[8] – that would be a Wilsonian critique); the insistence on state sovereignty that goes with your legalist paradigm (which they find problematic: sovereignty may lead to violations of individual rights); and, lastly and paradoxically, your respect for politics.[9]

What is your opinion on these questions today? People need states to protect their rights on the one hand, but new states are hard to squeeze into the international territorial grammar on the other hand, and many scholars actively combat the legitimacy of nation-states guilty of nationalism and exclusion. You wrote somewhere that this skepticism *vis-à-vis* the state, and the US in particular is somehow related to the "ideological fury'" at the state of Israel.[10]

Walzer: The hostility to Israel, not to the occupation or to the policies of the current far right government, but to the existence of the state is indeed a leftist pathology.[11] It probably goes some way toward explaining the ideological rejection of states and borders, but there are obviously more general explanations. Yes, the state is an exclusive community in this sense: it has special obligations to its own citizens. It is precisely those obligations that lead to the creation of welfare states which can't be imagined without boundaries and some restriction of immigration. But a liberal state can still be generous in its reception of refugees and in its willingness to naturalize aliens within its borders. And it can have a foreign policy aimed at reducing global inequality through foreign aid and fair trade. The best place to fight for policies like that is within the state, whose political space is the only space where the left has been able to win political victories.

So special obligations to fellow citizens don't exclude obligations to others. There are liberal philosophers and leftist ideologues who claim to reject any kind of commitment limited to particular people or groups of people. But I have a hard time imagining, and I suspect that they do too, what a world without commitments of those kinds would be like. I think it is perfectly possible to be a statist and an internationalist at the same time. In fact, my claim that everybody needs a state is an internationalist claim.

Busekist: The "default position of the left"[12] is at once a classical leftist-internationalist position, and a biblical ought: be good at home, be a "light unto the nations," and you will be rewarded for your righteousness.

Walzer: That is indeed a characteristic left position, but it is not my position. I mean, it is good to have a good domestic policy. I often think of the origins of the left in the writings of the biblical prophets, or at least, those texts from the biblical prophets that we most like (because there is a lot that doesn't fit any left account). Their doctrine was, you find it explicitly in Jeremiah, all you have to do is stop grinding the faces of the poor, create a just society, stop worshiping idols, treat widows and orphans the way they are supposed to be treated, remember that you were slaves in Egypt, and if you do all that, you will be safe in your land forever.[13] That's a good domestic policy. So the idea is that in order to be a light onto the nations, all you have to do is sit still and shine. That's been . . . It's not the only left position but it's a characteristic left position and that was, effectively, Bernie Sanders' politics. "America should be an example," he seemed to be saying: "I don't have to talk about the use of force abroad, I don't want to talk about it. If we create a just society, we would be serving the world."

Busekist: Your *Introduction to the Democratiya Project*[14] is a condensed version of your hope for internationalist politics, a critique of the "old internationalist left," and an analysis of the new self-declared internationalist left whose agenda amounts to being anti-American and defending the oppressed wherever they come from or stand for.[15] It summarizes positions that you have taken in "What is Left Internationalism?" and more generally in the chapters composing *A Foreign Policy for the Left*. We spoke of International Brigades that could supplement the shortcomings of international organizations and contribute to a fairer global politics. Could you elaborate on the "choice of comrades" that you associate with the international solidarity of leftist?[16]

Walzer: "The choice of comrades" is a phrase from an article in *Dissent* by the Italian novelist (and socialist) Ignazio Silone – a hero among Dissentniks. For me, what internationalism requires is that we support our comrades abroad – that is, leftists in other countries who need our moral, political, maybe financial help. But we have to choose our comrades abroad: who are they? They are men and women who share our commitment to equality and democracy – for that's what any genuine socialism requires. People who call themselves leftists but who support or apologize for authoritarian regimes and terrorist politics: these are not our comrades. Many leftists insist that "we have no enemies on our left." But we do, or we should, for the left has its own pathologies, as we have seen in the long history of Stalinist apologetics and support for third world dictators. Socialist internationalism has to be an internationalism of socialists.

Busekist: Allow me to digress and ask you a question related to what I asked earlier on the relationship between culture and politics. In "The Left and Religion"[17] you contest two of the common (not only leftist) explanations for religious ideology or zealotry. The "sociological" or materialist explanation: zealotry is the result of poverty, oppression, and (Western) imperialism; and the ideological or "culturalist" explanation: cultural relativism is considered to be a desirable intellectual quality, but it prevents the left from reflecting on Islamism. Islamophobia is politically incorrect and morally wrong. The task is very difficult, however, even for the insiders such as Kamel Daoud,[18] who acts as a whistle-blower, but who has been accused of recycling "Orientalist clichés" by a group of French intellectuals because he mentioned the profound sexism embedded in the Arab culture.[19] The left has a hard time condemning Islamism because they "understand" the Islamist opposition to Western alienation: fundamentalism is equated with resistance to the West, or even with post-modernism (Hardt and Negri) and capitalist globalization (Žižek), but not just any West: America – and its understudy: Israel. The left is also eager to condemn the crimes of the West that supposedly lie at the roots of

Islamist violence (as in Iraq, Pakistan, or Afghanistan). You argue for selective judgments – what you call a "politics of distinction" – and "ideological war" against Islamism in the name of pluralism, liberty, democracy, and gender equality. But the chapter ends on a pessimistic note: "The International Brigade of left intellectuals is still waiting to take shape." While waiting for the Brigade to take shape, what is the most urgent political answer to the specific threat of Islamism in your view?

Walzer: The first thing is to recognize, and talk plainly about, the fact that Islamic texts, like the texts of every other religion, can be interpreted in ways that justify violence against infidels and heretics – and that right now there are Islamist zealots engaged in an interpretation of that sort. We have to work out a strong, critical response – an intellectual response. Second, we have to figure out when it might be necessary to urge or defend a forceful response. We will naturally prefer political to military responses, but sometimes, as in the case of ISIS in Iraq and Syria, a military response is justified, and people on the left shouldn't pretend that that can never be true. Third, we have to oppose religious zealotry without becoming the enemies of religious men and women generally – and especially right now without becoming enemies of Islam. It is especially important, then, to support religious Muslims and also secular or lapsed Muslims who criticize the zealots, who defend liberalism, or democracy, or gender equality, from inside the Muslim community. They are our comrades.

Busekist: Let's go back to what you said earlier: the fact that everybody needs a state is an internationalist claim. This argument, to be heard, should precisely involve a multilateral effort.

Walzer: It should, and the enforcement of the no-fly zones in Iraq, for example, started multilaterally, the Brits were involved, I think the French also for a while ... but in the end it was mostly an American operation. It made possible, not a Kurdish state, but a strong autonomy.

Busekist: This is part of the problem, isn't it? As you wrote in "Regime Change and Just War": "had containment been an international project, American power might also have been contained within it." The fact that the US is doing the work without consulting its partners lead to overly critical positions from the left in particular.

Walzer: You are right, I do believe in a global division of labor on issues like humanitarian intervention and the use of force short of war[20] and that's why I have argued in various informal talks and papers that the Europeans should spend more money on military preparation, so that they are less dependent on the US and can handle something like the wars of the former Yugoslavia on their own. Those wars should have been dealt with from the beginning by the Europeans and not by the US.

Busekist: In your last book, *A Foreign Policy for the Left*, you argue, as you do more and more in your recent works, in favor of alliances, multilateral agreements, coordinated regional forces, and better organized ones than the current European Community. In your 1995 article, "The Politics of Rescue,"[21] however, you argued for a "concurrence of multilateral authorization and individual initiative [by states]; the first for the sake of moral legitimacy, the second for the sake of political effectiveness"; and you compare coordinated decision making to Rousseau's general will theory, bound to fail internationally. You now seem to endorse – or rather: you call for – a more robust practice of multilateralism.

This leads us back to my questions about normative claims and empirical situations we addressed in another chapter. You argue that, in principle, we have the tools (the UN, the Security Council, the IMF) to foster cooperation and alliances, but they do not do the work because many laws simply cannot be enforced. There is no global civil or political society that can elect or remove leaders from office, and the members of the Security Council reason in terms of national interests. "The political leaders of states strong enough to intervene in a humanitarian crisis can refuse to intervene, look to the UN, and escape any responsibility for the disasters that follow. Pretending that the UN can act effectively is a very effective way of closing one's eyes and turning one's back,"[22] you write.

Walzer: And that is exactly the way I've discussed interventions. We don't have the institutions, or we don't have the political will to use the institutions we have, for a global, an international enforcement regime. So, for example, what was going on in Rwanda was a massacre and, since the UN couldn't or wouldn't act, the massacre should have been stopped by anyone, any state or coalition of states, that could stop it. I don't believe that you can oppose unilateralism in situations of that sort. But I've also argued that if you go in to a place like Rwanda where the regime is conducting the massacre and has

97

to be overthrown, and you then get involved in political reconstruction – that might be a good time to seek multilateral cooperation. So, unilateralism first but then an effort to find multilateral support, which would also mean some kind of multilateral regulation of the reconstruction project, which wouldn't be all in the hands of one country.

Busekist: What you suggest here is related to what you once called the difference between a trusteeship ("where the intervening power actually rules the country it has 'rescued', acting in trust for the inhabitants, seeking to establish a stable and more or less consensual politics") and a protectorate ("where the intervention brings some local group or coalition of groups to power and is then sustained only defensively, to ensure that there is no return of the defeated regime or the old lawlessness and that minority rights are respected") in "The Politics of Rescue,"[23] and you suggest a "utopian and politically incorrect solution": that current war zones that account for many hundreds of thousands of refugees, should become not-independent and not-sovereign, in other words international protectorates.[24] Do you still believe this? And which are the countries that would be candidates for becoming international protectorates today?

Walzer: The idea is still utopian and politically incorrect, given that trusteeships and protectorates were generally cover for some sort of neo-colonial rule. But properly understood they could provide not cover but control. Imagine that there had been an intervention, say by France, to stop the Rwandan genocide. The government of Rwanda, since it was conducting the genocide, would be overthrown. What then? One possibility would be for the UN to establish a French, or EU, or NATO protectorate over the country, entrusting the protectors with maintaining the peace, rebuilding the country, and establishing some locally legitimate political regime, and then getting out. The protectorate would be authorized and constrained by an agency that had international legitimacy and resources at its disposal, and that could guarantee the eventual exit. There have been a number of failed states that would have benefited from an arrangement of this sort. I think of it as an example of internationalism in action. But it would require an international organization with a lot more legitimacy, and a lot more authority, than the UN as we know it possesses.

Busekist: So you are a statist because you believe that the state is still the most relevant unit to protect people and make them less vulnerable. However, in one of your last pieces, "World Government and the Politics of Pretending," which is a plea for multilateralism and international cooperation, you argue that statehood and/or nationhood actually *prevent* these international or multilateral institutions from functioning. I was wondering about the circularity of the argument. On the one hand, we need the state; on the other hand, when heads of states negotiate in international instances they protect their own interests first: either because the international organizations are not sufficiently integrated (even the EU is not a model on that behalf if you think about the failure to distribute migrants fairly), or because state sovereignty classically conceived inhibits multilateral policies, given that political leaders are accountable only to their domestic constituency. So, we would need a global civil society to empower legitimate international institutions, create a global responsibility, accountability, and voice – but there is nothing like a global civil society (yet). We have to rely on state-actors or international civil servants, and that doesn't seem to be enough.

Walzer: But we do! We do have the beginnings of a global civil society in organizations like Human Rights Watch and Amnesty International, Doctors without Borders . . . Actually, I think of those organizations in analogy with the International Brigades in Spain. We, on the liberal left, the good people of the Western world, can no longer recruit people to fight in distant countries. There was actually talk, at the very beginning of the Syrian uprising and the civil war about an international brigade. I went looking on the internet, thinking this was my idea, but there were hundreds of pieces there, and one writer, from England, said: "well, the truth is that people like me would rather run a marathon for charity than pick up a gun and go to Syria." And that is a problem. ISIS is an international brigade, they can do what we can't. But our brigadiers, our international brigadiers, are the people who work for Human Rights Watch, Doctors without Borders, and groups like that. To go into countries like Syria, they have to claim to be neutral. Human Rights Watch documents the atrocities, it doesn't prevent them, but that is still an important function and it involves risk for their people. That's as far as we can go, but those are important organizations. If there were more of them, that would be good. That's the beginning. You can see what an international civil society might look like. And these organizations recruit people from many different countries – although they usually raise money in only a few countries.

99

Busekist: I agree, but wouldn't you say that this is more of a parallel civil society? These organizations are very useful, in many places indispensable, but they are self-appointed, they are not politically accountable. They do not represent what we would like a global civil society to look like in the future, or rather, they are only a small part of it.

Walzer: Right, right. We would need other kinds of organizations, representing partisan interests and policies. There are American trade unions that call themselves international, but they aren't. Still, you can imagine unions that function internationally, and you can imagine political parties that function internationally. To some extent, there is a little of that in Europe today. The right-wing and the left-wing parties have formed coalitions across boundaries to function together in the European parliament. And there are organizations like the World Trade Organization that function, semi-coercively, to regulate economic activity across borders. Formed after the Second World War, these groups were supposed to be different from what they are now. The World Labor Organization was supposed to be parallel to, and as powerful as the World Trade Organization, but it never achieved that status, and in the era of neo-liberal economics, has hardly any impact. But those organizations are also intimations of global government of a kind. And yes, you are right, sovereignty interferes with what they do. You can see this clearly when you get someone like Trump who is opposed to any form of international cooperation and regulation.

Busekist: Do you think we should change the UN laws about the role and scope of the Security council? Elect or appoint more members, and which ones?

Walzer: Well, the problem is . . . you can't have global governance until there is a much larger sense among political leaders, across all the boundaries – a sense that they need to be concerned about the way the world goes, and not just about the interests of their own country. In Security Council debates, there is very rarely any concern about how the world goes. You saw that very clearly in the debate on the genocide in Rwanda when the Americans simply refused to call it "genocide" because they didn't want to have to invest resources in stopping it. Of course, politicians at home also think about their own interests, but there is at least some engagement with the well-being of the country. They do have ideas about what the country needs, about what it can or can't accept in, say, environmental damage or growing

100

inequality, and the political parties have to have programs about all that. And internationally, we aren't there. That's what I called the "politics of pretending"[25] – when we pretend that we are much farther along than we actually are. The example I always use is what happened after 9/11 when a lot of American globalists said: you have to go to the UN, you can't act unilaterally. Now, in the United States, 911 is the phone number for emergency calls. So, this was the 911 response to 9/11, except that there was, and still is, no one answering the phone.[26]

6

Israel–Palestine

Busekist: You are an intellectual, American, and Jewish, you have a long and close relationship with Israel, but you are also very critical of the occupation and the current politics of the Israeli government.

Walzer: I was a Zionist from the beginning – because my parents were, and because I was Bar Mitzvah'd in 1948, a year of high emotion, and because Judy and I went to Israel in 1957 and made connections there. 1967 was for me, as for everyone else, the moment when I got deeply engaged.[1] Around 1971, I started coming to Israel often, and I think I have been in Israel every year since then. You know that I first started as a tourist guide?

Busekist: You, a tourist guide?

Walzer: Well, it was political tourism. After the 1973 war,[2] my friend Marty Peretz[3] and I became tourist guides. We were very good friends then and we still are despite some political disagreements. We organized a very big ad in the *New York Times* calling on the US to help Israel. We really worked very hard to get it signed by all kinds of leading American academics, intellectuals and literary people.[4] After the war, Yigal Allon,[5] who was then foreign minister, invited us to bring groups of Americans to Israel – like the ones we got to sign the ad, but also younger people who might grow up to be important ad-signers in the future.

We brought a group of people every year for the next three or four years. We recruited them, half Jewish, half non-Jewish, some older recognizable figures and some people we thought might become recognizable, bright young people in international politics. We brought

102

them to Israel, we told them they would be paid for by the Israeli foreign ministry and the tour was organized by the ministry, with our advice. Most of the people we invited were happy to come. We had interviews with the foreign minister and sometimes with the Prime Minister and other members of the government, with members of the Knesset, and always with leaders of the opposition. We went to the Sinai, to the Golan. Marty and I were the people taking care of the group – so we were tour guides of a sort, though we were also doing what we thought of as political work. We aimed to create a cadre of academics and intellectuals who were friendly to Israel – but not uncritical; our own friends were already some of the leading critics of the (very new) settlement movement.

We brought the groups from 1973 to 1977. In 1977 [Moshe] Dayan was the foreign minister, he wasn't so much interested in us, but we had an interesting interview with [Menachem] Begin where I made the mistake of referring to "the occupied territories" and he yelled at us: I should have said Judea and Samaria. And I decided not to do this anymore. But I did continue to be a guide for another few years with the Federation of Jewish Philanthropies. I would bring all-Jewish groups, with the aim of gathering people on campus who could speak for Israel. And I did that without Marty I think, for another few years, avoiding the Prime Minister.

Busekist: Has moving to Israel for good with your family, leaving the US, ever been a plan?

Walzer: Well when we came in 1957, we certainly thought about it, but that summer was the summer I got admitted to Harvard with a big fellowship, and Judy hadn't finished Brandeis, she was in her last year – and the experience of her friends in the kibbutz had not always been so great ... No concerts in the evenings ... Certainly one of the things that influenced me was my monolingualism. I have studied many languages, but I did not function well in any of them. I always thought of English as ... well my ability to write a comprehensible English sentence was one of my talents. When I came to Israel for a semester in 1983, my daughter was a high-school junior, she took the semester off, came before me, and stayed with a family for a couple of months, and then found an apartment and I came over. And she was chattering away on the phone in Hebrew after two months. I took an ulpan[6] that year, that semester. And I got "tov me'od" [very good] on all my written assignments, but my tongue and my ear never picked up the language. I couldn't, I just ... it may have something to do with being shy about trying out the language when you know you are doing it badly. Some people do that, I couldn't. Maybe I was too old by 1983.

Busekist: When you brought groups to Israel in the 1970s, you made many connections with political activists and leaders from the left. With whom in particular?

Walzer: Our friends from the 1970s (Judy and I were together on most of our visits to Israel) are our friends still. I think of them as old Mapai-niks (then the main labor party), though in fact they came from all the left parties. The old differences (over the Soviet Union, for example) were fading and new differences (over how to oppose the occupation) were surfacing, but basically they were all at odds with the post-1967 euphoria and against the settlements. We were very close to the founders of "Shalom Achshav" (Peace Now), especially to Janet Aviad. Our oldest friends were Gur and Dahlia Ofer, he an economist who studied the Soviet economy, she a Holocaust historian; then the political theorists Brian Knei-paz and Yuli Tamir; the philosophers Yeri Yovel (and his wife, the novelist Shoshana Yovel), Avishai and Edna Margalit, and Menachem Brinker; the law professor Ruth Gavison. And many others: we had more friends in Israel than in Cambridge, New York, and Princeton together. Starting in the 1980s, we acquired an entirely new set of Israeli friends, not all of them leftists, because of the Hartman Institute philosophy conferences and my work on *The Jewish Political Tradition*. I was never engaged in party politics in Israel; that was for citizens, I thought. Our connections were always with particular people, who had different party affiliations or who moved around depending on the particular shape of left politics in any given year. I went with them to political demonstrations, but not to party meetings.

Busekist: You said earlier that you were very much against the Vietnam War but very pleased by the outcome of the 1967 war in Israel. You were not the only one, the 1967 war was supported and praised by many Western countries, parties, and intellectuals. But the left is worried – to say the least – about the consequences of the war today. Would the current situation be different had the Israeli leadership ordered a withdrawal from the occupied territories in the aftermath of the war? Do you believe they could they have done? Or is this a reasonable expectation with hindsight only? After all, Israel withdrew from Gaza (also a heavily criticized move), and has evacuated parts of Lebanon where the IDF was replaced by the Hezbollah.

Walzer: I think they could have prepared for withdrawal by rejecting, from the beginning, demands for settlement, and by announcing their readiness to return to the old lines in exchange for peace. And that stance could have been maintained for as long as necessary – but this would have taken a strong political will, a group of leaders capable of resisting the euphoria that followed upon the dramatic victory of 1967. Looking back, that certainly seems the path of wisdom. Even just pulling out, inviting the Egyptians and the Jordanians to come back without a proper peace agreement, would probably have been better than the ongoing occupation and the settlements.

So, yes, there was a period when it would have been possible to insist that in return for full peace, all the territories would go back, and Israel would hold them back only for that purpose. One of the difficulties was that there were people in the Labor Party itself, or in allied parties, who wanted to settle in at least some part of the territories. Remember Yigal Allon's idea that there should be a series of settlements in the Jordan valley . . . and we thought he was one of the good guys! Again, it would have taken very strong leaders at that moment to say "no" to eager Jews and to be ready to say "yes" to (what turned out to be very few) Arabs seeking peace. The rejectionists on the Arab side were met by the settlers on the Israeli side. You could say that they joined together to make withdrawal impossible.

Judy and I recently saw a movie, "The Lost Interview,"[7] a documentary about an interview with Ben Gurion that was done by Clinton Bailey in 1968, a very young Clinton Bailey, two or three years before Ben Gurion died, and a year after Paula's [Ben Gurion's wife] death. He is in Sde Boker (the kibbutz he retired to) by himself. Bailey did this interview, which was lost for some reason and found only a couple of years ago and edited into a documentary film. It's a six-hour interview, the film is one hour and a half, so there is a lot of cutting. It's wonderful! I never imagined Ben Gurion was a man with wit and humor. He is very funny sometimes. And very smart. And he insists in this interview that it was wrong to hold on to the territories. He was not in charge then, and I don't know if that was his view, private or public, in 1967; in any case, he didn't interfere. But they should have acted differently.

Busekist: Let's skip a couple of decades. You argued earlier for international alliances and cooperation in general. After the "Return

Marches" in 2018,[8] the International community harshly criticized Israel's reaction to the Marches (the IDF intervened forcefully to stop the Palestinians from Gaza to storm the border), but forgot to mention the role of important neighboring states who have the power to relieve the pressure on the Gaza strip: Egypt for example.[9] The constraints on the Palestinian civilians are brutal. Israeli policies about food and water supply, electricity, and so on, in short embargo policies that resemble politics short of war only from a distance (the situation is very different from the one you described regarding Iraq). But Egypt has a close-by airport, and the Egyptians could at least supply Palestine with food to relieve the civilian population, and to relieve – to put it from an Israeli perspective – Israel from some of its guilt and the international shaming for the way they treat the Palestinians. In other words, Egypt should also be held responsible for its lack of action. Would you agree?

Walzer: It's true. This is something you have to say again and again, when people condemn the Israeli siege of Gaza, you have to say it's a joint Israeli Egyptian siege and it has at least some secret support from the Palestine Authority (PA). That makes it a very complicated situation; the Egyptians as well as the Israelis can end the siege. But, still, the largest responsibility rests with Israel, which is the chief enforcer of the siege – at sea, for example. Any significant relief will have to be negotiated among the three siege partners. There was an article in *Haaretz* recently about some IDF officers who had come up with a program for relieving the siege, creating an industrial area in Northern Gaza, building a desalinization plant, extending the range for Gazan fishermen, allowing more travel out of the Strip, and much more – with the aim of avoiding another war.[10] According to the paper, the Egyptians were reluctant. The Israeli political echelon is more than reluctant; they seem either unwilling or unable to do anything on that scale, because it might look like a victory for Hamas, and I suspect that the PA [Palestinian Authority] would be reluctant as well because it would strengthen their rivals. The Egyptians believe, probably rightly, that Hamas or some elements in Hamas are helping the Islamist fighters in the Sinai, so they are not eager to strengthen Hamas. It is a difficult situation – and yet we need to argue forcefully for a radical change in Gaza; it is morally and politically important to improve living conditions there. This is something Israel could do, and it probably could force the PA and Egypt to go along.

Busekist: War, asymmetric war, involves smart leadership, we have mentioned this earlier. You are very critical of Israeli leadership, you have written about this many times,[11] and you have co-signed a petition encouraging economic boycott and non-recognition of the settlements in 2016.[12] What is your opinion on boycotts today and what would you say about Palestinian leadership?

Walzer: I would not support boycotts aimed at the state of Israel, but insofar as we can focus on the occupied territories and on the occupation itself, and insofar as we can act together with comrades in Israel, I do favor a boycott of commodities produced in the West Bank settlements. Academic boycotts, not. Free exchange is crucial to the intellectual life of the academy.

The Palestinian story is very sad; they have had, for reasons partly of their own making, a difficult history. I think that the PLO has probably been the worst national liberation movement in the history of national liberations. Its leaders have been so ideologically driven that any concern for the well-being of their own people has not figured in either tactical or strategic decision making. Not in day-to-day decision making and not in long-term decision making. Only now, so I am told, has life on the West Bank, especially compared to Gaza, gotten better, most clearly in the cities. But only a state of their own will allow real improvement in the life of ordinary Palestinians. And do their leaders really want a state of their own, alongside Israel?

Busekist: In Ramallah life is obviously easier than in Gaza. But Ramallah is far from comparing to Tel Aviv. Modernity and capitalism, access to goods and leisure may help to mitigate ideology, although they are not always conducive to secularism or democratization.

Walzer: The PA today, almost defined by its corruption, is more attentive to the well-being of its own people than in the past. But the ideological commitment from the beginning has been totalizing, aimed at the whole thing: Palestine from the River to the Sea – a mirror image of the totalizing ideology of the Israeli right. One aims at the elimination of Israel, the other at the avoidance of Palestine and the subordination of the Palestinians. I remember the moment of the Rabin–Arafat handshake; I was on the White House lawn; I was one of the people invited as a representative of Americans for Peace Now to come and watch. It was a moment of high optimism.

But looking back, I do not believe that Arafat ever conceived of himself as the president of a mini-state on the West Bank, concerned

107

about garbage collection in Nablus or the supply of fresh water in Jericho. I don't think he ever envisioned himself in that role. In most national liberation movements, there are people who imagine themselves as the future civil servants of a state. And there are some Palestinians like that, serious and competent people committed to state-building. But I don't think that the top leadership was ever like that. They thought of themselves as the leaders of a revolutionary movement committed to the destruction of the crusader state, and they were confident that even if it took a thousand years (they expected that it would be many years less), the crusader state would be destroyed. That has been a disastrous politics for their own people.

Busekist: You are referring to the over-ideologized Fatah, secular and Marxist in principle. But how does the Palestinian movement fit your *Paradox of Liberation*? Alongside the religious revival, embodied by the Hamas and the Hezbollah, there still exists a deep ideological, say leftist, liberation ideology, which has many supporters and representatives abroad.

Walzer: Yes, but the Palestinian story is similar to the stories I tell in *Paradox* – about India, Israel, and Algeria. Both Fatah and the groups to its left, like the PFLP (Popular Front for the Liberation of Palestine) – all of them were secular, and they described themselves as Marxist or, more generally, leftist. All of them were, in part at least, imitative of the FLN in Algeria – which I guess is also an example of a not very good liberation movement. There is a connection, which I tried to write about in one of my pieces on terrorism, between the choice of terror, as it was made in the FLN and the PLO (Palestine Liberation Organization), and the establishment later on of an authoritarian state or, as in the Palestinian case, an authoritarian semi-state.[13]

Initially, the Palestinian movement was quite radically secular, and then, on roughly the same time schedule as in the Arab world generally, there was a religious revival, which didn't entirely displace the old leftism, but has made it increasingly marginal (except, maybe, in the diaspora, about which I know much less). We now have two Palestines in the West Bank and Gaza; one of them is brutal, authoritarian and corrupt, the corruption being a mitigating factor, and the other one is brutal, authoritarian, and (at least in appearance) righteous. The righteousness, I am afraid, is worse. I don't know how strong the religious revival is on the West Bank; I suspect stronger than in Fatah itself. The PA regime is not repressive in the same way as Hamas. The attack on the freedom of women is not the same, in fact it doesn't exist in the West Bank. So the Fatah is still, mostly, a secular movement.

Busekist: What are the chances of an appeasement in the region? The idea of a negotiated solution seems to recede at the same pace as new territories are settled in the West Bank. Part of the Israeli opinion does take note of this evolution; but many Israelis, mostly on the right, argue that even if they cede territories in the West bank, which I believe they are hardly willing to do, there will be no improvement in the Israeli-Palestinian relations. The dream of an accord on the Green line is a nice dream, but a dream nevertheless today.

The situation evolves toward a one-state "solution" which is not a negotiated solution, but the result of the ongoing settlement policy combined with some kind of realism on behalf of the Israeli Palestinians, in Jaffa, Haifa, and in other towns where there is a strong proportion of Palestinian citizens, who do not necessarily love Israel – many of them have indeed resigned themselves to a life without a state of their own, many do not vote (as we have seen in the last elections) – maybe because they prefer sending their kids to school and making a decent living over the uncertainty of a Palestinian state. What role should the Israeli Arabs play in the negotiations in your view? Should they act as informal ambassadors for example and how?

Walzer: It seems to me that, without some kind of external intervention, the drift is toward one state, excluding Gaza, but one state: Israel and the West Bank. I think that a right-wing government, like the current one, would want to postpone making "one state" formal and final. Its members would prefer the current situation, but with ongoing settlement, more and more encroachment on Palestinian land, the intent being to make the two-state option impossible. What's going on, with strong governmental support, is the increasing Israelization of the West Bank – and at some point, soon maybe, Israel is going to look like one state with a disenfranchised Palestinian population. I suppose that's sustainable for a while; assuming that Gaza is not included, the Jews would be a majority for years to come. But it would be an ugly situation, universally condemned, and not sustainable over the long run. I don't know what would change that. I have heard murmurs and talks again, as I remember from the 1970s, about a "Jordanian solution." But why would the King and his government want anything like that? It would be very dangerous for their regime to bring in the West Bank. And yet, it does make a lot of sense: with the West Bank incorporated, Jordan would be a Palestinian state.

Busekist: Would it be more coherent if it were Jordan instead of a shaky one-state solution?

Walzer: Yes. I will tell you one more story. In the 1970s, I was coming to Israel often. Sometimes when I went back to the States, I would meet with former colleagues now in power, a few times with Kissinger when he was National Security adviser, and once with Brzezinski who held the same position in the Carter administration. Brzezinski had been a teacher of mine. So, I came back from a trip to Israel and we sat and talked about what was going on. And he told me this story. At one point, in his discussions about a possible Jordanian solution, he asked King Hussein what would happen if there was an election in the West Bank. And the King said, "If I run the election, I will win the election." A memorable line. I think of it often because in 2005, the Americans ran an election in Iraq, and our man came in third. Americans are imperial incompetents. But I don't think there is any eagerness, probably no willingness, in Jordan to take on the West Bank.

Busekist: For the past forty years, except for a short period of six years, the Israeli left has not been in power. As a social democrat and a supporter of the Israeli left, what do you think is the reason for this, and what changes would enable the left to return to power?

Walzer: What we now see as the rightward turn across the West began earlier in Israel, for reasons pretty specific to Israel. Firstly, the security situation and terrorism, both of which play into the hands of the right. Two decisive moments: the terrorist attacks during the election that followed Rabin's death and the rockets from Gaza after the Israeli withdrawal. Secondly, Sephardic resentment and Ashkenazi hubris – with the result that much of the left's natural constituency is hostile to the old left parties. Thirdly, the Russian immigrants, whose secularism should put them on the left but whose nationalism and uneasiness with anything that smacks of socialism put them on the right. Fourthly, the doubled religious revival – the zealotry of the settler movement and the growth of the Haredi sects[14] strengthens right-wing politics. And lastly, the lack of imagination and strength of will among the left's leaders (this is true also in much of Europe); they are nice people, smart people, with the right positions, but without fire. We've always been told that bad times bring forth great leaders – Lincoln, Churchill, etc. So, the times seem bad enough: we're waiting.

Busekist: What is your opinion on the "nation-state law"?[15]

Walzer: It's a vile law. David Grossman got it right. It has no operational clauses; it's purely gestural – giving the finger to the Arabs (and, maybe unintentionally, to the Druse, too). It has a history, going all the way back to Jabotinski,[16] who loved uniforms, and marching, and shaking the fist. But, still, he might not have loved this. It doesn't do anything, but it will be used as a cover to do things in the future – unless the anger it has produced has political results.

Busekist: We talked about nations and states, but not really about nationalism. Zionism is obviously a version of nationalism. In her book *Liberal Nationalism*,[17] Yuli Tamir (Professor and ex-Minister of Culture and Education), in a very Rawlsian fashion, writes that social justice and democratic debate are possible only if there is a shared value system, a common citizenship, a historically shared national identity. For all these reasons, national belonging should be a relevant information disclosed to the people under the veil of ignorance. She believes that we should perpetuate and not abandon nationhood, but in an open, a "thin" way, permeable to specific cultures, legally recognized and culturally valued. This sounds quite close to what you say in *Thick and Thin* for example. What would a defensible version of Zionism–nationalism be in your view?

Walzer: I am indeed a liberal nationalist, like Yuli Tamir. I am also an international nationalist – I recognize a universal right to national self-determination; I believe that every nation that needs a state, for the sake of physical security or cultural expression, should have one. Not only the Jews, but also the Palestinians and the Kurds. Not only the Palestinians and the Kurds, but also the Jews. I am suspicious of anyone who supports every national liberation movement in the world except the Jewish one. That kind of anti-Zionism does cross the line into antisemitism.[18] Brutal criticism of Israeli policies is well short of the line.

Liberal nationalist and nationalist; but why any kind of nationalism? Why do I love the Jewish people in exactly the way Hannah Arendt said she couldn't? The explanation is difficult for modern, secular, emancipated men and women. It has something to do with the fact that my grandparents lived in a certain way, with memories, celebrations, rituals, and moral commitments that are still part of my life and that I want to be part of my grandchildren's life. And all this I share with other people, who have similar grandparents and similar hopes for their grandchildren. And these people, across the generations, share my obsessions and laugh at my jokes. (But I am not sure that Hannah Arendt would laugh at some of the best Jewish jokes.)

Busekist: What role should the diaspora play ideally? You have mentioned in several places[19] that the attitude of the American public in general, and the American Jewry in particular, has changed in the last decade(s), especially among the younger generations and on College campuses. How do you explain this growing criticism toward Israel? In France, we witness a new and uninhibited antisemitism that leads many Jewish families to make Aliyah, and an "Israelization" of the French Jews,[20] which pertains mainly to a strong identification with Israel, and namely the Israeli right. In the "exportation of the conflict" from its original place – the Middle East – to France (but I believe this is true elsewhere), a significant part of the French Jewry virtually lives in Israel (this is particularly true for the Sephardic Jews) and takes part in the Israeli debates. Is that true in the US also? Or is the American Jewry a specific community? And in how far has the American society (Jewish and non-Jewish) changed *vis-à-vis* Israel? Is there a sociological/generational explanation? Religious? (the respective numbers of orthodox v. reformed /liberal Jews?), a fatigue about the conflict? No peace in sight, etc.?

Walzer: I will begin with "ideally." Jews in the diaspora have benefited (often when the benefit was life itself) from liberalism, pluralism, religious toleration, church/state separation, and all that. So, ideally, we should be engaged supporters of all that in Israel. However proud we are of Israel and however concerned we are about Israel's safety, we should feel empathy with the Arab minority and with the refugees arriving from Africa. And we should be critical of Israel as an occupying power. But I want to say something about the nature of our support and our criticism, given that we are not Israeli citizens and that our children are not, or only rarely, serving in the army. That's not a bar to criticism; I have criticized the political policies of many countries even though I don't share the life, good or bad, of their citizens. But in none of those countries is the survival of the state at risk, and Israel, despite its military might, lives with that risk. It not only has conventional enemies; it has enemies committed to its destruction. So, when I criticize Israeli policies, I always align myself with people in the country who are making the same critique. I don't stand on some imaginary mountaintop and wag my finger at the bad Israelis; I stand with my Israeli comrades.

Most American Jews simply stand with the Israeli government. And since the government has moved so far to the right, this is a difficult position to defend – especially difficult given that these same American Jews are mostly liberals at home. Young people are increasingly unwilling to defend that position; some of them join far left anti-Israel groups; more of them simply withdraw, focus their politics on other things. I continue to support groups like APN (Americans for Peace Now)[21] because I believe that if American Jews, especially the young ones, knew more about Israeli leftists, they would join me in joining with them.

Busekist: In an open letter to the supporters of APN in 2005 you exhort them to join the many APN grassroots initiatives and even quote the Exodus story to remind the supporters that "the way to liberation is not easy – it is a long march through the wilderness. Please join me in helping Israel and her Arab neighbors secure a better, brighter future for themselves. There is no way to get from here to there except by marching together."[22] In 2006 again, your tone is even more urgent, as you start out with very concrete facts about impoverished middle classes due to the government's channeling of funds to the settlements: "The settlement movement is a folly and a failure. It has helped to impoverish ordinary Israelis. And it is time for it to end."[23] And a couple of years later, in 2008, Israel celebrates its sixtieth anniversary (you mention the "misused triumph of 1967") – again: "The role of the Israeli peace movement isn't to make peace. It takes a government to do that, and the government that finally does it may or may not be a 'peacenik' government. The peace movement builds and sustains the readiness for peace, the openness to opportunities when they arise, the sense of a possible future settlement. The more vulnerable ordinary Israelis feel, the more fragile that sense of possibility will become, and the more crucial the work of those who want to keep it alive. No peace without a trustworthy partner – that maxim is true enough. But it is also true that there won't be peace without an Israeli readiness to trust a trustworthy partner." So why do you say that only the Israeli left can pave the road for peace? ("The real challenge for Israel, which only the left can meet, is to defend the physical safety of Israel's citizens forcefully since force is unavoidable, while at the same time preparing the ground for peace"),[24] as you argued that even a non "peacenik" government could do the job. We do know that the safety argument, has been key to Netanyahu's success in all the last elections.

113

Walzer: Actually, it would take a very strong left government to make peace – given the character of the other side and the legitimate fearfulness of so many Israelis. A leader from the right, like Begin, would have an easier, though not an easy, time. But right now, the right-wing government is doing everything it can to make a negotiated peace impossible, and only the left can hold open the possibility of an agreement with the Palestinians. That should be the task of Israeli leftists, a minimalist task but critically important – and the international left should support them, which means holding on to the idea of two states. The ideological leaders of the BDS movement (Boycott, Divestment, Sanctions) are one-staters; they are actually opposed to the existence of anything like the state of Israel – and that, obviously, doesn't help, isn't intended to help, the Israeli left.

Busekist: What is your position on BDS? You have called for a boycott yourself once.[25] I guess "targeted" boycott is the important notion (maybe as in "smart sanctions" we talked about earlier?) The International movement has many ramifications on college campuses (and in the economy: in France stores are being targeted for selling Israeli products – and not only from the settlements, some universities, unlike the Modern Language Association, indeed either boycott Israeli universities, or decline invitations to participate in conferences). Israel is accused of apartheid, colonialism, imperialism, human rights violations, segregation in important sectors such as housing and the workplace, etc. the list is long, and the supporters are growing, on the far left in particular, but not only: the movement seems to spread beyond the usual activism against Israel.[26] In light of Israel's travel ban on BDS supporters, you argue that Israel in fact strengthens the BDS movement by eliminating the distinction between those who support boycotts aimed at the settlements and supporters of boycotts aimed at Israel in general.[27] Do you participate in the campus debates? And in which way?

Walzer: I have talked with student leaders in New York urging them to oppose an academic boycott; I spoke at a large meeting on the Princeton campus just before a vote on BDS (the BDS resolution was defeated), and I am a member of a group of liberal and left academics who fight against BDS on every campus where we have people and in all the professional associations. Academic boycotts are never justified – they are an offense against the necessary freedom of the intellectual community. Economic boycotts are harder. Some of us support a boycott carefully targeted at products of the occupied

114

territories, even while fighting against a boycott that would undercut the strength and security of the state (Israel, again, has real enemies). As you suggest above, the fight gets harder and harder as the policies of the Israeli government get worse and worse. In principle, it is an easy line to draw: we oppose the policies of the government; we believe in the existence, and hope for the well-being, of the state. I am old enough to remember opposing the policies of the French government in Algeria without calling for the elimination of France. In the Israeli case, it isn't easy to draw that line – and though everyone is reluctant to say so, this has something to do, perhaps a lot to do, with antisemitism.

7

Political Theory

Busekist: An intellectual is, ever since the Dreyfus Affair, an academic, writer, or artist who is engaged, who intervenes in the public debate and accepts, at least for a while, to give up the comfort of his or her office or studio. You are no doubt an intellectual: you have taken risks, you have exposed yourself to contradiction and dispute, in academia and as editor of *Dissent* without ever giving up on your deepest convictions. How has your political activism beginning in the 1960s, and its potential contradictions – defending the Six Day War in 1967 while opposing the Vietnam War – shaped your work and your identity as a professor, as a political theorist?

Walzer: In American academic life, from about the 1980s on, students were pressed to become very professional. I used to argue with political scientists, economists, or sociologists, and with my students, telling them that even if there was no obvious politics at the moment, they should at least be writing for *Dissent* or other political magazines alongside what they were doing academically – because their academic work would be better, and because they would be acting as citizens; the left needs activist citizens. For me the experience of politics was a limited experience: a decade of activity on the left at a time when the left was oppositional. We could hardly imagine being in power. But my political work did shape the way I write political theory; it shaped my commitment to avoid abstraction, to write as concretely as possible, to use historical examples instead of weird hypotheticals the way analytic philosophers do. And it led me to take maximal advantage of the political theorist's "license." Political theorists have a license to take and to defend political positions explicitly, which political scientists are not supposed to do.

116

One of my last courses in Harvard was called simply "Socialism," and it was a defense of my version of socialist theory and practice. And the only commitment I felt I had to live up to in the classroom was to tell the students about the strongest arguments against socialism. I wouldn't have to do this at a political rally. All my books are political arguments, they are not high theory. In each case, I was trying to make an argument about how things should be. *Just and Unjust Wars* is an argument in favor of certain wars and against others; *Spheres of Justice* was an argument for a version of social democracy, against the more radical egalitarianism of the left and the libertarianism of the right. My last book is an openly political book. It's called *A Foreign Policy for the Left.*[1] It derives directly from Bernie Sanders' campaign for president of the US; he aspired to lead the world's hegemonic power, and he had nothing to say about foreign policy. The left generally has not been very good on foreign policy. In this book, I describe what I think the left should be saying, above all about the use of force abroad.

My book on *Secular Revolutions and Religious Counterrevolutions*[2] is an effort to address, in a way that I think the left hasn't done, the unexpected revival of religious politics around the world: Hindutva in India, Buddhist zealotry in Myanmar, the settlers' movement in Israel, Islamist zealotry, all of this . . . We didn't expect it. Secularization was supposed to be an inevitable process, a triumph of science and reason, and now we are face to face with religious craziness . . . How did it happen? I looked at three cases, India, Israel, and Algeria: what remains of the nationalist liberation movements that succeeded in establishing a state in each of these countries? The state is being challenged thirty or forty years later by a militant religious revival and we have to deal with that. So yes, I think of my academic engagement as a continuation of my political engagement.

Busekist: You are sensitive to context, and you are a pragmatic reasoner, but it seems to me that there is also an ethical foundation, a deep system of morality in your writings. Do you recognize yourself in this description?

Walzer: Yes, . . . but I have never tried to write about the foundations of ethics. And it's not because I believe that there are no arguments that could be made. I suspect that the ethical argument goes back to human vulnerability. We are all vulnerable to pain and death, something like Hobbes' statement that any human being can kill any other human being . . . if not by strength, then by cunning and so on.

And out of shared vulnerability we have constructed moral rules that protect us from each other. But I have never tried to work that out. For me, the moral universe simply exists, we inhabit it.

The metaphor I have always used is: we are living in a house. We assume the house has a foundation, but I've never gone down there. I am trying to describe the living space, the shape of the rooms – and to suggest better ways of furnishing the house; sometimes I make suggestions for renovation. Morality is a social construction but it's not, it's not their social construction or our social construction, it's a social construction over many, many centuries and it reflects our humanity, our common humanity, and so the basic rules of our morality are universal rules.

When I read military history before writing *Just and Unjust Wars*, I also read some anthropology, but I didn't do extensive reading in the literature of other religions or civilizations. I did enough however to find that the basic rules about aggression and noncombatant immunity are indeed universal: the basic conception that war should be a combat between combatants from which noncombatants are shielded – that conception you find in every major religion, in all civilizations; and it makes sense because wars are fought across cultural and political boundaries; so the arguments about what to do and what not to do have to be comprehensible across those boundaries. This universal morality exists and we can find it by living in the house and investigating the structure of the house which our ancestors have built over a very long period of time. And some of the critical prohibitions – because morality comes mostly in prohibitions – are very strong. I have tried in everything I write to sustain that forcefulness: don't commit aggression, don't kill civilians, don't torture.

Busekist: The house metaphor is a telling one and it is present throughout your work. I have mentioned it earlier. What I believe your readers may struggle with, those who are critical in particular, is the pendulum between normative principles, the prohibitions you just mentioned, and the necessary subjectivity of empirical evaluations in specific situations. There is no fixed system: the house changes with new owners and new interior designers, even though the deep foundation remains relatively stable. We talked about this when we mentioned your relationship with the analytic philosophers and the use of thought experiments.[3] From a constructivist perspective, to put it very simply, you begin with say the veil of ignorance – modeling irrelevance by ignorance – and you end up with two general principles.

You argue in a very different way. You start from within the house, you don't invent the house,[4] you live in the house, you are talking to the other residents, and to the residents from other houses with a different architecture. But that is, paradoxically, an uneasy way of thinking about morality and justice. You need to be morally, politically reasonable in a singular – or rather in a universal – way, beyond the internal coherence of the argument. If you look at the "just-war industry" your book has generated, it seems much easier to have a clear-cut and defined ethical program you can stick to in every case.

Walzer: Yes, I guess so. I've never been a systematic thinker, I write about politics and I write about the political issues that seem to me of great concern, at the moment, and I hope that what I say about these different issues isn't inconsistent, but I've never thought in systematic terms. Each of my books has a political purpose. *Just and Unjust Wars* begins as an argument against Vietnam (and in support of the Israeli pre-emptive attack on Egypt) and an argument for making distinctions, and, above all, an argument about how to fight and how not. I think the *in bello* is the part of the book I was the most invested in.

Spheres of Justice is an effort to say that we need, we should work for, a more egalitarian society; but that the radical egalitarianism of some leftists in the 1960s doesn't make sense. We have to be able to recognize that human beings are different and will excel in different spheres of life, and we have to be able to recognize their achievements. When you are thinking of the best novel of the year, you will have to pick one book, and that's very inegalitarian, but book reviewers are not required to give the same amount of praise and blame to every book.

So . . . all of my books are written that way; they are not systematic – I mean, they are not different elements of a single system. When I wrote *Just and Unjust Wars*, it seemed obvious that a principle like noncombatant immunity was a universal principle. And later on, when I wrote *Spheres of Justice*, it seemed equally obvious that the principle, "careers should be open to talent," depends on what having a "career" means in the society in which you live. So anyway, there is no system. That's right.

Busekist: You believe that we need "small theories."[5] I was wondering how you would define small theories and also how we should teach them. Are small theories "small" because they are modest in scope, or are they "small" because they do not call for dramatic changes, paradigm shifts, but are supposed to be an input for incremental social change? Karl Popper has this line about piecemeal social engineering I quite like,[6] and you often write about progress "here and there," at a slow but steady pace.[7]

Walzer: You need to have some coherent ideas about how the world works if you are to act in the world. The grandiosity of Marxist historical materialism never appealed to me. However, I do think it is important to understand, and to understand means to have some small theories, about how the class struggle works, how people are mobilized for political action, how coalitions are formed, what the economy is likely to look like ten years from now, what kind of responses people have had and may have in the future to growing (or declining) inequality. We need to understand, and these are more social science theories, based on empirical work, than political theories of the Hobbes–Locke–Hegel sort. We need to have some ideas about when insurrections or uprisings occur, how they are different from things like the medieval jacqueries, uprisings that come and go very fast and leave no residue. What kind of political action produces possibilities for the future, the chance of ongoing action. And I also think of something like noncombatant immunity as a small theory. It is a moral doctrine, but it requires some exposition and it requires historical examples. When you put all that together, you have a small theory about why civilians should be immune, and what the qualifications for that immunity are, when civilian injury ("collateral damage") can be justified – as in the doctrine of "double effect," for example.

Double effect is a small theory that I have defended – and also revised. The doctrine holds that if you are aiming at a legitimate military target but know that the attack will produce death or injury to civilians living nearby, the second effect, since it is unintentional, is allowed, so long as the injury it produces isn't disproportionate to the value of the military target. I argued that there must also be a second intention: to minimize the injury to civilians as much as possible. A lot of philosophers don't like the original doctrine; some have endorsed the revision. And I guess humanitarian intervention is another example of a small theory. It is often debated in the context of very big theories about imperialism and neocolonialism, about Western powers with malign reasons to intervene in the third world.

I think it was my innovation to insist that the key examples of humanitarian intervention, the ones that makes the idea clearest, are examples like Vietnam and Cambodia, India and East Pakistan (now Bangladesh), Tanzania and Uganda, precisely examples that do not involve the big powers. I am sure there are strategic interests in each of these cases – but they do not involve what is standardly called imperialism and Western neocolonialism.[8] If you look closely at examples like that, I think you get a much clearer understanding of what humanitarianism is and when it is justified. Or even, and that's another key issue: is it something that is right to do, or is it something that is obligatory to do? I have argued, very simply: if you can stop a massacre, you should.

Busekist: You told me that you do not consider yourself as a philosopher (I beg to differ), but that you nevertheless became friends with a group of philosophers doing "normative political theory."

Walzer: Yes, this was at Princeton in the early and mid 1960s. The group included Bob Nozick,[9] Tom Nagel,[10] and, very importantly for me, Stuart Hampshire,[11] the English philosopher, who was a visiting professor in Princeton in one of those years. It was then that I gave my first talk on political obligation – the talk was later included in *Obligations*.[12] I gave this talk and Stuart Hampshire came up to me afterwards and urged me to do more "normative" work. That was very important for me because I really wasn't a philosopher. I'm still not a philosopher, at least not of the analytic sort. I don't have an analytical mind of the kind that Bob Nozick, for example, had to a high degree. Later when we taught a course together at Harvard, our two different styles were very apparent.

Busekist: Is that when you became allergic to "weird thought experiments"?

Walzer: Yes. It started either when I was in Princeton or when I went back to Harvard and joined a group of philosophers (I was included, I think as an act of generosity), who were inspired by [John] Rawls, who published his *Theory of Justice* in 1971.[13] We had all read his book before that; versions of the chapters in mimeographed form circulated in the late 1960s. That is also when we founded SELF whose official name was the Society for Ethical and Legal Philosophy. The unofficial name – a sign of our youthful arrogance – was the Society for the Elimination of Lousy Philosophy.

Busekist: (*laughs*) How did you fit into this group of analytics? You do not share their approach, and you still don't, as you have just noted.

Walzer: This was my philosophical education nonetheless, but it was also the time when I learned that I was not the same kind of writer as the others – although I admired them. They were trying to write an engaged philosophy, and that was my project, too. Together we founded *Philosophy and Public Affairs*. Marshall Cohen, one of the SELFers, was the first editor. I contributed my piece on the Second World War[14] to the first issue.

Busekist: You were – and you are – a philosopher of another kind. Why do you stress that you are not a philosopher? You have said this many times during our conversation. But analytical philosophy is not the only way of doing philosophy, even if this specific style seems to have won among the Anglo-American philosophers. What you do is "practice oriented," and I mean this in the most positive way: you do not like theory without practice (hence the allergy to thought experiments). Instead of starting out with grand principles, instead of doing "constructivist work," you first look at how things work in the real world, you begin with empirical work, as in *Just and Unjust Wars* for example. Your philosophy, compared to the analytics, reaches conclusions from another end. The analytics are "inventors" in your language, you belong to the "interpreters" . . .[15] But the discussions were friendly and interesting nonetheless, although you didn't belong to the same club?

Walzer: They were friendly and certainly interesting. I was writing *Just and Unjust Wars* in those years. This is a book the others very much approved, even though I was using historical rather than hypothetical examples. It was when I wrote *Spheres of Justice* that some of them thought I had become an apostate.

Busekist: *Spheres* deserves a chapter of its own, we will talk about it. In those years at Harvard, you co-taught a class with Bob Nozick. How did that work? You are obviously from two different philosophical planets, so how did you manage to teach a comprehensive class? He probably did Libertarianism and you Socialism?

Walzer: Yes, the course was called "Capitalism and Socialism"; he did the capitalist part. His version of capitalism was, well, different from the standard American variety . . . he believed that capitalism, as he described it, was a just economic system and that a revolution to establish capitalism in the United States would be justified (*laughs*). So, he was in his own way a radical.

Busekist: So his book, *Anarchy, State and Utopia*[16] was the result of that class? It was published in 1974, and it immediately reached a wide audience. It is still an influential book. Almost every course on libertarianism starts with *Anarchy, State and Utopia*.

Walzer: Yes, it's an impressive book. We taught the course together as an extended argument. This was the format: he would give two lectures, laying out an argument on some issue, I would respond with one lecture. He would respond to my lecture with one more lecture. Then I would give two lectures, he would respond, and I would respond. That's the way we went for the semester . . .

Busekist: The kids must have loved it!

Walzer: The kids did love it. Yes. The students who were there liked the course, definitely. I worked harder than for any other course in my life. Bob was very, very, quick in a way that the best philosophers are quick. He also had a great wit. Not quite like Sydney Morgenbesser,[17] but that kind of smartness. You know the Morgenbesser story? Can we digress? Sydney Morgenbesser was . . . He wasn't part of our group, but he was a philosopher at Columbia during this time. He died some years ago. He was a very Jewish philosopher, with a wonderful wit whose witticisms were repeated all across the philosophical world.[18] In fact, he didn't write much, if anything. But he was famous for asking questions like: "What is the most important philosophical question?" His answer: "Are there Jews on other planets?'" (*laughs*). He was also famous because during a lecture on linguistics in Columbia, somebody was explaining how [according to J. L. Austin] in the English language a double negative makes a positive, but a double positive doesn't make a negative. And Sydney called out from the audience: "Yeah, yeah"! He came to the Hartman Institute, he was a regular at the annual philosophy conference[19] from the beginning. Very, very smart, more Jewish than leftist, though he would have been a lefty if he had ever written about politics.[20]

But I should have said more about the Harvard course: Nozick's book came directly out of it, and some ten years later, I published *Spheres of Justice*, whose key arguments were first tried out in the course with Nozick. I learned a lot about what I believed in that course, going back and forth with Bob.

Busekist: Did you, your group of philosophers, read any French philosophy at that time? In Europe there was a big renewal in philosophic

123

style, with a new generation of post-war philosophers. Where did you take your inspiration from? Britain? Only the American historical and philosophical literature? I mean not you specifically because I know that you have an interest in French history. You wrote about Louis XVI and the French Revolution. But the rest of your group: was Sartre studied in the philosophy or in the literature departments?

Walzer: No, not at all. No French philosophy. Well, I read Sartre's fiction and his plays – and admired particularly the play about "Dirty Hands"; I think that I wrote somewhere about Merleau Ponty who was in the *Temps Modernes* crowd, and who defended terrorism.[21] But I also had a connection in the 1960s with *Esprit*.[22] Joël Roman was my connection there.

Busekist: So, no currency for French philosophy? You do mention continental philosophy regularly however – at least in the geographical sense. In a very critical text "The Lonely Politics of Michel Foucault" you call Foucault an "infantile leftist"[23] . . .

Walzer: Did I call him that? (*laughs*). You know, that was originally supposed to be a lecture at Princeton University to which he was going to respond. That's the way I wrote it, and then he canceled the visit and I just gave the lecture. It was supposed to be an encounter, but that never happened, and I never met him. Reading him, I thought that there was some kind of deep political irresponsibility in Foucault. His call for "resistance" at every micro-point in the disciplinary system doesn't add up to a resistance movement, doesn't help us shape a left politics – in fact, again and again, he repudiates any such project.

Busekist: Foucault is very popular in France. Our students read him, and I guess there is a certain "Foucault industry" among philosophy and social sciences students. What my students and colleagues mostly write about in the last decade or so, after many books and articles on the surveillance society, is about "neoliberalism" and the way Foucault understood the term.

Walzer: He seems to have become a supporter of neo-liberalism toward the end of his life. I have read Daniel Zamora's analysis and critique of the pieces in which Foucault takes that position. It does make sense, given Foucault's earlier work. The "social security state" (what we call the welfare state) is one more modern institution that traps people in its disciplinary net. So, in Foucauldian terms, deregulation and the dismantling of social security must have an emancipatory effect. I would be surprised, however, if he didn't have some sense that liberating men and women from the state exposes them to the micro- (and macro-) power of capitalist entrepreneurs, managers, and bankers. But maybe he thought the free market to be more free than the liberal or democratic state. Obviously, I don't. What has become French "postmodernism" and made such a splash in the US – that was not part of my world. Not at all.

Busekist: How do you explain this split among the students? These very dissimilar preferences? Those who went for Rawlsian ideas and style, "realist utopias," analytical philosophy, theories of justice (and the epigones who participate in the post-Rawlsian industry), and those who chose postmodernism and "French theory."

Walzer: Yes, those were certainly two very different groups. I confess that it's much easier for me to sympathize with the first group than the second. Agree or disagree, there is no difficulty in understanding the arguments of the analytic philosophers. But I have encountered passionate defenders of Derrida, say, who cannot tell me in simple English what he is arguing. It is very exciting to be the member of a group of people expounding to each other an esoteric doctrine – a doctrine that is very deep (but the depths are murky). The splits among students in the 1960s and 1970s extended further: don't forget the Straussians,[24] who played a significant part in academic political theory, and in my life. When I was re-hired, when I was brought back from Princeton to the Harvard government department, the department was divided. Half of the department wanted to hire Harvey Mansfield,[25] and half of the department was for me! And that was clearly a left–right division. The department chair went to the dean and asked if they could make two appointments.

In those days, that was the easiest way to solve the problem, there was a lot of money around, and that's what they did. They hired both of us. We were careful colleagues. We got along well enough, but very carefully. Mansfield's students took my courses and my students took his courses, but as I must have said somewhere, his students in my courses were ... they combined deference and condescension. Odd combination! They were deferential because I was a professor and they believed in hierarchy; they believed in authority; and they were condescending because I didn't know the truth! One or two of them broke free from that and actually became friends. Cliff Orwin,[26] who comes now regularly to the Hartman conferences, teaches in Toronto. He is a liberal and flexible Straussian; we have overlapping commitments. Another one, who wasn't a student of mine, but who became a friend later on, is Steven Smith,[27] now at Yale, who also comes to Hartman. He is very much a Straussian, a student of Cropsey[28] in Chicago. But he is also a liberal, with a native sweetness.

Busekist: There is evidently a big difference between your thinking, your approach, and Leo Strauss' style. But I do find that there is an echo in your work, especially on Judaism, regarding Strauss' critique of modernity: moral relativism, the rift between ethics and politics, and the trade-off between the ancient *phronesis* and science and technique. You do not share the common idea that political modernity can only be achieved through forgetting the Ancients. That the moderns have nothing to learn from the ancients.

Ancient Judaism namely has a lot to teach us, if only through the social critique of the prophets. Modern politics cannot be fully understood without going back to the Book. In this light, faith, and hence truth, must be considered seriously, even though we are well aware that the Hebrew Bible opens a path of infinite readings and interpretations. Your writings on religion take faith very seriously – religion is about truth claims – even if they are debated in the Jewish tradition. It seems to me that you share part of these convictions with the Straussians.

Walzer: Well, I was certainly closer to the Straussians than to the post-modernists – for one thing I could understand what the Straussians were saying. They read texts carefully, and they expanded the canon – to include Shakespeare's plays, for example, and biblical texts, too, long before I got to them. They were politically engaged, though somewhere to my right. Their cultural conservatism had some appeal to me; I did believe in great books – though I didn't share their excessive admiration for Great Men (and I mean Men). Yes, as you say, Strauss and all the Straussians were committed to Truth, but – and this is critical – not for the masses. They imagined that all true philosophers wrote truthfully only for each other, in ways hidden from ordinary readers (like me).

Finally, I am quite ready to admire the Ancients, but I have never thought that Athens in its classical moment represents the human heights, never reached again. Hannah Arendt and her followers seem to think that when the Athenians met in assembly and voted on whether to invade Sicily, they were citizens and free political actors in a way that we moderns can only dream about (no matter that they made the wrong decision). The Straussians attribute the same unmatched excellence to the philosophers of ancient Greece, and I don't see it. To me, it is a kind of idolatry. I never met Strauss himself. Harvey [Mansfield] had studied with him; he was a first generation Straussian. The second, third generations, were sometimes just disciples in the bad sense of that word. Those are the ones I argued with; some of them became the intellectuals of the neocons. So my greatest disagreement was with the Straussian epigones, who were just too happy with their secret knowledge.

Busekist: It seems *Dissent* coined the term "neocon."

Walzer: We may have done that. It wasn't me. Who would it have been?

Busekist: According to Maurice Isserman, it was Michael Harrington.[29] His pieces on the history of *Dissent* like "Steady Work: Sixty Years of *Dissent*," are very well-informed papers which give the reader a sense of the different generations of editorship.

Walzer: Oh yes! I thought they were good.

Busekist: So around at that time gravitated the Rawlsians, the Postmodernists, and the Straussians. What about members of the Frankfurt school?

Walzer: There was an American group of people who called themselves critical theorists and who identified with the German idealist tradition and, more specifically, with Habermas and his friends. Writing that unpublished book on continental political thought, I did read all the Germans. I wrote a chapter on Kant and another one on Hegel, but I wrote about Kant's essays, like *Perpetual Peace*. I couldn't read the big books; I never did. I became a political theorist without reading Kant's *Critique*. And I struggled with the *Phenomenology*,[30] (*laughs*) but I wrote essentially on some of the smaller and easier things that Hegel wrote at various times.

I read the early Habermas, I was sympathetic to the civil society stuff and what he wrote about the coffee houses of eighteenth-century London.[31] I did write one critique of ideal speech theory, a piece on what I called "philosophical conversations"[32] – where you know in advance the agreement you are supposed to reach. But this was almost my only engagement. I didn't think that was the right way to write about politics. And then on the 75th anniversary of the founding of the Institute for Social Research in Princeton, in 1999, I was invited to come to Frankfurt and speak at the celebration. I spoke admiringly of the critical theorists and of the arguments they generated, but I insisted that social criticism, as I imagined it, did not require anything quite like Critical Theory – in fact, big theories like Marx's or like the theory of mass society or false consciousness often made for very bad social criticism. Axel Honneth later responded to my lecture, and I replied in a festschrift for Axel. So – a friendly disagreement but still pretty deep. Another example of my preference for "small" theories.

Busekist: When I asked Axel Honneth about your argument, he responded exactly like you: a friendly disagreement, but a disagreement nevertheless. But it seems to me that there are bridges between your work: both of you are worried about a kind of social justice that takes concrete individuals into account, their subjective realization and the recognition of their specific identities. Honneth looks at the "struggle for recognition," not only in terms of class, and not only within grand theories (Marxism or post-Marxism); he studies moral and political cultures that allow agents to express their experiences in their own language. While you take your inspiration and your references in different texts (the Bible versus Hegel . . .), you seem to share a certain way of doing social critique. Can these disagreements be explained by the differences in your philosophical or theoretical training? Between philosophy – reading the big books – and political science or political theory (although many theorists are actually trained in philosophy, in the US especially but also in France and in Europe in general). Or is it the way you read these texts and write about them that distinguishes you?

Walzer: Partly, I guess, it's the texts I *don't* read that make the difference. But it is also the *Dissent* training. Trying to write English the way Orwell taught us to write English or like Irving Howe wrote English. For Irving as an editor, writing was a commitment to democracy: to write in a prose that would be accessible for ordinary people.

Busekist: In French there is a nice line by Boileau, known to all French pupils, that has less to do with the democratic aspect of clarity, than with the intellectual facet. "What is clearly thought out is clearly

128

expressed" (*ce que l'on conçoit bien s'énonce clairement*). You always write in a very clear style. Maybe that is the reason you identified less or not at all with French theory, because some of the representatives use unnecessary complicated language?

Walzer: That indeed made me hostile to a lot of them. Derrida was not writing in my language, even when he was translated into English, it wasn't my English . . . (*laughs*). I sat with Avishai Margalit[33] while we were in Jerusalem recently. He was sick and weak at the time and talked very softly, but he was himself in every other way, intellectually lively, and he described a meeting with Derrida when they were both together in some conference in Norway. He talked with Derrida at breakfast and they went for a walk and Derrida was, Avishai thought, a good Jewish social democrat. It was so nice to talk to him, he said, and then Derrida stood up to lecture, and there was this radical transformation, suddenly he was talking in a totally different language . . .

Busekist: There is one book which you would probably like – very inspiring, I like it very much – it is a great book about language, about Derrida's struggle to speak an authentic language and about deconstruction in relation with language skills.[34] He argues that he has only *one* language, but it is not *his* language (he refers to the colonial French, and the language of high culture): he describes himself as monolingual (as you do), but says that he needs more than one language to do philosophy (which is a way of defining deconstruction). I am not an expert on Derrida, but he described very beautifully how you have to appropriate a language without being able to fully do so.

Walzer: We should fill in the argument with Jeff McMahan here. Because one of the differences between us has to do with why I said I am not a philosopher. One of Jeff's colleagues, now at Oxford, is David Rodin.[35] Rodin is originally from New Zealand; he taught in Australia, but he now lives and teaches in Oxford. He is a very smart philosopher. He runs or did run the Oxford group that studies war and the ethics of war. He wrote a book on *War and Self-Defense*, and it's a smart book, which pushes just-war theory very close to pacifism. But what was most striking to me is that this is a book written in Britain, discussing all the problematics of national defense, and it does not mention the Battle of Britain, one of the most important twentieth-century examples of national defense. The book has an extensive bibliography, in which the only book about war is

Thucydides'. Everything else is moral philosophy. By contrast, I spent five years reading military history before I wrote *Just and Unjust Wars*; I am afraid that I read very little moral philosophy. I read Aquinas and the Spanish Dominicans, who are really heroic figures in the history of just-war theory. Did you know that the faculty of the University of Salamanca met in solemn assembly and voted that the Spanish occupation of Central America was a violation of natural law (*laughs*)?

Busekist: Well at the same time, the Spaniards were discussing whether Indians were really human beings . . .

Walzer: Yes, yes. And they were burning heretics. Yes, I recognize all that. Still, it was a great moment!

Busekist: From what I understand, you think that what you call the "just-war industry" has become completely detached from reality?

Walzer: Most of the scholars working in the industry are really not interested in war. It's a strange phenomenon! They are interested in moral philosophy; they are interested in just-war theory – and the subject of just-war theory is just-war theory.

Busekist: Sometimes, the subject of philosophy of justice is philosophy of justice also – it is the same kind of industry I guess where "real" justice is overshadowed by sophisticated arguments that are really internal discussions. But there are many philosophers who try very convincingly to write about actual "experiences" of justice or injustice, as in Judith Shklar's account for example,[36] or in feminism, or in race studies, or in Honneth's account of recognition we have mentioned. More worrisome in my view is that in many instances political theorists or philosophers seem to have abandoned politics to sociologists; the big topics that were so prominent and so important in the past – class, parties, unions – are no longer hot topics in political theory. So what is true for the just-war industry seems to be true for moral philosophy in general: political reality, politics, has been somehow swallowed by the discipline.

Walzer: I think that often happens – perhaps in English and Comparative Literature departments, also, where many professors seem to have lost interest in novels and poems and choose instead to write about literary theory. I worked in the same way on *Spheres of Justice* as I did on the just-war book. Before I wrote about meritocracy, for example, I read three or four books about the Chinese exam system. I love that kind of research; I can't think abstractly about these kinds of questions: who is entitled to a civil service position? Who should be admitted to graduate school? How much welfare is the state bound to supply? Who should do the hard work, the dirty work, that society requires? I need to think very concretely about these questions, and I am reluctant to provide singular, abstract, or foundational answers to them – which is again why I think I am not a philosopher.

Busekist: I don't think that is true. Or else we should redefine philosophy. Speculation and metaphysics are part of the discipline of course, but social criticism is part of the noblesse of philosophizing, and it starts with being connected, "having an openness to the real world,"[37] and calling on your people for the highest ideals as you often noted. The prophets are such critics, but so is Socrates, who, undoubtedly, was a true philosopher.

Walzer: Yes, yes, but why are most contemporary philosophical arguments so different, and not only analytic philosophy with its weird hypotheticals? There are whole books on the trolley car case . . .[38]

Busekist: Yes, there are even dedicated websites on the trolley car case to find out what kind of a moral philosopher you are; but there is also an ongoing debate on the usefulness of thought experiments. Some are quite illuminating and challenge our philosophical imagination. Judith J. Thompson's story in "A Defense of Abortion" about the famous violinist plugged into you by the Society for Music Lovers for example,[39] or Anthony Appiah's "experimental philosophy," which confronts virtue ethics with psychological findings about our innate good or bad character.[40] The problem with these studies is, as Jeremy Waldron rightly notes, that "if all they show is that we need to examine our spontaneous judgments using our existing moral sensibility, then we beg the question of the origin and reliability of that sensibility itself."[41] In other words, even though our spontaneous reactions to hard cases are sometimes counterintuitive, applied philosophy eschews the question of "moral socialization." But it is an alternative, or an addendum rather to analytic philosophy, and it is quite popular in classrooms.

131

So, you are not a philosopher, you do not like thought experiments, you do not feel close to any of the styles of philosophy we have talked about (continental, applied, analytic, critical). But someone still believes in you (*laughs*) . . . and has described you, I think it was Michael Kazin, as a "supremely rational man," a "decent leftist." There is this small piece in *Dissent* called "A Decent Leftist"[42] that uses the title of a controversial article you wrote after the 9/11 attacks.[43] Are you a decent leftist Michael?

Walzer: I hope so . . . I am still a leftist but determined to resist the thugs of the left, which is a minimalist definition of decency. Michael Kazin is my successor at *Dissent*. We have the same politics, but maybe not the same passions. He once said to me: "I don't have your gut feeling about Israel." He is Jewish, raised in a secular family, with a position on the Middle East much like mine, but without the same deep sense of attachment. So, to answer your question, I guess I am not completely rational! (*laughs*) I am also not rational in the way that analytic philosophers are rational. I think I mean to be reasonable. Which is different.

Busekist: What are your greatest disappointments in your career as a political theorist, and your greatest pleasures in politics and in academia?

Walzer: Oh . . . Yes, I probably should think about that. As I told you, my biggest surprise was the reception by the US Military Academy of *Just and Unjust Wars*. And I guess my greatest disappointment is simply that my political views have remained the views of a small minority – most of whom were convinced before I arrived to convince them. I don't miss applause; I do miss agreement.

Busekist: Let me ask about your career as a whole. From the early articles we talked about, published in the 1960s, to the latest ones in 2018, what is the common denominator?

Walzer: Well, the moment when I decided that I didn't want to write the history of political thought, but that I wanted to think politically about contemporary politics. As I told you, that came when I was an Assistant Professor at Princeton talking to [Robert] Nozick and Tom Nagel; but I was very importantly encouraged by Stuart Hampshire.

Busekist: And what are the main evolutions, shifts in your career? Events that have given a new orientation to your work?

Walzer: I don't know, I often thought that I was boringly consistent. I started as a social democrat, I will end as a social democrat. I know so many people who moved right or left, I watched them move but I was pretty steady.

8

Spheres of Justice

Busekist: *Spheres of Justice. A Defense of Pluralism and Equality,* is a milestone in your career. Written and published between *JUW* and *Exodus and Revolution,* the book is paradigmatic of your reflections on justice and reads like a masterplan of your work in general. In *Spheres,* as in *JUW* you use many historical examples and empirical situations, but you also inaugurate a new philosophical method by looking separately at different spheres of our social life (ranging from money to political power via education, divine grace and meritocracy),[1] at specific experiences of justice, and the way communities understand and negotiate the distribution of rights and duties within the relevant spheres.

The main thesis could be briefly summarized as follows: there is no single overarching system of justice but a plurality of spheres in which the requirements for a just distribution of goods differ; there are no primary goods conceivable across all moral or material worlds. Within the spheres, the fairness of distribution depends on the value of the goods to be distributed and the shared meanings attached to these goods that vary over time; because all goods are social goods – individuals interact through goods – each sphere has its own criteria of distribution. In other words, justice is contextual and depends on specific rules of legitimate distribution within each sphere. The general requirement is that access to goods should not be monopolistic and usurped by the powerful, and that possession of goods in one sphere (say money) should not lead to domination of goods in other spheres (say political office).[2] The equity of distribution and the autonomy of the different spheres serve what you call "complex equality" and are aimed at non-domination.[3]

Like Charles Taylor – who talks about "frameworks" (who provide the background, explicit or implicit for our moral judgments)[4] – you believe that a society is best characterized not by the pursuit of interests and needs, but by a set of shared understandings that allow us to make sense of our practices: we cannot and should not conceive of justice as an independent variable, but should refer just practices to shared social values. So justice is also an "art of differentiation" ("distributive justice is – unlike utilitarianism – not a full science, but an art of differentiation"), as you once said about liberalism,[5] and justice is relative to social meanings: "the best account of distributive justice is an account of its parts."[6] Maybe we should begin with the date of publication: 1983. Part of the (short) history of theories of justice has been written. Rawls has published his *Theory of Justice* a decade earlier, around the time you published *JUW*. Maybe *Spheres* joins the debate a little late?

Walzer: [John] Rawls published his big book on justice in 1971 and [Robert] Nozick his own in 1974. It was a time when distributive justice was a big theme, a lot of people writing about it, maybe inspired by 1960s politics. And then the theme faded; there are some very good books on distributive justice that came a little too late. They didn't get the kind of attention they should have gotten in the academic world. I guess it's like that, it's not exactly fashion but it's something like fashion.

Busekist: This is not the case of *Spheres* however. The book has gotten a lot of attention and generated much debate – and still does; I cannot imagine a course on Justice without *Spheres*. You said somewhere that you are "more willing than your colleagues to be wrong"; but you defended your book very vigorously, and very elegantly: you responded to many critics, including the most aggressive ones.[7] Some questioned its structure and theses; some were angry with your vision of distributive justice. In my view the diversity and the vigor of the debates are a tribute to the originality and the profoundness of your thought. *Spheres* is regularly quoted and discussed, in relation with new emerging problems which proves its renewed topicality: by scholars who write on commodification for example, like Michael Sandel, on immigration like Joseph Carens or David Miller,[8] and many others. The latter go back to your chapter on belonging, the former to the one on money. I will get back to David Miller who always quotes you admiringly in his reflections on justice and immigration in a moment. One of the most debated chapters was – and is – the one on "Membership." Membership in

135

a political community is a social good, a primary good that needs to be distributed fairly. But membership you say, is always already there, we are members of communities, that is a given of our social and political life. You defend three ideas usually associated with communitarianism: membership is the basic condition for the existence of political communities; communities need a territory; social justice is possible only within a community of values and shared understandings.

Walzer: Yes, that's it. The chapter on belonging and membership is probably the most contested. But I think I was the first to treat membership as a good to be distributed. And as the first good that we distribute.

Busekist: I would like to go back to the question of neighbors and boundaries in this context – with a long question. You are not interested in the original delineation of boundaries (as in the "boundary problem" . . .), but you ask two questions: firstly who is entitled to decide whether to grant membership (to newcomers, migrants for example, or refugees); and secondly how we should frame the debate on the justice of boundaries: when and under what circumstance should we open the boundaries of political communities and share membership. In your reflections on the state you argue that a territory founds the bonds of common membership, shared understandings and special commitments. But you are interested in the despair of those who would like to join the political community, especially the most vulnerable individuals or families – refugees or migrants.

The question of neighbors, boundaries, and borders is obviously related to what you have written on wars and the legitimacy of humanitarian interventions. But the question of boundaries has also become a huge debate in political theory, especially around questions of migration, and the chapter on "Membership" in *Spheres* is very often quoted in the debate on the justice of immigration policies. You are close to David Miller in this debate (although I believe his "doorstep example" metaphor is not necessarily the best comparison):[9] both of you argue for a just immigration policy, and you insist on the injustice that a "band of citizen-tyrants" would rule "modern metics."[10]

Most cosmopolitans *a priori* reject the legitimacy of boundaries. As a coherent liberal, so they say, boundaries are incompatible with fairness. Joseph Carens or Charles Beitz among others argue along these lines.[11] They basically say that being subjected to the law or affected by a law (which is the case for migrants) requires, in a democracy, that you must also participate in elaborating the law. Hence the circularity problem and the illegitimacy of boundaries: migrants are subjected to a law they have not authored. You have a much more empirical or presentist approach to boundaries: boundaries exist, but we should make them as fair as possible while protecting the shared culture of the national community.

Walzer: Yes. boundaries exist, and we sometimes need to defend them. But we have obligations to people on the other side who are in desperate trouble. That's very hard because there are so many people in desperate trouble, but David Miller and I would defend a generous policy toward refugees. That boundaries of any sort are illegitimate seems to me obviously wrong. If there is to be a political community, and groups of people committed to each other, if there is to be a common good, there have to be boundaries. You can't have social democracy or a welfare state without boundaries. And if there is to be self-determination, the "self" has to be visible as a self, capable of acting in the world.

I learned some of this at Princeton in 1964 when I was a faculty adviser to SDS. The first time SDS was founded at the university, it was founded as a naturally open organization: no closed borders. Everybody was invited, and so all the Young Republicans joined and voted to shut down SDS. So then it was re-established with boundaries: members had to express their commitment to the principles of SDS. That's where my idea of a "community of character" came from. There have to be limits if our country is to be a country of a particular kind. That doesn't preclude welcoming immigrants who are coming because they admire the country and also refugees who are coming because they have no choice. The really hard question comes when there are masses of refugees, as in recent years and probably also in years to come. Germany takes a million of them in, and almost no other European country accepts its share. And then you have the problem that Merkel has faced in Germany and the question: are you obligated, if you are the good country, if you are the country ready to accept refugees, do you have to accept all of them because everyone else is saying no? That's one of the places where, it seems to me, you can make the clearest case for limits. Merkel at some point, probably for her own political good but also for the sake of the process of integration, should have said to France, to Britain, to Poland, to whomever: now it's your turn.

Busekist: If membership is the first good that we distribute, and if all the other goods are distributed among members in a second instance, wouldn't that entail that membership be a dominant good, determining all the others?

Walzer: Well, yes and no. It is the precondition of the other distributions, but it doesn't corrupt them. None of the goods come to members simply because they are members: they get welfare only if they meet the criterion of need; they attain offices only if they qualify; they get the book prize only if they write a great book. I guess that the vote comes with membership, with citizenship, and that does make members dominant over, say, resident aliens – which is why I have argued so hard for a path to citizenship for guest workers. In the US, I also support making citizenship available to the millions of so-called "undocumented" immigrants and to their children.

Busekist: David Miller argues in favor of general (European perhaps) distributive principles to host migrants, and vindicates that states do not have any specific duties of hospitality (except for refugees). He tries to figure out what fair "particularity claims" may be, and he discusses the case of the Gurkhas for example. He does acknowledge that Britain owes them something ("the conditions for a comfortable life"), but not doesn't seem to believe that desert should translate into immigration rights.[12] What is your opinion on this?

Walzer: I think this is a very important issue. You know our book on *Getting Out*?[13] That's where some colleagues and I addressed this question. After an imperial adventure, after a war, even a just war, after any kind of occupation, just or unjust, there are going to be people compromised, people vulnerable because of what you did, and you have to take them out with you. I think that's one of the absolute obligations. The numbers are not going to be too high. They are not going to endanger any integration process in your society. It's just, and you have to do it. The people who did it best – we have a lot of examples in that book – are the Brits after the American revolution. In these little boats that held a couple of hundred people, they took out forty or fifty thousand Tories who might have been ill-treated or who wanted to leave, or thought they had to leave the new republic. They gathered them in New York over many months and they took them all. They took most of them, the ordinary ones, to Canada, and the rich ones to England; they made a class distinction but still they took them all out. The French in Algeria left behind people who had worked with them, whom the FLN simply killed, and we did the same thing in Vietnam and again in Iraq. There are a lot of people, not just collaborators, informants, but also truck drivers and cooks and secretaries – people who cooperated with the Americans and who were certainly going to be treated very badly when the Americans left. So yes, I think there are obligations to people outside, people with particular claims on us, as the result of both good and bad activities abroad.

Busekist: This poses the question of reparations. Do you believe there should be reparations, and in what form, to make up for colonial crimes? Territorial rights, and the restitution of land are part of a current debate on post-colonial restorative justice.

Walzer: Reparations are a hard subject. The argument in favor is made in America because of slavery. But the people who would pay the reparations are people who have had absolutely nothing to do with slavery – and yet that's true of all reparations. Reparations to Israel from Germany were paid by people who weren't . . .

Busekist: But this was in 1952–1953 so the people who paid were still alive and were indirectly guilty to say the least.[14]

Walzer: Okay, but the money was collected from people who might have been opponents to the regime . . . Yeah, okay. That's not the best example.

Busekist: We don't know of that many opponents to the regime unfortunately.

Walzer: But with America, I would prefer spending public money in ways that create a more egalitarian society rather than handing reparations to particular people for injustices committed more than a hundred and fifty years ago. In a place like Afghanistan, the Americans ought to have invested in political reconstruction. We had a lot to do with the destruction of the country, beginning when we were supporting the people fighting against the Soviet Union. The Bush administration was so committed to the next war, to Iraq, that they never thought about their responsibility to make Afghanistan work, to help rebuild the society. And we see what Afghanistan is like now because of what they didn't do then.

139

Busekist: Let's go back to *Spheres of Justice*. I had you digress on boundaries and interventions because the chapter on Membership is still lively and discussed by our colleagues today. The content of the debates has shifted however: the critics were worried about relativism in the 1980s, they are rather worried about nationalism today. In the 1980s, Ronald Dworkin for example wrote a very harsh piece in the *New York Review of Books* to which you replied, and he answered.[15] Dworkin paradoxically describes your work as follows: "He [Michael Walzer] hopes to break the grip that the formal style has lately had on Anglo-American political philosophy. Such philosophers try to find some inclusive formula that can be used to measure social justice in any society, and that can therefore serve as a test rather than simply as an elaboration of our own conventional social arrangements."

Walzer: Yes. Partly because they thought, Dworkin definitely thought, that I had endorsed a relativist position that they believed was both dumb and morally wrong.

Busekist: Not only relativist ("Walzer's deep relativism about justice," writes Dworkin), too conservative, too communitarian also ("The idea that the world is divided into distinct moral cultures, and that it should be the goal of politics to foster the value of 'community' by respecting the differences, has for a long time been associated with political conservatism and moral relativism.")

Your reply however is quite explicit: "[. . .] most relativists would think me just as tiresomely judgmental as he is. Indeed, we share a desire to reach moral conclusions. We only disagree about the force or, better, the scope of our conclusions. I don't hope to make arguments that are conclusive for all human beings in all societies that exist or will exist or have ever existed. I don't subscribe to the idea – it seems to me distinctly odd – that the principles of justice appropriate to Americans must be appropriate as well to ancient Babylonians. Not that such an idea makes it impossibly hard to arrive at principles of justice; it makes it too easy, for the principles need not apply to anyone in particular. The hard task is to find principles latent in the lives of the people Dworkin and I live with, principles that they can recognize and adopt." Would you sign *Spheres* today?

Walzer: Oh yes. Yes, yes. Well, as to the accusation of being a relativist, let's start with the fact that I believe the principle of noncombat-

140

ant immunity to be a universal principle. Actually, even the idea that distributive justice is relative to the meaning of the goods being distributed is a universalist idea: it is meant to shape the distributive rules everywhere. *Thick and Thin*[16] is the book in which I tried to make clear what my actual position was. The attention to particular histories and to local circumstances and to the different social goods, all of that, starts before *Spheres* with the book on *Just and Unjust Wars*. That book had, as my friends recognized, a universalist doctrine. Since wars are fought across political and cultural boundaries, you have to argue in terms comprehensible to people on both sides. But I was also attentive to history and to the experience of soldiers – an approach different from that of the analytical philosophers. The difference became much more apparent when just-war theory became a "philosophical industry."

Busekist: But you just said they very much approved of your book *Just and Unjust Wars*, so why is it that it established a distance between you and the analytical philosophers? Was it *Spheres* or *Just and Unjust Wars* that signed the end of your *entente cordiale*?

Walzer: You are right: it was *Spheres*. But I experienced the difference before they did, I guess. I knew that I was doing something different.

Busekist: Some feminists have also argued against *Spheres*, Susan Okin in particular, your former student.[17] She thought that the way you described shared meanings, or rather the way they operate in society, is patriarchal, and therefore inadequate to argue in favor of justice.

Walzer: Susan wrote her dissertation with me, because Judith [Shklar] was concerned that Susan's project was too big for a dissertation, for a first book. I thought Susan was smart enough to pull it off. And she did. You do know that I wrote a piece in *Dissent* called "Feminism and Me,"[18] which was addressed to Susan's criticism.

Busekist: Yes, and I liked the end of the article where you seem to say that we haven't found a way of securing justice or "complex equality" within families.[19] In *Spheres*, when you mention neighborhoods, clubs, and families in the chapter on Membership, you did say that none of them is an adequate way of describing a political community. Family however is important for your reflections on belonging and membership, right? You don't choose your family.

141

Walzer: Right, right. Well, when you marry you join a family, and you choose at least one new relative, but you get a lot more, unchosen. Consent is not the key to family relationships. Susan was dead by the time I wrote the article; she died much too young. So, in part that piece was an homage. I had these wonderful graduate students at Harvard in late 1960s and early 1970s. Young women who were very smart, very determined, and very ambitious. I think I must say in that essay "Feminism and Me" that it was criticism by people like Susan that most affected me after *Spheres* came out.

Busekist: Do you think she was unfair?

Walzer: No, no! I think it is at least one possible reading and I did have to address it. I did that in a number of places, arguing (we've discussed this already) that the "shared meanings" Susan and others objected to weren't really shared – that is, their objections weren't as new as they thought. Just as "happy slaves" are a myth of the masters, so women eager to submit to the rule of men are a patriarchal invention. There is also an article in a book edited by Martha Nussbaum and Amartya Sen[20] that makes this argument. Trying to think how I came to write it, it was at their invitation.

Busekist: The critics of *Spheres* mostly stress that because distributive justice ultimately depends on "shared meanings," your account of justice is conservative (although you never wrote that shared meanings are the shared meanings of the past, meant to remain in some original form, quite the contrary). It is also relativist because there is not one single standard to measure the fairness of distributive principles (to me your "relativism" only translates the fact that the nature of the goods is not comparable and that the spheres are incommensurable). Lastly, some of your readers have questioned the status of the most important or the most powerful sphere, political power: is political power a sphere among others or the decisive one? (I believe you are quite explicit on the role of political power: "[state power] is the crucial agency of distributive justice; it guards the boundaries within which every social good is distributed and deployed."）[21]

My question pertains to a critique I haven't really read in this form. Against the contractualist version of justice, whether in the classical or in the contemporary form as in Rawls for example, is not hypothetical, it is meant to achieve something like real consent, much in the same way "real talk" in democracies is more valuable and more

142

complicated than ideal speech situations. If I am right, this may be what readers had a hard time figuring out.

Walzer: Well, the argument was that shared meanings aren't shared very often in societies radically unequal or societies where there is subordination. And I picked that up! That is part of the argument. If they aren't shared, then they don't have the effect that I claim for them on my account of distributive justice. If they aren't shared, then we have to look beyond them to other shared values and then try to resolve the disagreements here by some deeper set of agreements. That's the way I tried to address arguments about the subordination of Blacks and women. Martin Luther King appealed to shared meanings in the struggle for civil rights. What does citizenship mean in our society? He also goes back to the biblical creation story and the image of God. That's a line he quotes often. You know, one of the implications of Rawls' theory of rational argument is that you can't appeal to doctrines that aren't fully . . .

Busekist: "Comprehensive moral doctrines."

Walzer: Yes, you can't appeal to comprehensive moral doctrines or religious doctrines. There are people who say that therefore you can't quote the Bible.

Busekist: You can't quote comprehensive moral doctrines or religious arguments for political purposes because they are not shared or sharable. "Public reason" should only include arguments that other citizens could reasonably be expected to accept as Rawls says.

Walzer: And yet Martin Luther King . . .

Busekist: Yes, you are right, the abolitionists too made use of these kinds of arguments. Michael Sandel is right to stress this in his critique of Rawls: slavery has been fought with religious arguments.[22] Maybe this is a good moment to ask you about the "minority experience" you have often mentioned. Does *Spheres* owe to your own experience of being part of a minority, to your commitment to pluralism, to your reading of the Hebrew Bible?

Walzer: It comes first from the minority experience. I discovered the pluralism of the Bible much later, reading the three law codes of the Torah, for example, and realizing that they were different,

143

but they are all there, sitting side by side. They are all "the words of the living God," as it says somewhere in the Talmud. I suppose that my pluralist commitments are clearest in a little book that an Italian friend put together: *What it Means to be an American*[23] – the book was published in Italian before it was published in English. But I do believe that America is the best diaspora place, the best host nation. I thought a lot about what makes it work; the fact that it's an immigrant society, therefore a pluralist society, and not a single nation-state, has a lot to do with its success.

Busekist: When you were a boy, Judaism and socialism, you said, were the same . . .

Walzer: Yes, but that's a common idea, at least on the New York left. A lot of red diaper babies with whom I went to college had the same view about Judaism. They didn't know much, but what they knew was that Judaism was a religion of concern for the stranger, of a passion for justice, and I remain convinced that the Jewish response to the Civil Rights Movement, to the Black kids in the South, had a lot to do with the Seder,[24] with the way Passover was celebrated even, or especially, in secular Jewish families. There are many different Passover hagadahs, including five or six "liberation" hagadahs. I don't know if that's true in France. Probably it is. But in America, I really think it was this idea: we were slaves in Egypt and they were slaves in Mississippi, and we have to connect – that brought so many young Jews South. As I said to you the other day, that didn't make for a permanent alliance, but it did make early civil rights something of a Jewish/Black coalition.

Busekist: This leads me back to my earlier question about the relationship between Judaism and your academic work. You just confirmed that there is a mutual enrichment between your identity as a Jew, and your intellectual work.

Walzer: But the argument for *Spheres of Justice* comes out of Pascal. The quote from Pascal is at the very beginning of the book[25] – and was its actual inspiration. Why Pascal? I don't know; maybe somebody told me to read the *Pensées*. I probably found it on my own when I was writing that book, never published, about continental political thought. Yes, I'm sure that's when I read Pascal. And that quotation just stuck in my head. Then I later combined it with a similar line from Marx. They both appear in the first chapter of *Spheres*.[26] That's the origin of the idea of different spheres of distribution. And working it out, the idea that . . . first, that it all depends on the meaning of the goods that are being distributed to the people among whom they are being distributed – and so distributive justice works differently for different goods, in different distributive spheres and then in different societies at different times, with different cultures and religions as you said. The goods have different meanings, and different principles of distribution will follow. All that emphasis on "difference" – that's the part that my philosopher friends hated.[27] I should add another influence – in addition to Pascal and Marx; I was greatly helped in working out the argument of *Spheres* by Clifford Geertz, who was my colleague at the Institute for Advanced Study from 1980 on, though I began reading him before that. Cliff's version of cultural anthropology fits well with my commitment to "shared understandings." You could say that, under his influence, I produced an anthropological theory of distributive justice.

Busekist: Pascal, the Bible, Judaism. Maybe we should move on to some of your latest publications: *In God's Shadow* and *The Jewish Political Tradition*.

9

In God's Shadow and
The Jewish Political Tradition

Busekist: *In God's Shadow* is a political reading of a religious text. It is wonderfully paradoxical book: although you believe that the religion of Israel is "deeply indifferent" to politics, you nonetheless write about the "politics in the Hebrew Bible" (the subtitle of the book). I suppose the paradox has two possible explanations: either God's shadow is so mighty that there can be no politics in the modern – or in the Greek – understanding of politics, or that worldly politics (if that means anything in ancient Israel) are "free" and "open to prudential and pragmatic determination."

Walzer: The Bible has always been read selectively. Since it was written in pieces, we now think that this is not a counterintuitive way of reading it. What has always struck me about the Hebrew Bible is the fact that the pieces are often inconsistent, and the editors didn't try to resolve the inconsistencies. They just let it all appear. And that's the distant origin of the rabbinic saying which appears somewhere in the Talmud: "these and these" – contradictory statements – "these and these are the words of the living God."[1] The fact that they don't leave out or harmonize contradictory statements means that there is a kind of openness in the texts,[2] which invites interpretation – and while there are efforts to restrict interpretation to the priests and then the rabbis, in fact this is an open invitation.[3]

Busekist: Saying, as you just did, that there are "inconsistencies" in the Hebrew Bible, that the "editors" did not try to resolve these inconsistencies, appears to me as a "scientific" statement as opposed to a "faithful" reading. An esoteric reading, a rabbinic reading, in short, an insider reading would never mention "inconsistencies." A

146

true believer would argue that the Torah has been given to us by God; that differences in the text are meant to be explained within that general framework and matched for good reasons, but there can't be any inconsistency.

Walzer: That's the official version, but the editors of the biblical text must have known that they were incorporating different legal statements and different historical accounts. In the retelling of Israel's history in the first three chapters of Deuteronomy, for example, there are six clear differences with the account in Exodus and Numbers (which I won't try to describe here; readers can look it up). The rabbis of the Talmudic age did try to harmonize the biblical contradictions, but then they disagreed among themselves, and those disagreements are openly presented in the text. Often one view is followed by "another view," with no attempt to decide which one is right.

Busekist: The way you read the Hebrew Bible recalls, *ceteris paribus,* the way you proceed in your more "secular" texts: you look at classical and contemporary political categories – belonging, covenant, loyalty, authority, justice – and you trace the origins of these notions through the complex meanders of the Bible: two covenants, three legal codes . . . *In God's Shadow* is the culmination of a long journey, starting, as it were, with Exodus, and Ki Tisa, your Bar Mitzvah. This book and the four volumes on *The Jewish Political Tradition* you are co-editing are an important step in your writings.[4] *In God's Shadow* comes late in your career; it is a bold book, an ambitious project. What carried the decision to go ahead and write this one?

Walzer: The book comes out now because when you reach a certain age, you can do anything you want! I've been writing these chapters, struggling with them, giving them as lectures here and there for twenty years without the courage to put them into a book. Biblical scholarship is so vast, and the scholars are so erudite; you have to know six ancient languages, and here I am, I'm reading the Bible in English. When there are disputed passages, I can look at the Hebrew text, and I can pretend to act like a scholar, but in fact I'm working from a couple of different English translations – mostly from the King James Version simply because that's the King's English, Shakespeare's English!

Busekist: But you have read a lot of biblical scholarship?

147

Walzer: Yes, I've read a lot over the years, and I did once teach a course, way back in the early 1990s, when Judy (my wife) was provost of the New School. She persuaded me to teach a course, and I taught "biblical politics." I gave a series of lectures; that's when I wrote out most of what later came into the book, though there has been lots of rewriting since. The biblical scholarship that I know best is the work of scholars from my generation. At the Hebrew University, Moshe Greenberg was very important – also for *Exodus and Revolution*. I came to Israel in the early 1980s carrying the manuscript of *Exodus and Revolution*,[5] which I gave as a set of lectures at Princeton. And the question was: should I publish this?

Moshe Greenberg sat with me, we went through the Exodus text, he read some of what I had written, and he encouraged me. He was a lovely man – one of those scholars who knew the requisite six languages. And he told me "look, the perspective of a political theorist is also interesting." The truth is that most biblical scholars no longer read the text as if it's a text. They break it up into little pieces, and they argue about whether this piece was written two hundred or four hundred years before this other piece . . . I can't join those arguments. I did have to make a few assumptions about which parts of the book are older than other parts. The lines in Deuteronomy about kingship, for example: is that a commentary on the reign of King Solomon or does it come earlier? Not likely, in my view. I don't have the courage to join the scholarly debates, so I just describe the assumptions that underlie my arguments.

Busekist: Your education as a political theorist has contributed to the "political" reading of the Bible, and probably to selecting the most topical passages. The parts on the covenant for example: you stress inclusion and voluntary participation in the covenant – the "almost democracy" in the Bible – as opposed to the hierarchical interpretation where only the Israelites count. The religion of ancient Israel "anticipates certain features of democratic culture" (the term is obviously anachronistic): "equality and lay participation" you write, and, although God's rule is absolute, he rules by law, and "the Israelite's choice of their God presumably reflects their conceptions of freedom and will."[6] Israel's "almost democracy" has three features: the covenant (the Mosaic one); the law (everyone, including the "stranger in our gates" and the Kings who did not make the law, but were subjects to the law); and prophecy: the prophets were the social critics of their time, and their criticism, at once licit and listened to, is a sign of religious democracy according to you. I wonder whether there is

148

some "wishful reading" on your part? Isn't the "almost democracy" of ancient Israel exactly what you wanted to discover?

Walzer: For me, both the covenant and the law come near to (they are not the same as) modern democratic understandings: both of them are inclusive, as you say; they rely on consent. The other democratic moment in the Bible is the moment when the prophet leaves the palace, walks out into the street and prophecies and argues there. What is he doing? Why does he think it's important to argue in the streets? He is talking to ordinary people, in a language that seems to us so figurative that we have difficulty understanding it, but presumably it was comprehensible at the time. So that is a democratic moment. There are also antidemocratic moments in the biblical text. There is, for example, the establishment of the monarchy, which initially is at the request of the people, so we can call that another democratic moment, but once there is a monarchy, the Kings develop a royalist ideology which sounds very much like the ideology of their neighbors. Although I tried not to read social democracy into the biblical text, I do believe that there are statements in the prophets, perhaps especially in Amos, that could inspire contemporary social democrats. But mostly the position I stress in my own interpretation is very far from my own political position: in the chapter on the prophets and international politics, especially, I acknowledge the very strong *anti-political* character of some major biblical writers.

Busekist: But there are also strong countercurrents. You recall frequently that there is no political theory in the Bible, that there's no "program" and there can't be, but on the other hand the Bible is full of politics, and you seem to say that if you read carefully, this is what the Bible is about: politics! "God's engagement makes for human impatience. Prophetic passivity is in tension with this impatience, but they are two sides of the same coin. The cast of mind needed to confront a world from which God is disengaged, a world where politics is ambiguous and contingent, is wholly different."[7]

Walzer: There is politics and there is at least one effort at constructing a political ideology – a royalist effort, reflected in some of the Psalms. The Kings have to claim that they are in charge, that they are political agents acting in the world. Prophets like Isaiah deny that this is possible. To try to act as political agents is to usurp God's position, and that can't succeed. The experience of kingship did produce one of the most remarkable books in the Bible – the book of Samuel, describing the reigns of Saul and David. Moshe Halbertal and Stephen Holmes have written a fine book about Samuel and its author, whom they regard as the inventor of something like political theory.[8] Indeed, the author, whoever he is, has a keen sense of how monarchic politics works. His account is pretty much godless; it is a secular history (or maybe a secular novella), unlike anything that comes after in the biblical history books, First and Second Kings or the Chronicles. I am not sure how to place Samuel; it is a biblical outlier. It doesn't challenge what I take to be the Bible's central religious/political arguments about how God's people should conduct themselves at home or about how God acts in the world. It has no teaching, though there is much that we can learn by reading it.

You might say that the story Samuel tells has to be overcome or forgotten if David's line is to bring us the messiah. In any case, the messianic David won't lust after Bathsheba or face a rebellious Absalom. Royalist theology replaces royalist experience. I try to tell that story, but my focus is, as you say, on biblical anti-politics, which opposes anything like the autonomy of kings. One version of anti-politics is the idea, which becomes a general idea in Jewish political thought, that the gentiles, the goyim, need politics, but we don't – because God takes care of us. The Joseph story is a key example of this. Joseph predicts that there will be a famine in Egypt; he is appointed by Pharaoh to deal with it. He organizes the storage of grain; he creates the first welfare state, he guarantees the food supply. Two or three hundred years later, the Israelite slaves march into the desert with no one in charge of supply. They don't need a Joseph, because God will deliver manna from heaven. That's a classic example of the contrast. The goyim need Joseph, or someone like that, and we don't.

And this theme is reiterated again and again. I talked about this at the Shalom Hartman Institute in 2018, about the story of Nahshon at the Red Sea. The Bible tells us that the people, the fleeing slaves, come to Moses in despair; they are at the sea, and they hear the Egyptian chariots approaching. Nobody thinks of organizing resistance, digging what we now call tank traps, for example, which would stop the chariots; there is no idea of self-defense. And Moses says to the people: be quiet, stand still, watch the deliverance of God. And that's it! You don't have to do anything. The story of Nahshon is invented because even some Jewish writers were uneasy with the passivity and despair of the people.[9] It isn't in the Bible; it is a midrash: Nahshon dives into the sea, without waiting for God's deliverance. He alone isn't frightened and passive.

Busekist: You have often mentioned this passivity and what you call the deference of the Israelites. The "*Galut* mentality"[10] that you spot among contemporary (orthodox) Jews and Israelis is a state of mind that exists since the destruction of the Temple. Its consequences for today are important, however. According to you, the lack of experience and the lack of tradition in governing other nations, despite the king's rule over what we would call a multinational empire today, has inhibited the sense of political responsibility over other ethnic, national, and religious groups in the state of Israel today. You often quote Ben Gurion's speech at a Mapai meeting in 1947,[11] and the desire he had for a country living in peace with its (future) Arab citizens, but we also know that his dream did not really come true, and that the Founding fathers had little to say about a Jewish state taking care of other people.

Walzer: Yes, in the biblical story, if you take it seriously, King David and King Solomon ruled over other people. We don't know how effectively or with what regard for their well-being, but they did, they ruled over a (small) multicultural, multi-ethnic empire. In exile, in *Galut*, starting in Babylonia or maybe with the Patriarch in Palestine, the Jews govern, when they are able to govern, only themselves. The exilic communities are radically homogenous; there are no non-Jews. And so the experience of Jewry, the political experience of Jewry over some eighteen hundred years never involved being responsible for other people. And then, suddenly, you have a state and a lot of the Jewish leaders don't have any sense of that kind of responsibility. I've told the story somewhere of a minister of Labor, in the first Netanyahu government. I was in Israel for a semester and one day I read in *Haaretz* that the ministry of Labor had sued a restaurant, I think it was in Eilat, for requiring its Jewish workers to work on Shabbat. The restaurant was fined about 200,000 shekels and they appealed, and the appeals court reduced the fine to 18 shekels (5 dollars) and sharply rebuked the minister of Labor because he had pursued one case after another of this kind but had never, never pursued a case involving factory safety or the well-being of guest workers. Never! Nothing! This guy was one of the ultraorthodox Knesset members, and he had a conception of Israel as a state like any state in the exilic world, that could be used whenever it was useful but that entailed no obligations. He had no conception of a state in which people like him were citizens and civil servants responsible for the common good. That's the *Galut* mentality. You don't get that in the Bible, because the Egypt story is so important; you are told there are

151

strangers among you and that you must not mistreat them – because you were strangers in Egypt. Again and again and again. We have no notion, of course, about how strangers, aliens, were in fact treated, but the text is clear.

Busekist: Yes, the "Ger" (the stranger) is a very important notion; the Bible continuously repeats the respect owed to the stranger in Exodus, Leviticus, and Deuteronomy. It includes the Jews themselves who are said to be strangers on a "land that cannot be sold because it is God's land" (Lv 25, 23). You wrote or said somewhere, I believe in a talk at the Shalom Hartman Institute about the state of Israel and the meaning of sovereignty,[12] that the Jewish people, East and West, and the historical Zionists had a shtetl mentality on the one hand, and a radically secularist ideology on the other hand, and that these two groups really couldn't understand each other. Although the Galutnik community has tremendously gained in power, the two groups still exist in the state of Israel today according to you. You also argue for a reconciliation between tradition and secularism: you told me that the secular Israelis in particular have a lot to learn from the Jewish tradition. Could you explain?

Walzer: Yes. Yes. I think Ben Gurion had a sense of the necessary moral treatment of strangers, that is, of minorities in a modern nation-state. If not for the war, he and the early leaders of the new state would have had a large Palestinian minority to deal with; I assume some efforts at decency, if not full equality (as mandated in the Declaration of Independence) would have been made. That is obviously easier if you have a secular understanding of statehood. Ben Gurion thought of Israel as the state of the Jewish people, not of the Jewish religion – the model was France as the state of the French people or Norway as the state of the Norwegians – and then the problem of minorities would have been a common problem, with well-known difficulties and a long history of failures but still a problem that everyone knows, in principle, how to deal with. But this is not what happened. The secular Zionists found themselves governing a people of whom large numbers were religious, either in a traditional or in an "ultra" way, for whom fear and hatred of non-Jews was almost a reflex. I have argued that they tried to deny or override the religious feelings of their people, "to negate the *Galut*," when it might have been better to engage those feelings directly. What was necessary – I would say morally as well as politically necessary – was a critical, but also an appreciative engagement. Think of how religious feminists (not only among the Jews but among Muslims too) argue from within their community, re-interpreting the authoritative texts. That can also be done from the outside, by studying the old texts and arguing from them and with them.

Busekist: You use another term, closely related to *Galut* in my understanding, to describe a specific type of mentality that resurfaces in Israel today: "shtadlanut." That made me think of the debate between Yerushalmi and Arendt.[13] Reading the literature of shtadlanut provides, you say, "a strong justification for statehood," but requires that we look back at the biblical teachings instead of being prisoners of a *Galut* mentality – embattled, humiliated, and persecuted (the "all the world is against us mentality.") Entering the world of states means entering a world of formal equality among states and acquiring new responsibilities. I was wondering whether you could say a word or two about the biblical teachings pertaining to the interaction between nations, the "biblical foreign policy."

Walzer: I think of shtadlanut as the foreign policy of the *kahal* [community] or of the exilic communities generally, and it is a policy of deference, fearfulness, humble appeals for protection – typified by the traditional prayer for the king (some orthodox synagogues in the US simply substitute "president"): that "he deal kindly with us." The point of having a state is to have rulers before whom we aren't beggars, rulers who are committed to our welfare. And a state like that has to have a statelike foreign policy, claiming its rights, acknowledging its responsibilities in the society of states. In the bible, there are many descriptions of imperial politics, much writing about the conquests of Assyria and Babylonia, but there is only one description of a society of more or less equal states – that comes in the first two chapters of the book of Amos, where the prophet castigates the "transgressions" of the mini-states that are the neighbors and sometime rivals of the two Israelite kingdoms. The list of transgressions adds up to a kind of international legal code, as Max Weber argued in *Ancient Judaism*.[14] It suggests the responsibilities that we would expect the modern state of Israel to accept as its own.

Busekist: Is it possible to overcome the "paradox of national liberation"? It seems to me that religious revival is not a necessary reaction to secular nationalism, but rather the negation of secular values, the quest for answers and solutions beyond politics and the lack of

153

dialogue you often deplore between the new messianic leaders and the resolutely secular political personnel.

Walzer: Yes, "solutions beyond politics," or, better, "beyond human politics" is what the contemporary Jewish zealots aim at; I sometimes think that their political arguments only make sense if you assume that divine intervention is near. They seem to me like the zealots of ancient times who expected God to break the Roman siege of Jerusalem. And secularism is, compared to that, just a version of common sense. But of course, the argument runs deeper. Secularists are committed, for example, to equality between Jews and non-Jews and between men and women, and the religious revivalists don't accept either of these – in fact their rejection is central to the revival. But both of these equalities can be defended not only rationally, in the secular mode, but also religiously, from within the tradition. We have to make both defenses, for both moral (democratic) reasons and for pragmatic reasons.

Busekist: Let's go back to *God's Shadow*. The Israelites have invented two covenants as we said earlier – Abrahamic and Mosaic – the former is exclusive, based on the "birthright" model, the latter is about choice and consent: the law, it is "passed on with words, not with knives," and serves as model for modern contract theories. Would you say that the two covenants are good analogies for communitarianism and liberalism?

Walzer: The covenant really is, for sixteenth and seventeenth-century writers, English and Dutch writers, the beginning of serious thinking about the social contract. And, of course, it is the consent version that they adopt. Shalem – do you know this right-wing think tank?[15] It is less right wing now than it was when it was founded by Yoram Hazony,[16] who grew up in New Jersey; I knew him when he was a student, he used to come to heckle whenever I was giving a talk at Princeton Hillel. He came to Israel and he set up the Shalem Institute with money from American right wingers. I have to say that he is very smart, and he brought some smart people with him into Shalem who made Shalem into something rather different. They published a journal called *Hebraic Political Studies*, which I wrote for a couple of times. In fact, several of the chapters in *God's Shadow* appeared in that journal.[17] Meirav Jones was the managing editor – also very smart. The journal was committed to the idea that pretty much all of Western liberal political thought, constitutional thought, it all comes from the Jews. I am probably exaggerating, but I thought that the journal's guiding principle was: the poor Goyim, they couldn't think of anything by themselves!

However, there were some very good people who did work along these lines, though with more qualification, like Fania Oz-Salzberger[18] in Haifa and Eric Nelson, a political theorist at Harvard who wrote a very good book called *The Hebrew Republic*.[19] It turns out that there are about a hundred or more treatises published in the late sixteenth and in the seventeenth century with titles like "the Hebrew Commonwealth." And they are all efforts to extract political thinking from the biblical text and sometimes from later rabbinic texts, too. A lot of it is based on the idea of a contract between the government and the people, a revision of the biblical covenant between God and the Israelites. So, I didn't make it up. It's a very influential idea.

The biblical covenant is importantly different from earlier Middle Eastern covenantal ideas which describe agreements between a King and other subordinate Kings. It is a kind of alliance politics. The superior King accepts the tribute of a kind of vassal – and it's called a "Brit" or some cognate term.[20] But it seems to be a biblical innovation that all of the people join in the covenant. Although they don't get an item veto over its parts, they have to take the whole thing! And they do, and their consent is important. The rabbis built on that idea, insisting on its necessity. There is a midrash where the rabbis say: Yes, the Israelites consented, but why did they consent? God lifted the mountain up, held it over their heads and said: "Accept my covenant or I will bury you under the mountain." And they said yes! But then another rabbi comments: "if that's what happened, then the covenant is not binding, because the people's agreement was coerced. The whole idea of government by consent is not always upheld or ever fully developed in the Jewish tradition, but it's there. At least some of the rabbis understood it in a very concrete way.[21]

The other covenant – God's eternal commitment to the people of Israel or to the House of David – I wouldn't call it communitarian (some communitarians are also consent theorists!) – is unconditional; it is not dependent on the people's or the king's behavior. The political purposes it might serve in later times are monarchist or nationalist. And the problem with this second covenant is, obviously, that God's eternal commitment hasn't always or even often been visible or, so to speak, helpful.

Busekist: You argue that there is free will and consent despite God's shadow. There is "politics in the shadow."[22] In the sixteenth and seventeenth centuries when consent theories were elaborated (another) God's shadow was very present in the minds of the Europeans. This is prior to the French Revolution, but even at the eve of the French Revolution I doubt that God's shadow was entirely absent.

Walzer: Right, right. Although I should tell you my French Revolution story which I discovered when I traced the history of my Bar Mitzvah parasha. My first academic article was based on a few lines from my parasha, when Moses comes down from the mountain, sees the golden calf and the people dancing around it, and he says: "Thus saith the Lord: take every man, his sword, and go through the camp, and kill every man, his friends, his neighbors."[23] Not a democratic moment. I traced the history of that text, and I wrote an article that was published in the *Harvard Theological Review* called "The history of a citation."[24] The text was used to justify religious persecution by Christian writers, again and again, but it was also commented on by non-Christian writers, Hobbes and Machiavelli, for example. You would think the comments would end with the Enlightenment, but they don't.

In the English revolution, it's a common theme, justifying the purge of insufficiently zealous people. In the American revolution not so much, and you would expect nothing at all in the French Revolution, where classical rather than biblical references were required. But Collot d'Herbois, one of the members of the Committee of Public Safety, a Jacobin, was asked how long the Terror will go on. His response was: "thirty to fifty years," which I take to mean forty years. It's a biblical reference to the years in the desert during which the slave generation died out and was succeeded by men and women with no memory of Egyptian slavery. He can't make the reference explicitly, but he is telling the people: our forty years! I had a lot of fun with that text. I used it again in a longer version for a Hebrew University biblical politics conference.

I ended my talk there with Lincoln Steffens. Did you ever hear of him? He was an American radical, a progressive journalist in the early twentieth century, a fairly important figure of the American left as it then was. He published a book in 1926 called *Moses in Red*.[25] The red Moses was Lenin. And he quoted "my" text [Exodus 32] to justify what he called the Red Terror and the purge of the Mensheviks. The text resonates. I tell everybody who has had a Bar or Bat Mitzvah that since you have studied your parasha for months, you have to make use of it.

156

Busekist: In principle, you have to re-say it every year. Do you do that?

Walzer: No, but this year I had a second Bar Mitzvah.[26] I was called to the Torah, and I gave the drash, the commentary, on this same text.

Busekist: In *God's Shadow* you say that God did not "decree a politics but an ethics." Could you explain? For the ancient Greeks, there would be no difference between politics and ethics; how is this different in ancient Judaism?

Walzer: Well, they are obviously related but politics in the Greek sense is importantly about the regime. What is the best regime, how do you list and describe and judge the different regimes? That, the Bible doesn't do. It gives you a history of regime change, from the Judges to the Kings to the commonwealth of the Priests after Babylonia. But it doesn't elaborate in a theoretical way on regime change, and it doesn't describe the different regimes; it certainly doesn't rank them, except to indicate that redemption will come with a king in the Davidic line. So there isn't an explicit political teaching in the sense, say, of Aristotle's *Politics*. But there are ethical teachings. So, somebody, a moral philosopher, could write a book like mine focused on biblical ethics, which would work from the legal texts of the Five Books and then the prophetic lines that we all love to quote – but it would also have to include some of the oracles to the Nations, which are often brutal.[27]

Busekist: To my knowledge no one has done this kind of explicitly political reading of the Hebrew Bible as you have done. Your book was translated into French and probably other languages immediately.[28] You talk about the place Israel holds among the nations and I was wondering whether your judgment could apply to contemporary Israel: "should Israel's foreign policy be governed by the principle of self-defense, the principle of territorial expansion or the principle of appeasement and accommodation, or should Israel have no foreign policy at all? Is Israel best conceived as a political nation or as community of faith?" This is a quote from *God's Shadow*, and you pose the question after having studied the history of the Israelites.

Walzer: Yes, I guess it is, although I think the idea that Israel should have no foreign policy at all, which the prophets urge, isn't . . .

Busekist: But self-defense, territorial expansion, faith or politics . . . everything is already there in a sense.

Walzer: Yes, yes. It's all there, which is why the devil can cite scripture for his purposes, as Shakespeare wrote. And the good guys, too. But I would stress the "no foreign policy at all" as a central theme.

Busekist: Do you believe that there is a hidden biblical script in Israeli politics today?

Walzer: Well, Ben Gurion lived with the Bible in a way that I don't think Bibi [Netanyahu] does, or [Ehud] Barak before him. There is a collection in English of all Ben Gurion's writings on the Bible;[29] I was disappointed when I read it. The text he was mostly interested in is the Book of Joshua, which suggests[30] . . . (*laughs*). That may be the most important book for some Israelis on the right today.

Busekist: Some of the people who have written about you suggest that Judaism is the key to your work, that your Jewish identity and your interest in Jewish scholarship and the Hebrew Bible is the thread that renders your writings intelligible. Would you agree or is that an overstatement?

Walzer: I think it is an overstatement, although I can't give an account of why I've written what I've written. I do think that the commitment to pluralism, present in so much of my work, has to be in some sense a reflection of the diaspora experience. And it is after all consistent with a lot of American Jewish writing, including the books and articles of Horace Kallen,[31] who is quite important to me.

Busekist: You didn't make an important space for "biblical" wars in *Just and Unjust Wars*. But there is a chapter on holy war in *God's Shadow*, and you gave a talk at the Hartman Institute about the biblical and rabbinical legacy regarding warfare.[32] The rabbis, you recall, had to work with the two commandments of "command" and "permission." God "commands," and the Kings are "permitted" to enhance their greatness and their territory through war. The "natural third" however, "prohibited wars" is missing. Haim Herschensohn,[33] whom you quote, made an attempt to integrate prohibited wars into the halacha, but he seems to be an exception. Without this third category, "there can't be an explicit and coherent debate about when it is right to fight a war, when war is just."

Collateral damage for instance was not a moral problem for the rabbis (except maybe for Maimonides who argues in favor of escape routes for the victims of siege warfare). You explicitly mention contemporary rabbis in Israel who believe exactly that: civilian victims are not a "halakhic" problem. Secular Israelis on the other hand, who debate in the language and against the background of international law and just-war theory, are not – even critically – engaged with the halakha of war: "they haven't naturalized just-war theory within the Jewish tradition [. . .] so they can't argue usefully with their fellow religious citizens." In short, it is necessary to engage with the Jewish history and the Jewish tradition.

Walzer: You are right. God does most of the fighting in the Bible. It is noteworthy that the Kings of the Northern and Southern kingdoms fight wars but they never describe their campaigns; nor are they portrayed as military leaders. With the exception of the young David, there is no glorification of the warrior in classical Jewish texts. There are some midrashim where the young David figures in a certain style that we associate with Greece, as a warrior. Solomon is never portrayed as a warrior. Hezekiah, Josiah . . . They did fight but they didn't celebrate their fighting. The only discussion of tactics is in the book of Joshua, but it's always God who tells you to do this or that.

Judah the Macabee and Bar Kokhba are warriors,[34] and there is some discussion of both the tactics of war and the ethics of war in texts dealing with them. But after that, for almost 2,000 years, there are no Jewish armies and only a few Jewish officers fighting for Gentile rulers. So, the Jewish literature on when to fight and how to fight is fairly thin; as you just said, halacha doesn't provide much guidance for contemporary soldiers. Some Israeli writers turn to international law and just-war theory; some try to make do with whatever they can find in halachic texts – sometimes with frightening results, since the existing Jewish laws don't have anything to say about the rights or obligations of non-Jewish fighters. What seems to me necessary is something like what Maimonides did philosophically: he brought Greek and Jewish ideas together in a synthesis that is his own. It is time to bring just-war theory together with halacha and come up with a doctrine that can be read and understood by religious and non-religious Jews, and by anyone else who wants to understand.

Busekist: *Politics in the Hebrew Bible* is part of the constellation of the four collective volumes on *The Jewish Political Tradition* (*JPT*); three volumes have been published, the last one is under preparation.[35] The project of the four volumes on *JPT* has been developed at the Shalom Hartman Institute in Jerusalem. It was your idea, it dates back to the early 1980s, and one fully understands why reading your introduction to volume 1. How did you get involved with the Institute and what is your relationship with the institute?

Walzer: I met David Hartman sometime around 1983. I had recently left Harvard, settled in at the Institute for Advanced Study. I must have been looking, not entirely consciously, for a big project that would justify leaving teaching. The Institute is a good place for big projects. David was a charismatic teacher – a learned orthodox Jew who was at the same time a master of irony, self-mockery, and Borsht circuit humor. And he had a project or, better, a couple of projects: first, to liberalize the orthodox community and teach it to recognize the value of Jewish pluralism, and, second, to make Jewish learning accessible to secular Jews and to convince secular Jews of the value of that learning. I attended the first "philosophy" conferences that he organized – a week of study: Talmud in the morning, philosophy (mostly Maimonides) in the afternoon; politics in the evening. It was at those conferences that I first imagined *The Jewish Political Tradition* volumes. David quickly endorsed the project, and the Institute in Jerusalem helped move it along (as did the IAS in Princeton, which provided significant funding). All my co-workers were Hartman Institute scholars, and that's one reason I have been back so often to Jerusalem. It's been a long road, and we are not yet finished: the fourth and last volume is still to come. As Pirke Avot says,[36] we are not obliged to finish, but I would like to live to see the end. My mother called the work my "opus gadol,"[37] and I am very glad that she lived to hold volume 1 in her hands.

Busekist: You have asked many well-known scholars (and practitioners such as Aharon Barak the former chief justice) to write commentaries: Michael Sandel, Bonnie Honig, Yael Tamir, Hilary Putnam, Martha Minow, Amy Gutman, Nancy L. Rosenblum, to name only a few, to participate. The aim of the volumes, writes David Hartman, is "to retrieve a Jewish political discourse concerned with issues like authority, distributive justice, membership, and welfare. They help to correct the mistaken notion that the Jewish tradition was concerned only with ritual celebration, laws of purity, daily worship, the study of Torah. They make the political arguments that have gone on for more than three millennia accessible, so that readers can gain a new appreciation of the traditional

160

meaning of covenantal engagement – which encompassed not only the life of worship but also the building of a just and compassionate community."[38] Would you say that this is a good summary of the project of the volumes: the dialogue between tradition and modernity we just mentioned?

Walzer: David's summary is a good one, though I would put things a little differently. I think of *JPT* (which is how we refer to the volumes) as a project in Jewish cultural nationalism – a liberal and pluralist project, which fits David's commitments, and the commitments of my fellow editors, and my own, too. I have always believed that the two political answers to "the Jewish question" – democratic citizenship in the West and sovereignty in the Middle East – must be accompanied by a cultural revival. I don't think it is accidental that *JPT* appears first in English (the first two volumes have been translated into Hebrew). Israel's greatest cultural achievements have come in literature, not, unhappily, in politics. Retrieving and re-imagining Jewish political culture should be, and will have to be, an Israeli project, but it may well begin in the Diaspora. In any case, we want Jews to engage with the tradition, engage critically, as a way of sustaining our common life. But we are definitely "liberal nationalists" – we also want to make the Jewish experience of politics available, accessible, to non-Jews. You don't have to be French to study French political history (I've actually done that); so you don't have to be Jewish to take an interest in how Jews sustained a national existence for so long without land or sovereignty.

Busekist: The volumes, as you present them, are faithful to the requirement of "probity, patience and the will to know,"[39] which means endless reading, commentary, cross-reference, intertextuality, and reinterpretation. As you just said, you wanted to make the content of the volumes, the selection of the topics and themes, available for non-Jews. The entries you have chosen are indeed relevant not only for Bible scholars, but also for political readers across the board, political theorists, political philosophers. The architecture of the volumes strikes me as very "Walzerian" – many chapters reflect your intellectual preferences – but maybe the reverse is true: your own thinking has indeed been influenced by the way biblical commentary works. There are many examples of this. The image of the house you are particularly fond of;[40] reiterations that, in your view, characterize the difference between "thick and thin" moralities;[41] social critique, civic responsibility, and moral probity.[42] I could add that you do not resist quoting the great authors from another canon: Shakespeare, Whitman, and others.

Walzer: The work on *JPT* has been genuinely collaborative; Menachem Lorberbaum, Noam Zohar, and I have worked very closely together (with others, too, all of whom spent two or three years at the Institute in Princeton: they would do their own work in the mornings, and we would read Jewish texts in the afternoon). We worked so closely that it would be hard to attribute this or that idea to any one of us. I wrote all the introductions, but then I rewrote them, more than once, after receiving critical comments and suggestions from the others. Our deepest political commitments are shared – without that, we could not have stuck together for over three decades. I assume that some of my earlier writing is reflected in the pieces I wrote for *JPT*, but most of what I have written since we started working on volume 1 reflects the experience of reading in the tradition. This is particularly true of what I have written about interpretation and about social criticism from close up. And, of course, the argument of my book *The Paradox of Liberation* is also one of the underlying arguments of *JPT*: that secular liberals and leftists need to connect with the tradition if they are to create a sustainable politics and culture.

Busekist: The aim of the volumes, for you, is to educate ("retrieval"), publicize ("integration"), and debate ("criticism"). Would you like to comment on this? Are you a kind of contemporary *stam* within political theory?[43]

Walzer: We are collectively and individually more modest than that last question suggests. "Retrieval" implies that we accept the historical selection process that produced the canonical texts. Those are the ones we want to bring back into view and subject to critical reflection. With regard to contemporary writers, we are, I guess, participants in an ongoing selection process, but we aren't looking for the last word. Still, our ideas about criticism do reflect those that must have governed the work of the *stam*. Here is one critical voice, and here is another, very different voice, and both of these belong to the living tradition!

Busekist: In "Exiles and Citizens" (vol. 2), you comment on the prayer "For government and country" and the "Responsa" by Rabbi Ismael of Modena's to Napoleons questions to the Assembly of Notables in 1806.[44] Your (short) commentary ends with a hope and a question. The hope: that Jews as citizens have abandoned their submissive *Galut* mentality. The question: whether it is possible to retain Jewish distinctiveness in modern democratic societies, characterized for present purposes, at least by two of your four "mobilities": social and marital. What is the nature of Jewish distinctiveness you have in mind?

Walzer: This is the hardest question. There have been many versions of Judaism and Jewishness in our history, so, of course, I expect new versions. What makes my generation of American Jews distinctive is the experience of twentieth-century history – the Holocaust, the establishment of a Jewish state, the remarkable success of Jews here in the US. The last of these accounts for the radical absence of a "submissive *Galut* mentality" in my children and grandchildren.[45] But what kind of Jews will my great-grandchildren be, who will know very little about the twentieth century? What do I hope for? That they recognize themselves as Jews, spend some time in their lives studying the tradition (*JPT* is for them), visit Israel and find friends there, attach themselves to some Jewish communal organizations, and somehow learn to laugh at the same jokes that make me laugh.

Busekist: The general introduction to volume 2 (pp. 3–8) poses some interesting questions, albeit in an oblique way, on the interaction between tradition and modernity,[46] namely on changes in the law and adaptations of the law:[47] how far-reaching should the reinterpretation or adaptation of the halacha be in modernity?

Walzer: That is a question for orthodox Jews, like Rachel Adler (see her commentary on the marriage contract in *JPT*), who need a modern halakha to shape their everyday lives. I am interested in something else. Think of the Catholic bishops in the US who have issued pastoral letters on subjects like social justice and nuclear deterrence, drawing on Catholic understandings of natural law. I imagine Jewish scholars (without the ecclesiastical authority of the bishops) developing a kind of speculative halakha, drawing on the tradition to speak out on current issues. I am sure that there would be rival speculations, but this would be a way of recognizing what we might think of as the "ongoingness" of the tradition. Of course, some of the speculations would have to begin by acknowledging the thinness of the tradition on certain issues (like war) and the need to borrow from other traditions – as Saadia did, and Maimonides, and many others.

163

Busekist: Before closing our last chapter, I would like to get back to my first question, on the intriguing role of politics in the biblical text and in Jewish life. Your understanding of politics is very broad. Although you repeatedly write (in *God's Shadow* also) that politics has never been the "chief interest" of the Israelites, the Jews, or the rabbis, and that, in principle, on the classical understanding, "politics was for gentiles," the politics of the Jewish tradition is everywhere. It is practical and experience-based activity;[48] it is political both inside and outside of the community – in other words, it is much more than a mere "housekeeping" activity as Arendt once said.[49] The political experience of the Jews is closely related to the notion of *kahal*, to the exilic communities who have lasted, through study of course, but also because they had to rule themselves internally while interacting with the gentiles in the states they lived in.[50] Would you say that one of the distinctive features of Jewish politics is the experience of membership in the kehillot, and that this experience has invented politics? That politics, in other words, belongs rather to the exilic period? Lastly, Jewish "politics" entertains a specific relationship with knowledge. The tradition is a "Jewish politics of knowledge" argues Fishbane:[51] How would you translate this into contemporary language? And what conclusions would you draw from this relationship for modern Jewish politics?

Walzer: We had to define politics broadly in order to free it from any necessary connection to the state. But I think the broad definition is right. Everything having to do with the organization of the common life: who is recognized as a member, what ranks and orders are enforced among the members, what services the community provides, how it pays for whatever it does, how the members distribute power and honor among themselves, how they imagine their community (what it is and what it should be), how the community uses whatever coercive power it has, how the members think about their history, how they relate to strangers – all this is politics, and therefore grist for our mill. The last volume of *JPT*, which we are working on now, takes on the world-historical topics: land, war, exile, and redemption. Here too there are everyday matters, like whether or not you can "go up" to the land of Israel and leave your parents behind (whom you are commanded to honor), or whether you can pray or study in the local language, or whether you have to serve in the Czar's army. But we will also focus on some very big questions, at play mostly in the collective imagination: why are we in exile?, what might the rules of war be if there ever is (and now there is) a Jewish army?, what will the messianic kingdom be like?, is there anything we should be doing to bring it about?, and if the messiah isn't coming, how should we imagine a secular redemption? We won't answer those questions; we will just suggest some possible answers and some likely disagreements – so that our readers can join the arguments and sustain the tradition.

Coda

When does a life on the left begin? I might date it from when I was seven or eight years old and my parents taught me never to cross a picket line. But it was years later that I became a political activist and, later still, a social critic. Politics and criticism in my life, as in most left lives, are intermittent activities. We are also students, friends, lovers, husbands and wives, parents; we find work to do; we earn a living; we go to movies and baseball games; we read novels; we cook; we fix things around the house; we drink coffee and talk. Still, left politics keeps coming back. If it isn't "steady work" in one life, it is "steady work" across many lives. My comrades and I keep at it.

I have lived through victories and defeats – or, perhaps better, years of anticipated victories, never fully realized, and years of deep disappointment. As anti-Stalinist leftists, we had a hand, a small hand but morally important, in the defeat of Soviet Communism. As young radicals in the 1960s, we helped end a war, and we made America a more just society. As egalitarians and feminists, we moved the country closer to gender justice. I could go on, but, unhappily, not for long. We haven't transformed the class hierarchy, which may be steeper now than it has ever been. We haven't won the battle for universal health care. We have watched the erosion of public education, the weakening of the welfare state, the massive decline of the labor movement, and the increasing economic vulnerability of many Americans. We have failed to rouse the country to the dangers of global warming. We were surprised by, and are struggling to deal with, the rise of right-wing nationalism and the return of racial, ethnic, and religious bigotry.

Does the arc of history bend toward justice? Maybe, over the long haul. Through most of the twentieth century, however, the arc

166

seemed to be bending the other way. I am more inclined to think of history as a zig-zag line of victories and defeats – two steps forward, one step back or, sometimes, as Lenin once wrote, one step forward, two steps back. And what do we do then? Or, more urgently, what do we do now? What is the role of activists, critics, left intellectuals today? Actually, my question should be different: what do I want my younger friends and comrades to be doing, saying, writing? I will continue here as if I am still fully engaged with them, but I won't try to avoid sounding like an old man. Leftism right now, first of all, has to be a defensive politics. Yes, defense is sometimes helped by a surprise offense – like Bernie Sander's presidential campaign in 2016. But I worry about young radical enthusiasts who think that the US is ripe for a socialist transformation. There are indeed available victories. Some of the failures and defeats that I have just listed can be reversed or partially reversed. But what we call, in the aftermath of Trump's triumph, the "resistance" has a lot of resisting ahead of it, even if Trump is defeated in 2020 or before. Much damage has to be undone. The novelist Milan Kundera once described the image of the Grand March as "leftist kitsch." That's right; but the image is useful nonetheless. Two steps forward is, for example, a detail of the march, a good moment. Right now, we have to minimize backsliding and make up for lost ground.

We need to defend democracy and constitutional government; we need to resist anti-immigrant ethno-nationalism; we need to protect our most vulnerable fellow-citizens; we need to stop the exclusion of minority voters from the electorate; we need to prevent ecological disaster. And, most important, we need to build a coalition capable of doing all the things we need to do. This won't be a coalition of leftists with other leftists – though we have to find some way to bridge the gap between class and identity politics on the left. An effective coalition has to include liberals and (for some of the necessary battles) decent conservatives. And it has to involve the kind of compromises that good politics can produce – not the "rotten compromises" that Avishai Margalit has identified and condemned,[1] but ones that provide benefits for different political groupings, including our own.

The Jewish left is also on the defensive these days. It needs to fight against other leftists who have, ignorantly or maliciously, singled out the Zionist project and the state of Israel as the world's great evils. And it needs to support the embattled Israeli left as it struggles to oppose the occupation of the West Bank, end the siege of Gaza, and hold open the possibility of two states. And this too requires coalitions and compromises – not with evangelical Christians who manage to combine antisemitism with support for right-wing nationalists in Israel, but with liberals and centrists who sympathize with Israel's security dilemmas and at the same time call for the establishment of a Palestinian state alongside Israel. This is the practical work of left intellectuals like me and like many of my comrades, who might wish for something more adventurous: we have to defend defensiveness and the compromises it requires against radical absolutists, many of them young, vibrant, and enthusiastic – the hope of our future. There is a lot more, however, that I think we should be doing for the sake of that future. Our work isn't only defensive; we also need to be engaged in the kind of political analysis and social criticism that opens transformative possibilities. I have never believed that these engagements require the guidance of an overarching, world-historical, totalizing theory such as Marxism was. Theories like that tend to produce a vanguard of knowers, whose views are always correct, dominating over the mass of men and women who are the victims of false consciousness. This makes for a bad politics, and, as it turns out, the big theories aren't so good either. Again and again, the knowers get the world wrong; vanguard militants also suffer from false consciousness. Still, our critical work requires a better understanding of the social order and its internal contradictions – theories, of course, but modest ones.

Getting the world wrong is an old story. Modern society doesn't divide into two classes as Marx predicted; nor is it a "mass society," whose members are atomized, lonely, "bowling alone." Modernity hasn't produced the disenchantment that Weber foresaw; the triumph of science and reason over religion is still to come, if it is coming at all. Capitalism continues to survive its crises. The final victory of liberal democracy isn't anything like final; democracy still needs advocates and fighters. All this we have to understand, and understanding requires empirical and theoretical work. But we know that this work will produce divergent analyses and fierce disagreements. We know that we will be forever bereft of what leftists once called The Correct Ideological Position. It is argument itself, the ongoing analysis of where we are and what needs to be done, to which we have to commit ourselves. And that means that social criticism can't depend on a definitive social theory. It is at least partially an independent activity. We criticize a society that we are simultaneously struggling to understand.

I have said enough about social criticism in these pages; I want to add only this. Just as criticism doesn't depend on a successful social analysis, it also isn't progressive in the sense that it advances along with the moral education of humankind or the historical realization of reason. It is more like a reiterative activity; again and again, we invoke the values of our fellow-citizens against their practices and institutions. Sometimes these are very old and deeply engrained values. Think about the idea of equality, a prime focus of social criticism in an America where inequality is more and more extreme. Perhaps the oldest argument against inequality is the assertion by the writers of the Hebrew bible that all human beings are created in the image of God. This simple sentence resonated in medieval peasant revolts, among radical Protestant reformers, in the American Declaration of Independence, and in the civil rights movement of the 1960s. It is still a line that calls upon Americans to live up to what we say we believe. We should keep repeating it, even if some of us have to revise the biblical sentence: all human beings are created in the image of God, *whether or not God exists*. That is also a line (I have found) that resonates with many Americans.

At the same time, there are more particular versions of equality that are central to American (and, more generally, to Western) political culture, like equality before the law and equality of opportunity, and with these also we can build a critique of capitalism – even if we can't provide a foundational account of these two equalities or a definitive argument for their rationality. And even if we don't have, as we don't, a full-scale analysis of modern capitalism – which some leftists optimistically call "late" capitalism, implying a history that they can't defend. But so long as the adjective helps the critique, it probably doesn't matter. I still hope for a transformative politics, but I am certain that transformation will be, should be, slow and steady work. There won't be a messianic moment or a final revolution. Jewish leftists who oppose the messianic Zionists of the settler movement don't have to give up on the idea of radical change, but we do have to insist on its limits. The establishment of the state of Israel was not the beginning of redemption; Israel only has to be a better, and a safer, place than czarist Russia was. That is a good enough beginning, and then we can dream of something still better. In the US, too, revolutionary talk is foolish and probably also dangerous, but reforms can add up (two steps forward . . .). One day, maybe, our social life will look very different, and we will live together without the arrogance of the powerful and the humiliation of the weak, in an egalitarian society. I still think of that achievement as democratic socialism, and the effort to get there, the experience of struggle and solidarity – that is what life on the left is really about. The struggle for democratic socialism has to be the work of the many, not the few. That is or should be the

169

absolute rule of left politics. I can illustrate what this means with two examples. Consider, again, Leninist vanguard politics, which also comes in religious versions, where zealots form the vanguard. The secular version goes like this: the workers of the world are supposed to band together and make the revolution, but they are trapped, at best, in the politics of trade unionism, fighting for a few more dollars, capitalist droppings. They are ignorant of their historical task; they lack revolutionary consciousness – so we, the vanguard of knowers, will make the revolution without them.

My second example is drawn from the feminist politics of the 1970s and after, when militant women committed themselves to "consciousness raising" – an activity they thought necessary to the defeat of patriarchy and the realization of gender equality. I don't think that this activity was based on the idea of false consciousness; at least, that wasn't its necessary basis. The better idea was that the key values of feminism were latent in the consciousness of many women; the values only needed to be brought out, made visible, so to speak, articulated. The political message of consciousness raising was clear: we can't make the revolution without you. No revolution, no trans-formation, no left politics, without you and me! That insistence is the best way to respond to the kind of arguments that once were common on the left – less so in these latter days, I hope. Tyranny is necessary now, it was said, for the sake of a brighter tomorrow, for the sake of generations to come. "We who wished to lay the foundations of kind-ness," Bertolt Brecht wrote, "could not ourselves be kind."[2] The truth is different: the postponement of kindness is actually its rejection – so "we" have learned. Leftists must pursue a politics of kindness right now, for our contemporaries and for ourselves: arguing softly (even when injustice makes us angry), raising consciousness, forming coali-tions, building a majority, making lives better, one step at a time. And if not now, when?[3]

Notes

Introduction

1 A Cheder is a traditional elementary school teaching children the rules and history of Judaism and the Hebrew language.
2 Michael Walzer wrote a short intellectual autobiography for the *Annual Review of Political Science* 16, 2013: 1–9 under the title "The Political Theory License," where he talks about his career, but also his childhood and the relationship between Judaism and socialism.
3 Michael Walzer, *The Revolution of the Saints: A Study in the Origins of Radical Politics*, Cambridge MA, Harvard University Press, 1965; *A Foreign Policy for the Left*, New Haven, Yale University Press, 2018.
4 Irving (Horenstein) Howe, 1920–1993, co-founder of *Dissent*. See the biographical note below, ch. 1.
5 See ch. 3, and Maurice Isserman, "Steady Work: Sixty Years of *Dissent*," *Dissent*, January 23, 2014.
6 Michael Walzer, "The Political Theory License," art. cit. See ch 7.
7 "Good prose was never an absolute value in itself, but writing clearly and directly about even the most complex of topics, spoke to a shared value of openness and respect for the reader. There was a vision of politics in such prose," Nicholas Howe (Irving Howe's son) about *Dissent* in an interview with Maurice Isserman, "Steady Work: Sixty Years of *Dissent*," art. cit.
8 "Theory is a very special field because it provides a license to do something that academics generally are not supposed to do: that is, defend a political position in the classroom and in the learned journals. I worked hard during my teaching years to distinguish what I said in the classroom from what I said at political meetings. But the distinction was not substantive; it was more a matter of style or of what these days is called 'discourse'. In the classroom, I tried to describe political positions opposed to my own as fairly as I could, in their strongest versions. I felt no need to do that at political meetings," Michael Walzer, "The Political Theory License," p. 2.
9 Michael Walzer, *Interpretation and Social Criticism*, Cambridge MA, Harvard University Press, 1987, p. 39. Henceforth ISC. Comp. *The Company of Critics*, Basic Books, 1988, 2nd edn., 2002, p. 18f. Henceforth CC.

10 "The Critic Protests From Within," *CC*, p. xi. Comp. *ISC*, pp. 16, 26, 48, 56, 72.
11 In the following books and articles in particular: *Interpretation and Social Criticism* (*The Tanner Lectures on Human Values*), Harvard University, November 13 and 14, 1985) published under the title *Interpretation and Social Criticism; The Company of Critics*, 1988; "Objectivity and Social Meaning," in M. Nussbaum and A. Sen (eds.), *The Quality of Life*, Oxford, 1993, pp. 165–177; "Shared Meanings in a Poly-Ethnic Democratic Setting. A Response," *Journal of Religious Ethics*, 22, 1994: 401–405.
12 Michael Walzer, *Thick and Thin: Moral Argument at Home and Abroad*, Notre Dame Press, 1994.
13 Michael Walzer, *Spheres of Justice. A Defense of Pluralism and Equality*, New York, Basic Books, 1983. Henceforth *SOJ*.
14 Michael Walzer, *Nation and Universe*, in G. B. Peterson (ed.), *The Tanner Lectures on Human Values*, vol. XI, Salt Lake City, UT, 1990, pp. 507–556; "A Particularism of My Own," *Religious Studies Review*, 16 (1990): 193–197; "Universalism and Jewish Values," Carnegie Council on Ethics and International Affairs, 2001.
15 Michael Walzer, *On Toleration*, New Haven, Yale University Press, 1997.
16 Michael Walzer, *Reformed Church and Holy Commonwealth: A Study in English Puritanism, 1652–1662*, Brandeis University. Dept. of History, 1956; *The Revolution of the Saints*, op. cit.
17 Michael Walzer, *In God's Shadow: Politics in the Hebrew Bible*, New Haven, Yale University Press, 2012.
18 Michael Walzer, Menachem Lorberbaum, Noam J. Zohar, and Yair Lorberbaum, *The Jewish Political Tradition*, vol. 1 *Authority*, New Haven, Yale University Press; Michael Walzer, Menachem Lorberbaum, Noam J. Zohar, Ari Ackerman, *The Jewish Political Tradition*, vol. 2 *Membership*, 2003; Michael Walzer, Menachem Lorberbaum, Noam J. Zohar, Madeline Kochen, *The Jewish Political Tradition*, vol. 3 *Community*, New Haven, Yale University Press, 2018. A fourth volume is in preparation.
19 *ISC*, p. 56. Comp. CC, p. 3.
20 CC, p. 4, and p. 16: "Complaint is one of the elementary forms of self-assertion, and the response to complaint is one of the elementary forms of recognition."
21 CC, pp. 10–11: "Mainstream criticism [. . .] that is critics who stand sufficiently close to their audience and are sufficiently confident of their standing so that they are not driven to use highly specialized or esoteric languages."
22 *ISC*, p. 33.
23 CC pp. xiv–xvii and 15.
24 CC, pp. xiii and 9.
25 CC, p. 8.
26 "It's not connection but authority and domination from which we must distance ourselves," *ISC*, p. 52.
27 "A little to the side, not outside: critical distance is measured in inches," *ISC*, p. 53; Comp. CC, pp. 20 and 226.
28 *ISC*, p. 16.
29 Michael Walzer, "Philosophy and Democracy," *Political Theory* 9 (3), 1981: 279–399, p. 389.
30 *ISC*, p. 12.

31 "Philosophical founding is an authoritarian business," "Philosophy and Democracy," p. 381; "The claim of the philosopher in such a case is that he knows 'the pattern set up in the heavens'. He knows what ought to be done," Ibid., p. 383.
32 *ISC*, p. 14.
33 *ISC*, p. 18.
34 "If [the poet] hopes to become a 'legislator for mankind', it is rather by moving his fellow citizens than by governing them. And even the moving is indirect. 'Poetry makes nothing happen'. But that is not quite the same thing as saying that it leaves everything as it is. Poetry leaves in the minds of its readers some intimation of the poet's truth. Nothing so coherent as a philosophical statement, nothing so explicit as a legal injunction: a poem is never more than a partial and unsystematic truth, surprising us by its excess, teasing us by its ellipsis, never arguing a case," "Philosophy and Democracy," p. 382.
35 "Working out the design is a major enterprise in contemporary moral and political philosophy. Curiously, once one has a conversational design, it is hardly necessary to have a conversation," Michael Walzer, "A Critique of Philosophical Conversation," *Philosophical Forum*, 21, 1989: 182–196, p. 184 (reprinted in M. Walzer, *Thinking Politically*, D. Miller (ed.), New Haven, Yale University Press, pp. 22–37).
36 "Real talk is unstable and restless, hence it is ultimately more radical than ideal speech. It reaches to reasons and arguments that none of its participants can anticipate, hence to reasons and arguments undreamt of (for better and for worse) by our philosophers," "A Critique of Philosophical Conversation," p. 195.
37 "While the necessary meetings go on and on, they will take long walks, play with their children, paint pictures, make love, and watch television. They will attend sometimes, when their interests are directly at stake or when they feel like it. But they won't make the full-scale commitment necessary for socialism or participatory democracy," Michael Walzer, "A Day in the Life of a Socialist Citizen. Two Cheers for Participatory Democracy," *Dissent*, June 1968: 245.
38 *Kibbitzers* (Yiddish) are spectators who offer undesired commentaries. "A Day in the Life of a Socialist Citizen. Two Cheers for Participatory Democracy," p. 247. Comp. CC, Introduction and 231.
39 *SOJ*, p. 4.
40 *SOJ*, p. 6.
41 Michael Walzer, "Liberalism and the Art of Separation," *Political Theory*, 12 (3), 1984: 315–330.
42 *SOJ*, p. 29. Differentiation is the "regime of complex equality."
43 "Equality is a complex relation of persons, mediated by the goods we make, share and divide among ourselves; it is not an identity of possession. It requires then, a diversity of distributive criteria that mirrors the diversity of social goods," "[. . .] It is the meaning pf goods that determines their movement. Distributive criteria are not intrinsic to the good-in-itself, but to the social good," *SOJ*, pp. 8–9.
44 This is the main claim of "Objectivity and Meaning," reprinted in *Thinking Politically*, pp. 38–53. Walzer also makes this claim in "Philosophy and Democracy" (p. 395): "It is not only the familiar products of their experience

173

that the people value, but the experience itself, the process through which the products were produced. And they will have some difficulty understanding why the hypothetical experience of abstract men and women should take precedence over their own history,"

45 *ISC*, p. 24.

46 "And that is [. . .] more a matter of (workmanlike) social criticism and political struggle, than it is of (paradigm-shattering) philosophical speculation," *ISC*, p. 25.

47 *ISC*, p. 24.

48 "[The] argument has no end. It has only temporary stopping points, moments of judgment," *ISC*, p. 42.

49 The three legal codes are in Exodus, Leviticus, and Deuteronomy.

50 Michael Walzer, *The Paradox of Liberation: Secular Revolutions and Religious Counterrevolutions*, New Haven, Yale University Press, 2015.

51 Walzer is mindful of culture, belonging and shared meanings. He favors a strong welfare state and "decentralized democratic socialism" (*SOJ*, p. 323). Rawls holds that the (capitalist) "so called" welfare state is ill equipped to realize the principles of justice precisely because it abstracts from political sociology, and doesn't recognize the equal value of political liberties and the principle of reciprocity (J. Rawls, *Justice as Fairness, a Restatement*, E. Kelly (ed.), The Belknap Press, Harvard University, 2001, see p. 8, n. 7 and part IV). Walzer, on the contrary, defends the welfare state precisely because it doesn't overlook political sociology.

52 "I want to argue that philosophers should not be too quick to seek out the judicial (or any other) instrument, and that judges, though they must to some extent be philosophers of the law, should not be too quick to turn themselves into political philosophers" (p. 392). Like Rousseau's legislator again, the judges have no direct coercive power of their own: in some ultimate sense, they must always look for support among the people or among alternative political elites. Hence the phrase "judicial tyranny," applied to the enforcement of some philosophically but not democratically validated position, is always a piece of hyperbole," "Philosophy and Democracy," p. 398, n. 21.

53 David Miller aptly summarizes this double colonization of political dispute in *Thinking Politically*, p. ix.

54 "The critical enterprise is founded on hope [. . .] critique is future oriented," *CC*, p. 17. For Walzer, having to face defeat or disappointment, critique of a too close proximity with the society that is the object of critique, or, reversely, of universalist pretensions, may lead to three consequences: ceasing to be a critical intellectual; becoming a general intellectual, a "critic-at-large" à la Herbert Marcuse who criticized everything, from political modernity to bureaucracy and pop culture and who incarnates a version of "collectivist misanthropy"; becoming, finally, the critic of the small circle, the "critic-in-the-small" as in closed circuit academic debates. *CC*, pp. 227–228.

55 *ISC*, p. 75; This is why the theories of historical determinism are not compatible with social criticism. When the people are the subjects of criticism however, as in Marx, the "revolt of the masses [becomes] the mobilization of common complaint. Now the critic participates in an enterprise that is no longer his alone; he agitates, teaches, counsels, challenges, protests from within. This is my own view of the proper location of contemporary social criticism," *CC*, p. 26.

56 "Men and women are driven to build and inhabit moral worlds by a moral motive: a passion for justification," *ISC*, p. 40.
57 *ISC*, p. 29.
58 *CC*, p. 232.
59 *ISC*, p. 57.
60 *CC*, p. 232.
61 *CC*, p. 226.
62 Distinguishing the good from the bad prophets is not a judgment on the philosophical quality, but a critique of their critical position.
63 *ISC*, p. 34. Comp. "Inside, another kind of knowledge is available, more limited, more particular in character. I shall call it political rather than philosophical knowledge. It answers the questions: What is the meaning and purpose of this association? What is the appropriate structure of our community and government?," "Philosophy and Democracy," p. 393.
64 *ISC*, p. 40.
65 *ISC*, pp. 35, 38, 45.
66 *On Toleration* is exemplary of a certain relativism Walzer commits to; however his relativism is not a moral relativism, he does not abandon general principles such as the canonical prohibitions not to kill, not to oppress, not to exploit, but postulates that historical context and different expressions of tolerance matter (the same is true for all values), and that it would be vain to put the general rule above particular manifestations of tolerance. It is sometimes by exhaustion that moral progress is obtained: observing the horrors of religious wars for example has eventually led to the toleration of the dissenters and peace between factions. The constructivist or procedural approach is unfit to grasp the thickness of specific historical moral constellations.
67 *On Toleration*, pp. 16–17.
68 *ISC*, p. 47. Michael Sandel's approach is quite similar when he evaluates licit arguments to condemn slavery. Against "public reason" in the Rawlsian understanding, Sandel shows that the abolitionist debate has been fought with the help of religious arguments. He looks at the Lincoln–Douglas debates of 1858. The focus of the debates is not firstly about the moral status of slavery but pertains to the question whether we should put our comprehensive moral doctrines on hold to reach a political agreement. Douglas argues from a "liberal" position: the state should remain neutral qua morality and not use comprehensive doctrines, whereas Lincoln speaks in the language of religious morality: it is amoral to reduce human beings to slaves, and a vote will not settle the issue; a vote merely records preferences and does not say anything substantial about morality. Michael Sandel, *Liberalism and the Limits of Justice*, Cambridge University Press, 2nd edn., 1998.
69 *CC*, on Camus: p. 139.
70 *CC*, p. 151.
71 See the passages on Camus in our conversation, below.
72 Sartre, *Plaidoyer pour les Intellectuels*, Paris, Gallimard, 1972.
73 *CC*, p. 140 quoted after J. P. Sartre, *A Plea for Intellectuals*, in *Between Existentialism and Marxism*, New York, William Morrow, pp. 228–285.
74 *CC*, p. 140 quoted after J. P. Sartre, *A Plea for Intellectuals*: "If he poses as the guardian of the universal, he lapses at once into the particular and again becomes a victim of the old illusion of the bourgeoisie that takes itself for a universal class," p. 260.

75 *CC*, p. 143.
76 *CC*, p. 141.
77 "The philosopher fears fellowship, for the ties of history and sentiment corrupt his thinking. He needs to look at the world from a distance, freshly, like a total stranger. His detachment is speculative, willful, always incomplete," Michael Walzer, "Philosophy and Democracy," p. 382.
78 *ISC*, p. 51.
79 See the passages on prophecy in our conversation below, ch. 9.
80 *ISC*, p. 59.
81 "The prophetic texts [. . .] are painfully obscure at many points, and I don't possess the historical or philological knowledge necessary to decipher them (or even to offer speculative readings of disputed passages," *ISC*, p. 58.
82 "Amos' prophecy is social criticism because it challenges the leaders, the conventions, the ritual practices of a particular society and because it does so in the name of values recognized and shared in that same society [. . .]. Jonah is a mere messenger who makes no appeal to social values [. . .]. He just represents the minimal code [. . .]. What makes the difference is Amos' membership. His criticism goes deeper than Jonah's because he knows the fundamental values of the men and women he criticizes (or because he tells them a plausible story about which of their values ought to be fundamental). And since he in turn is recognized as one of them, he can call them back to their 'true' path," *ISC*, pp. 75–76.
83 "Prophecy is a special kind of talking, not so much an educated as an inspired and poetic version of what must have been at least sometimes, among some significant part of the prophet's audience, ordinary discourse," *ISC*, p. 62.
84 Michael Walzer, *Nation and Universe*, p. 513f. "[. . .] Plurality may be consistent, at least in principle, with the single, omnipotent God of Israel who creates men and women in his own image. For then God himself must make some kind of peace with their plurality and creativity. The artists among them will not all paint the same picture; the playwrights will not write the same play; the philosophers will not produce the same account of the good; and the theologians will not call God by the same name. What human beings have in common is just this creative power, which is not the power to do the same thing in the same way but the power to do many different things in different ways: divine omnipotence (dimly) reflected, distributed, and particularized. Here is a creation story – it is not, I concede, the dominant version – that supports the doctrine of reiterative universalism," *Nation and Universe*, pp. 517–518.
85 Michael Walzer, "Philosophy and Democracy," p. 394.
86 Michael Walzer, *Nation and Universe*, pp. 520–521.
87 Michael Walzer, *Nation and Universe*, pp. 526 and 531.
88 Michael Walzer, *Nation and Universe*, p. 555.
89 Isaiah Berlin, "Does Political Theory still Exist?" in *Concepts and Categories: Philosophical Essays*, Henry Hardy (ed.), London, New York, Hogarth Press, 1979, pp. 143–172.
90 Michael Walzer, *Nation and Universe*, p. 555.
91 Ronald Dworkin, "To Each his Own" (Review of *Spheres of Justice*), *New York Review of Books*, April 14, 1983; "*Spheres of Justice*: An Exchange," response by Michael Walzer followed by a response by R. Dworkin, *New York Review of Books*, July 21, 1983.

92 Michael Walzer's "Objectivity and Social Meaning" deals exactly with this problem.
93 John Searle, *The Construction of Social Reality*, New York, Free Press, 1997.
94 "Majority rule does not govern arguments about social meanings; it only governs behavior. The rules of behavior, then, are objectively right relative to the prevailing meanings, but the prevailing meanings are not objectively right (or wrong). They are only objectively there, the objects that is, of more or less accurate reports," Michael Walzer, "Objectivity and Social Meaning," p. 170
95 "Reiterated social construction rather than diffusion from an authoritative center is the preferred explanation for the appearance of identical or similar used and valued objects in different societies. There is no authoritative center, no Jerusalem from which meanings go forth. The list of similarly constructed uses and values, the, constitutes -what we might think of as a universal and objective morality – relative to social construction where construction repetitively takes the same form, relative to the prevailing argument where the same argument always prevails," Michael Walzer, "Objectivity and Meaning," p. 171.
96 Michael Walzer, "Liberalism as an Art of Separation."

1 Who Are You Michael Walzer?

1 Herbert Hoover, Republican, secretary of commerce wins against the Democratic Governor of New York, Alfred E. Smith, a Roman Catholic.
2 Stephen Samuel (Weitsz) Wise (1874–1949), Reform rabbi and in favor of political Zionism. Born in Budapest, Wise was the co-founder of the NAACP, founder, in 1922, of the Jewish Institute for Religion (a center for Reform Judaism), president of ZOA (Zionist Organization of America), chairman of Keren haYesod, honorary president of the AJC (American Jewish Congress) who's first meeting in Philadelphia he organized with Louis Brandeis and Felix Frankfurter in 1918. He counseled President Roosevelt on Jewish issues, but has been criticized (namely by Saul Friedlander) for supporting the embargo on aid to be sent to Jews in Nazi occupied territories.
3 Ewa Morawska, *Insecure Prosperity: Small-Town Jews in Industrial America, 1890–1940*, Princeton University Press, 1999.
4 Ewa Morawska, *For Bread with Butter: The Life-Worlds of East Central Europeans in Johnstown, Pennsylvania, 1890–1940* (Interdisciplinary Perspectives on Modern History), Cambridge University Press, 1985.
5 Bethlehem Steel, founded in 1904, was America's second-largest steel producer and largest shipbuilder.
6 See chs 4, 7, and 9.
7 *PM*, was a left-wing journal founded in 1940 by Ralph Ingersoll (who first employed I. F. Stone). The paper campaigned for the US involvement in the Second World War, fought against racial discrimination, fascism, and anti-semitism, making use of Dr Seuss' (Theodor Geisel) cartoons. The journal was published until 1948.
8 Isador Feinstein Stone (1907–1989) was a Russian born American writer, left-wing radical journalist, member of the Popular Front in the 1930s. He worked for *The New York Post*, *The Nation*, *PM*, then founded his own

newspaper: *I. F. Stone's Weekly*, published from 1953 to 1971. He was a Zionist, urged President Roosevelt to rescue the European Jews, and a strong supporter of the state of Israel. He wrote against the wars in Korea and Vietnam. He is said (almost certainly wrongly) to have been a spy for the Soviets.

9 I. F. Stone, *Underground to Palestine*, New York, Boni & Gaer, 1946, first published as a series of articles in *PM* (paperback edn., CreateSpace Independent Publishing Platform, 2017), is an eyewitness account of the voyage of the Holocaust survivors to Israel. It was reprinted in 1978 under the title *Underground to Palestine and Reflections Thirty Years Later* with two additional chapters that had appeared in the *New York Review of Books* ("Confessions of a Jewish Dissident," "The Other Zionism"), reflections on the Arab–Israeli crises of 1948–1949 and the Suez war of 1956, and a new foreword by D. D. Guttenplan. *Dissent* published a review by Susie Linfield in 2012: "Zionism and its Discontent," Fall, 2012.

10 United Jewish Appeal (UJA), is a philanthropic organization founded in 1939.

11 Sam Rappaport has become Sam Shapiro in Michael Walzer's "On Humanitarianism. Is Helping Others Charity, or Duty, or Both?" *Foreign Affairs*, July–August 2011. "*Tzedakah*" means charity and justice in Hebrew; it is also the name of the box in which one puts the money to be distributed to the needy. "In the Jewish tradition, this view of *tzedakah* as an expression of justice was sometimes described in theological language. The idea is that God has heard and responded to the cries of the poor and, in principle at least, has given them what they need. You may possess some part of what they need, but you possess it only as an agent of God, and if you do not pass it on to the poor, if you do not contribute, say, to the communal charity fund, you are robbing the poor of what in fact already belongs to them. The negative act of not contributing is a positive theft. And since theft is unjust, you are acting not only uncharitably but also unjustly by not giving – which is why coerced *tzedakah* is legitimate. I called this a theological argument, but it is possible even for nonbelievers to accept that, in some sense, it is true and right. Or nonbelievers can translate the argument into secular language: some part of everyone's wealth belongs to the political community, which makes economic activity and peaceful accumulation possible – and it can and should be used to promote the well-being of all the members of the community [. . .]. What moral or philosophical principle was Sam enforcing? He probably could not have answered that question, but the answer seems obvious: 'from each according to his abilities, to each according to his needs'. That line is from Karl Marx's *Critique of the Gotha Program*. Sam was not a Marxist, not by a long shot, but he adjusted the demands he made on each of us to his knowledge of our ability to pay.

And we all believed that the UJA would distribute the money to those most in need. 'From each, to each' is another example of two in one, for it describes equally well charitable giving and justified taking. This is the principle that Marx believed would apply after the withering away of the state – that is, in a condition of statelessness [. . .]. Jewish statelessness can help us understand what charity more generally is or should be. It can also provide us with the crucial categories for thinking about humanitarianism in international society. When you do not have a state, charity and justice come two in one. Individuals decide which good deeds, out of many possible ones, they will undertake, which needs they will recognize and how much of their time, energy, and money they will give. But decisions of this sort cannot be made appropriately without understanding what justice requires.

This is the context in which we have to think about humanitarianism, which cannot in the circumstances of statelessness be a freely chosen gift, which has to respond to urgency and need. It is like *tzedakah*: if it does not connect with justice, it will not be what it should be. Religious men and women can reasonably think that God has already determined what we owe to the global poor, and the sick, and the hungry, and that our task is just to figure it out. And secular men and women can acknowledge that whether or not God exists, this is not a bad way of thinking about these things."

12　H. A. Wallace became F. D. Roosevelt's Vice-President after the 1940 presidential elections. In 1944, the Democrats selected H. S. Truman as Roosevelt's running mate. Wallace, who became the editor of the *New Republic* in the late 1940s was a fierce critic of Truman's foreign policy. Harry Truman served as President of the US (1945–1953) after the death of F. D. Roosevelt.

13　Harry Truman approved Ernest Bevin's plan to supply blockaded Berlin by air. He also supported the creation of the state of Israel. See D. McCullough, *Truman*, New York, Simon & Shuster, 1992.

14　From Michael Walzer's keynote at the 125th anniversary of Jewish life in Johnstown, courtesy of MW.

15　Joseph McCarthy (1908–1957), Senator of Wisconsin from 1947 to 1957. Violently anti-Communist, he fueled campaigns against alleged Communists, as well as alleged homosexuals in the US government, academia, the press, and the film industry. He was censored by the Senate in 1954. McCarthyism refers to his semi-legal or illegal attacks against alleged anti-American politics and behavior.

16　See ch. 2 on Michael Walzer's early political activism.

17　Marie Syrkin, *Golda Meir. Woman with a Cause*. New York, Putnam, 1963.

18　Marie Syrkin, 1899–1989. Daughter of Nachman Syrkin (1868–1924), the influential socialist Zionist and founder of Labor Zionism. Marie, who held a BA in English literature from Cornell, was an English teacher at the Textile High School in Manhattan before joining Brandeis. Author, poet, translator of Yiddish poetry, she also co-founded the Zionist journal Jewish Frontier. Her book, *Blessed Is the Match: The Story of Jewish Resistance*, New York, Knopf, 1948, is a story based on Holocaust survivors in Palestine.

19　Frank E. Manuel (1910–2003) was a Professor of History, known for his writings on utopia. He published *Utopian Thought in the Western World*, with his wife, Fritzie P. Manuel (Oxford, Blackwell, 1979), which won the National Book award in History in 1983 (paperback edn.).

20　Dr. Abram Leon Sachar was the founding president of Brandeis University. When it opened under his direction in 1948, Brandeis had 107 students and 13 faculty members. The university counts more than 6,000 students and more than 350 faculty members in 2018. Sachar was born in New York in 1899, to immigrant parents. Director and chairman of the Hillel Foundation, Sachar was a historian of Jewish history. See the *New York Times* obituary from July 25, 1993.

21　*Birth of a Nation*, a movie by D. W. Griffith released in 1915, tells the story of two families, Northern and Southern, during the civil war. The movie, based on two novels by Thomas F. Dixon (*The Clansman: A Historical Romance of the Ku Klux Khan* and *The Leopard's Spots*), includes an apology of the Ku Klux Klan and racist scenes. It was banned in many American cities.

22 "There was also a dance studio downtown, "Kelly's," where Gene Kelly's sister taught many of us to fox trot and waltz – nothing more complicated, though for me those two were hard enough. (We also learned the polka, and I remember the song we danced to: "Johnstown, Johnstown, city that flood waters couldn't kill.") From Michael Walzer's keynote at the 125th anniversary of Jewish life in Johnstown. Courtesy of MW.

23 From Michael Walzer's keynote at the 125th anniversary of Jewish life in Johnstown, courtesy of MW.

24 Hashomer Hatsaïr is a Jewish socialist and Zionist youth movement founded in 1913.

25 An example of Judith B. Walzer's contributions to *Dissent*: "The Breakthrough: Feminism and Literary Criticism," *Dissent*, Spring, 2008.

26 Geoffrey Rudolph Elton (1921–1994), British political and constitutional historian, Regius Professor of Modern History at Cambridge. Author of more than 20 books on the Tudor Revolution, Reformation, Modern British history, Henry VIII, Cromwell.

27 Victor Ehrenberg (1891–1976), German historian, specialist of ancient Greek history and thought, father of Geoffrey R. Elton.

28 Isaac Deutscher (1907–1967). Polish author and journalist, Communist (but not Bundist) in Warsaw, he moved to Britain at the outbreak of the Second World War. Known for his influential biographies of Stalin, *Stalin. A Political Biography* (1949), Oxford University Press, 2nd edn., 1967, and Trotsky, *The Prophet Armed* (1954), *The Prophet Unarmed* (1959) and *The Prophet Outcast* (1963), Three-volume set, Oxford University Press, 1963. Deutscher also wrote about Israel, *Non-Jewish Jew and Other Essays*, London, Oxford University Press, 1968.

29 Stuart Hall (1932–2014), co-founder of the *New Left Review*, is also the founder of "cultural studies," and has contributed to incorporate gender and race into the mainstream curricula in higher education. He wrote many essays and books influenced by continental – especially French – philosophy, post-modern and post-colonial theory and semiotics. Hall is well known for his conception of cultural identity as undergoing constant changes: "the different ways we are positioned by, and position ourselves within, the narratives of the past" (*Cultural Identity and Diaspora. Identity: Community, Culture, Difference*, London, Lawrence and Wishart, 1990). His works include, with P. Walton, *Situating Marx: Evaluations and Departures*, London, Human Context Books, 1972; *Encoding and Decoding in the Television Discourse*, Birmingham, Centre for Contemporary Cultural Studies, 1973; *Representation. Cultural Representations and Signifying Practices*, London Thousand Oaks, California, Sage in association with the Open University, 1997; *Selected Political Writings: The Great Moving Right Show and Other Essays*, London: Lawrence & Wishart, 2017.

30 Michael and Margaret Rustin are both scholars in psychoanalysis and experts on Melanie Klein. Michael Rustin has been a regular contributor to the *New Left Review*. A fine summary of the history of the Review can be retrieved here: https://newleftreview.org/history.

31 Catherine Hall, Professor of Modern British Social and Cultural History at

180

UCL. She married Stuart Hall in 1964. Her works include *White, Male, and Middle-Class: Explorations in Feminism and History* (1992); *Race, Nation and Empire: Making Histories, 1750 to the Present* (2010, editor, with Keith McClelland).

32 Charles Taylor is a well-known Canadian philosopher born in 1931, from a francophone mother and an English-speaking father. He was an early contributor to the *New Left Review* (with Alisdair MacIntyre). He has published more than twenty books on ethics and moral philosophy in particular, but he has also been active within the "Taylor-Bouchard Commission" in 2007 on accommodationist practices in Quebec (cultural integration, collective identity, church–state relations and appropriate procedures for handling religious differences). His major books include *Sources of the Self: The Making of the Modern Identity*, Cambridge MA, Harvard University Press, 1989; *The Malaise of Modernity*, Toronto, Anansi, 1991; *Multiculturalism: Examining the Politics of Recognition*, New Haven, Princeton University Press, 1992; *La Liberté des modernes*, Paris, PUF, 1999; *The Ethics of Authenticity*, Cambridge MA, Harvard University Press, 2005; *A Secular Age*, Belknat Harvard, 2007.

33 The piece is called "My Israel." (*Mein Israel – 21 erbetene Interventionen*, Micha Brumlik (ed.), Frankfurt a. M., Fischer-T. B., translation Ilse Strasmann). Below is an excerpt: "So what did we have in common with the Egyptians and the Poles? Of course, I had an intellectual answer to that question. I wouldn't have been on the ship if I hadn't already been in some sense a Zionist. I believed in the unity of the Jewish people and in the right of the Jews to national liberation and in the urgent importance, after the Holocaust, of Jewish statehood. What I came to understand between Piraeus and Haifa was the emotional correlate of those beliefs. My feeling of kinship with the people on board was so strong that even today I have no words to express it – nor, after forty-five years of writing, do I feel any need for words. Ever since that time, I have been a Zionist not only for all the other reasons but also because of that boy, who was so suddenly unsure about what it means to be a Jew and so suddenly caught up in the Jewish experience [. . .]. I have higher hopes for Israel than that it be a place where children like him can grow up safely and figure out who they are. But that is the first thing that it has to be. Whenever my hopes lead me to criticize this or that Israeli government or policy, which happens often, I remember the Egyptians and the Poles on that ship in 1957. I suppose they have made a home in Israel and because they have, because they could, their Israel is mine too."

34 A historical kibbutz in central Israel. Named after Nahshon, leader of the Judahites (Book of Numbers). "Operation Nahshon" was the name of a major Haganah initiative to relieve the siege of Jerusalem in the 1948 war by liberating the route from Tel Aviv to Jerusalem.

35 According to a Midrash, Nahshon (son of Amminadav) was the first to wade into the Red Sea before it parted during the escape from Egypt.

36 Kiryat Shmona ("City of the Eight") is a historical village on the Lebanese border. Founded on the grounds of an Arab village in 1949 (al-Khalisah), the village became a transition camp (*ma'abara*) for Yemenite Jews. It was given its name in memory of Joseph Trumpeldor and his seven comrades who were killed in 1920 defending Tel Haï.

37 See excerpts from the speech above.

181

38 In an interview with Harry Kreisler (*Conversations with History*, https://www.youtube.com/watch?v=t1_Z5SPIrs4), Michael Walzer speaks about the "narrowing down work" in graduate school and the welcome escape *Dissent* offered from research at graduate school.

39 Louis Hartz (1919–1986), American political scientist and Professor at Harvard. He wrote on American exceptionalism. His books include *The Liberal Tradition in America. An Interpretation of American Political Thought Since the Revolution*, Harcourt, Brace 1955; *The Founding of New Societies: Studies in the History of the United States, Latin America, South Africa, Canada, and Australia*, Harcourt, Brace & World, 1964.

40 Samuel Beer (1911–2009), American political scientist, Professor at Harvard. Speechwriter for F. D. Roosevelt, member of the Democratic National Committee and contributor to *The New York Post*. His books include *The City of Reason*, Cambridge MA, Harvard University Press, 1949; *Britain Against Itself: The Political Contradictions of Collectivism*, New York, W. W. Norton & Company, 1982; *To Make a Nation: The Rediscovery of American Federalism*, Cambridge MA, Harvard University Press, 1993.

41 Valdimer Orlando Key Jr. (1908–1963), American political scientist, expert on voting behavior. His books include *Politics, Parties, and Pressure Groups*, Springfield, Ohio, Crowell, 1942; *American State Politics: An Introduction*, Knopf, 1956, Westwood CT, Greenwood Press, 1983; *Public Opinion and American Democracy*, Knopf, 1961; co-authored with Milton C. Cummings, *The Responsible Electorate: Rationality in Presidential Voting, 1936–1960*, Belknap Harvard Press, 1966.

42 Zbigniew Brzezinski (1918–2017), American-Polish political scientist and international relations expert and "realist" scholar, diplomat, political counselor (to Lyndon B. Johnson) and National Security advisor (to Jimmy Carter). Brzezinski has had a long career in government and influenced US policy in Iran, China, Afghanistan, and the Middle East. Intellectual and Professor (Johns Hopkins, Columbia, and Harvard), he is the author of many books and articles, namely on totalitarianism. See *The Permanent Purge: Politics in Soviet Totalitarianism*, Cambridge MA, Harvard University Press, 1956; *Soviet Bloc: Unity and Conflict*, Cambridge MA, Harvard University Press, 1967; *Grand Failure: The Birth and Death of Communism in the Twentieth Century*, New York Collier Books (Simon & Shuster), 1990; the classic *Totalitarian Dictatorship and Autocracy*, co-authored with Carl J. Friedrich, Cambridge MA, Harvard University Press 1956.

43 Rupert Emerson (1899–1979), American political scientist, Professor of International Relations at Harvard. Expert on nationalism in Asia and Africa. His books include *From Empire to Nation: The Rise to Self-Assertion of Asian and African Peoples*, Cambridge MA, Harvard University Press, 1962; *Self-Determination Revisited in the Era of Decolonization*, Cambridge, MA, Center for International Affairs, Cambridge MA, Harvard University Press, 1964.

44 See Stuart Hall's piece on the early New Left, including comments on the New Left Club, "Life and Times of the First New Left," *New Left Review*, 61, January–February 2010, https://newleftreview.org/II/61/stuart-hall-life-and-times-of-the-first-new-left.

45 The statement was published on May 10, 1961 in the *New York Times*, 41M.

46 Stephan Thernstrom, born in 1934, was Professor of American History at Brandeis, Harvard and Cambridge. He co-authored many books with his wife Abigail (born in 1936), a political scientist, expert on race relations (*America in Black and White. One Nation, Indivisible*, New York, Simon & Schuster, 1997; *No Excuses: Closing the Racial Gap in Learning*, New York, Simon & Schuster, 2003).

47 Gabriel M. Kolko (1932–2014), American (revisionist) historian, expert on the history of war, capitalism, socialism, and the "progressive era." His books include *The Triumph of Conservatism: A Reinterpretation of American History, 1900–1916*, New York, The Free Press, 1963; *Vietnam: Anatomy of a Peace*, London and New York, Routledge, 1997; *Century of War: Politics, Conflicts, and Society since 1914*, New York, The New Press, 1994; *After Socialism: Reconstructing Critical Social Thought*, Abingdon, Routledge, 2006.

48 *The Revolution of the Saints. A Study in the Origins of Radical Politics* was published in 1965 by Harvard University Press.

49 Michael Walzer, "After the Landslide," *Views* (American Issue), *Quarterly* 6, Autumn, 1964 (Civil Rights, Goldwaterism, Cold War, Automation, Poverty, Mass Culture): 13–20.

50 Clancy Sigal (1926–2017) was an American novelist, journalist, screenwriter and filmmaker. His autobiographical novel *Going Away. A Report. A Memoir*, New York, Carroll & Graf, 1961 was nominated for the National Book Award.

51 *Soundings* was founded by Doreen Massey, Stuart Hall, and Michael Rustin. The current editor is Sally Davison (https://www.lwbooks.co.uk/soundings).

52 Perry Anderson (born 1938), is a British historian, Marxist, editor of the *New Left Review* (from 1962 to 1982, and again in the early 2000s). Author of many books on Western Marxism (*Considerations on Western Marxism*, London, Verso, 1976), and late capitalism, he also published a critical reading of postmodernism engaging with Frederik Jameson's theses (*The Origins of Postmodernity*, London, Verso, 1998). His books include *Arguments within English Marxism*, London, Verso, 1980, *Mapping the West European Left*, co-authored with Patrick Camiller, London, Verso, 1994. Paul Blackledge wrote a biography of P. Anderson: *Perry Anderson, Marxism, and the New Left*, London, Merlin Press, 2004.

53 Dr. Stanley Plastrik (1915–1981) was the co-founder and editor of *Dissent*. He taught American history at a branch of the City University in Staten Island before retiring in 1980. Both Plastrik and Howe were disenchanted with the Independent Socialist League (ISL, the former Workers party), which they left in 1952. "They complained in their letter of resignation that the ISL's 'shell of isolation' has begun to seem almost comfortable, and what was once felt to be the tragedy of sect life has now covertly become glorified in the psychology of the 'saving remnant'," writes M. Isserman in "Steady Work," art. cit. Plastrik became business manager at *Dissent*'s founding.

Upon Plastriks death, Irving Howe published a moving Obituary in *Dissent* (Winter 1981): "The other day I was asked to speak at a gathering on "the moral basis of socialism." I was somewhat taken aback since it was not clear to me whether socialism can claim a moral basis apart from that of other humane persuasions, and if it can, in which ways and to what extent. But then, after visiting the hospital in which Stanley lay dying, it struck me that the moral basis of socialism had been on the phone with me almost every day these past seventeen years, had been my friend for forty, and my collaborator on *Dissent* for twenty-seven years. In the experience we shared since the late 1930s the idea of socialism may have become increasingly problematical, but the rightness of being a socialist had remained clear. And to be one meant to be like Stanley; meant to stand fast in good times or bad; meant to be on call for whatever task was needed; meant to live by a code, largely unspoken yet not to be violated, of concern for the lives of men and women. Those of us near Stanley never had to talk about the moral basis of anything, since we felt through him its constant warming presence."

54 Emanuel (Manny) Geltman (1914–1995), also one of the founding Dissentniks and an ex-Trotskyst. Former editor of *Labor Action*, proofreader then editor for various publishers (The Free Press of Glencoe, Chicago University Press), he was executive editor and in charge of design and layout. An In Memoriam written by Brian Morton appeared in the *Dissent* Winter issue of 1996: "'Manny was a socialist for longer than most of us have lived. As a teenager, influenced by his radical older brothers and sister, he joined a young Communist group. By the time he entered Brooklyn College he had come to question the Communist accommodation with Hitler, and he joined the embryonic American Trotskyist movement. Soon he was a leading member of the youth group. Along with James P. Cannon and Max Shachtman, founders of American Trotskyism, and youth leader Nathan Gould, he attended the Paris meeting that resulted in the Fourth International in 1937. Manny used to joke that he joined movements just in time to leave them. Never one to follow a 'party line', he broke with the Trotskyist Socialist Workers party and went with the Shachtman group that had been disgusted by the Hitler–Stalin pact and the Soviet invasions of the Baltic countries. Before he was drafted, Manny edited *Labor Action*, the Shachtmanite group's weekly paper and served as an organizer on the West Coast. In the post-Second World War era the limits of sectarian politics became clearer, and in 1953 he left the Shachtmanites and joined Irving Howe, Stanley Plastrik, Lewis Coser, and Meyer Schapiro, among others, in founding a journal that, Howe and Coser wrote, would 'provide a rallying point for those who dissent from the bleak atmosphere of conformism that pervades the political and intellectual life of the United States'."

55 Lewis Coser, "Sects and Sectarianism," *Dissent* 4, Autumn, 1954.

56 Edward Palmer Thompson (1924–1993), was an important British socialist historian, expert on the British working class. Founder of the "new social history." His books include *The Making of the English Working Class*, London, 1963; *The Poverty of Theory and Other Essays*, London, Merlin Press, 1978; *Protest and Survive*, London, Penguin Books, 1980; *Making History: Writings on History and Culture*, London, The Free Press, 1994.

57 "The Great Moving Right Show," *Marxism Today*, January 1979 (available here: http://banmarchive.org.uk/collections/mt/index_frame.htm); Stuart Hall and Martin Jacques, *The Politics of Thatcherism*, London, Lawrence and Wishart, 1983.

58 John Schrecker (born 1937), is a Professor Emeritus of History at Brandeis. Expert on East Asian history and civilization. His books include *The Chinese Revolution in Historical Perspective*, 2nd edn., New York, Greenwood/ Praeger, 2004; with Paul Cohen, *Reform in Nineteenth-Century China*, Cambridge MA, Harvard University Press, 1976; *Imperialism and Chinese*

Nationalism: Germany in Shantung, Cambridge MA, Harvard University Press, 1971.

59 Michael Walzer, John Schrecker, "American Intervention and the Cold War," *Dissent*, Fall 1965, and "A Reply by Michael Walzer and John Schrecker," *Dissent*, March–April, 1966.

60 Jon Wiener (born 1944) is an American historian and a journalist. He contributed (as an editor) to *The Nation, New York Times Magazine, Guardian, New Republic*, etc. He is known for the legal battle he led against the FBI to expose the FBI surveillance of John Lennon and to get the John Lennon files released by the FBI. While he wrote his first book on Lennon, *Come Together: John Lennon in his Time*, New York, Random House, 1984, he discovered Lennon was under surveillance. In *Gimme Some Truth: The John Lennon FBI Files*, Berkeley, University of California Press, 2000 he recounts the story of his battle against the FBI. Wiener was very much involved in the anti-war movement and wrote on the Chicago Eight (*Conspiracy in the Streets: The Extraordinary Trial of the Chicago Eight*, edition and introduction Jon Wiener, afterword by Tom Hayden, drawings by Jules Feiffer, New York, The New Press, 2006).

61 https://simplecast.com/s/410f4b0e?t=0m0s.

62 Michael Walzer, "The State of Righteousness: Liberal Zionists Speak Out," Huffpost Blog, April 24, 2012, see https://www.huffingtonpost.com/michael-walzer/liberal-zionists-speak-out-state-of-righteousness_b_1447261.html?guccounter=2.

63 See Michael Walzer, "What Does it Mean to Be an American?," *Social Research*, 71 (3), Fall 2004: 633–654.

64 Michael Walzer, "A Day in the Life of a Socialist Citizen," *Dissent*, May–June, 1968.

2 Political Activism, Civil Rights, and the Anti-War Movement

1 Quoted by M. Isserman, "60 Years of *Dissent*, Steady Work," *Dissent*, January 23, 2014.

2 This is how Michael Walzer describes the state of mind of the first sit-inners: mobilized by "a day to day indignity," a certain happiness about the protest, "we were so happy"; a strong, spontaneous solidarity, and a good organization, "as if from a bureaucracy textbook," Michael Walzer, "The Young: A Cup of Coffee and a Seat," *Dissent*, Spring, 1960.

3 The Weather Underground Organization was founded by a faction of the SDS in 1969 when the SDS dissolved. Fighting for a classless society and for Black rights alongside the Black Panthers, opposed to the Vietnam War, the group declared war on American imperialism and organized bombings of government buildings in the 1970s and riots (three "Days of Rage" in October 1969 in Chicago).

4 Jürgen Habermas recounts the German experience in "20 Years Later. May '68 and the West-German Republic," *Dissent*, Spring, 1989.

5 *Dissent*, Symposium 68, Spring, 2008.

6 "Presidential politics seemed to them a universe apart from sitdown, picketing and student solidarity," Michael Walzer, "The Young: A Cup of Coffee and a Seat," art. cit.

7 Ralph Abernathy (1926–1990) was a minister and political activist during the Civil Rights Movement. In favor of nonviolence, co-organizer of the Montgomery Bus Boycott, co-founder and president of the SCLC after Martin Luther King Jr.'s assassination in 1968, board member of the Martin Luther King Jr. Center for Nonviolent Social Change. He wrote a controversial autobiography (*And the Walls Came Tumbling Down*, New York, Harper Collins, 1989) in which he discussed Martin Luther King Jr.'s private life.

8 "Can the Blacks do for Africa what the Jews did for Israel?" is an interesting article on the solidarity between Jews and Blacks, long gone by 1974. See Martin Weil, *Foreign Policy*, 15, Summer, 1974.

9 *Conversations with History*, November 12, 2013, https://conversations. berkeley.edu/walzer_2013.

10 Harvey Pressman, Brandeis alumni (class of 1958), founder of the Central Coast Children's Foundation. Deena Ecker interviewed Harvey Pressman in The Civil Rights History Project: Survey of Collections and Repositories [Massachusetts to Mississippi: Brandeis student involvement in the civil rights movement, 1960–1964], https://www.loc.gov/folklife/civilrights/survey/view_collection.php?coll_id=1500.

11 The article was never published. Walzer analyzes the student's discovery of politics and solidarity in the 1960s; the misunderstandings between generations in general, and between the political old-timers who wanted to recuperate the movement and the enthusiastic students resisting the enlistment in particular; the experience of picketing; the relatively calm behavior of the police ("The police were uncomfortably in the middle: for if their first instinct was to worry about disorder – and about Woolworth property rights – their second thoughts were political. The issue was potentially explosive, and Negroes had far more votes than did Woolworth managers. The result was a kind of compromise, in which the police shuffled back and forth between manager and picket captain and tried to keep everyone happy, and the street as quiet as possible"); the role of the local press ("newspapers which for years had piously thundered against student apathy and the silence of the 'silent generation' failed to comment on the end of apathy"); and lastly the civic education within the protest movements in the early 1960s.

12 R. F. Williams, *Negroes with Guns* (1962), Wayne State University Press, reed. 1998.

13 Michael Walzer, "Politics of nonviolent resistance," *Dissent*, Fall, 1960.

14 Ibid.

15 "When one wages a war 'without weapons' one appeals for restraint from men with weapons. It is not likely that these men, soldiers, will be converted by the creed of nonviolence," Michael Walzer, *Just and Unjust Wars*, p. 380.

16 The My Lai massacre took place on March 16, 1968. One of the most atrocious episodes of the Vietnam War (between 350 and 500 Vietnamese civilians, men, women, and children were murdered by US infantry soldiers) in the hamlets of My Lai and My Khe. The massacre became public knowledge in November 1969, and contributed to strengthen the domestic opposition to the war.

17 Martin Luther King Jr., "A Time to Break Silence," Riverside Church, New York City, April 4, 1967. An excerpt from this long and important speech by the 1964 Nobel Prize winner: "Somehow this madness must cease. I speak

as a child of God and brother to the suffering poor of Vietnam and the poor of America who are paying the double price of smashed hopes at home and death and corruption in Vietnam. I speak as a citizen of the world, for the world as it stands aghast at the path we have taken. I speak as an American to the leaders of my own nation. The great initiative in this war is ours. The initiative to stop must be ours."

18 "Yippies" refers to the Youth International Party founded by Abbie Hoffman and Jerry Rubin.

19 Tom Hayden (1939–2016) was an intellectual, author, politician and early influential political activist during the Civil Rights and Anti-War Movements; he was one of the founders of SDS (Students for a Democratic Society, a movement dissolved in 1969), and the author of SDS's "Port Huron statement." One of the major representatives of the New Left and of the Countercultural revolution in the US, Hayden, although denouncing the politics of the Soviet Union, did not wish to restrict the movement's members to non-Communists. He traveled to North Vietnam and Cambodia as early as 1965, founded the Indochina Peace Campaign (1972–1975), fought for women's rights, and entertained a difficult relationship with the Dissentniks, Irving Howe in particular who said about the New Left: "the movement (New Left) was something long hoped for, and when it came it came in forms that were sometimes quite wonderful, as in the early Civil Rights Movement, and then progressively more and more difficult for us to connect with," Irving Howe, "New Styles in 'Leftism'," *Dissent*, Summer 1965.

20 In early March of that year, Johnson leads in the polls by 49 percent against 42 percent for McCarthy; mid-March, Robert Kennedy announces his own candidacy, he is assassinated in June; the Chicago Convention nominates Vice President Hubert Humphrey.

21 M. Walzer, I. Howe, "Were we Wrong about Vietnam?," *New Republic*, August 18, 1979: 15–18.

22 M. Isserman, "60 Years of *Dissent*, Steady Work."

23 The 2018 Midterms.

24 *Dissent*, January 24, 2017.

25 Michael Walzer, "A Day in the Life of a Socialist Citizen. Two Cheers for Participatory Democracy," *Dissent*, May–June, 1968: 243–247.

26 Michael Walzer, *The Company of Critics*, New York, Basic Books, 1988. The chapter on Camus first appeared in *Dissent*: "Commitment and Social Criticism, Camus' Algerian War," *Dissent*, Fall 1986.

27 See for example M. Hadj, "A Voice from Algeria," *Dissent*, Spring, 1956; Stanley Plastrik wrote "On the Death of an Old Militant" after his death in 1974, *Dissent*, Fall 1974.

28 *Dissent*, Summer 1956 issue on Algeria, https://www.dissentmagazine.org/issue/summer-1956.

29 J. P. Sartre "The Frenchman in Algeria cannot be neutral or innocent. Every Frenchman [. . .] oppresses, despises, dominates" quoted by Michael Walzer in "Albert Camus' Algerian War," CC, pp. 142–143 after Frantz Fanon, *Toward the African Revolution. Political Essays*, trans. H. Chevalier, New York, Grove Press, 1965, p. 81.

The full quote reads as follows: "The rebel's weapon is the proof of his humanity. For in the first days of the revolt you must kill: to shoot down a European is to kill two birds with one stone, to destroy an oppressor and the man he oppresses at the same time: there remain a dead man, and a free man; the survivor, for the first time, feels a national soil under his foot. At this moment the Nation does not shrink from him; wherever he goes, wherever he may be, she is; she follows, and is never lost to view, for she is one with his liberty. But, after the first surprise, the colonial army strikes; and then all must unite or be slaughtered," Preface to Frantz Fanon, *The Wretched of the Earth*, New York, Grove Press, 1965.

30 Camus is supposed to have said "I believe in justice, but I will defend my mother before justice." The quote is indeed apocryphal. In reality he said: "Right now, bombs are being thrown at the tramway in Algiers. My mother may sit in one of the carriages. If that is justice, I prefer my mother." See the interview with Carl Gustav Bjurström, after the publication of Camus' Nobel Prize discourse, *Discours de Suède*, Paris, Gallimard, Folio, 1997, http://www.gallimard.fr/catalog/entretiens/01002289.htm.

3 Dissent

1 "The accent of *Dissent* will be radical. Its tradition will be the tradition of democratic socialism. We shall try to reassert the libertarian values of the socialist ideal, and at the same time, to discuss freely and honestly what in the socialist tradition remains alive and what needs to be discarded or modified." I. Howe, L. Coser, "A word to our readers," *Dissent*, January 1954.

2 Brown v. Board of Education, 1954.

3 *The Daily Worker*, founded in 1924, was the newspaper of the American Communist Party.

4 Khrushchev's "secret speech" to the 20th Congress of the Soviet Communist Party on February 25, 1956, denouncing Stalin's politics after 1934.

5 "Angry Young Men" was the name of a group of British novelists and playwrights in the 1950s.

6 John Osborne, *Look Back in Anger*, played at the Royal Court Theatre in London in 1956.

7 Michael Walzer, "The Hero in Limbo," *Perspective: A Quarterly of Literature and the Arts*, 10/3, Summer–Autumn, 1958.

8 Michael Walzer, "In Place of a Hero," *Dissent*, Spring 1960; reprinted, fifty years later, in January 2010, after the death of J. D. Salinger, https://www.dissentmagazine.org/online_articles/in-place-of-a-hero-spring-1960.

9 "For Howe and his comrades, socialism had instead become a kind of Kantian categorical imperative, a normative guide to moral duties in the everyday world. Without necessarily believing that one would ever see the dawn of a socialist society, one still needed to live one's life as a socialist, as if the goal of socialism were a real historical possibility [. . .]. Socialism, Howe and Coser wrote in the second issue of *Dissent*, in an article on utopian thought, 'is the name of our desire. And not merely because it is a vision which, for many people around the world, provides moral sustenance, but also in the sense that it is a vision which objectifies and gives urgency to their criticism of the human condition in our time' (emphasis in the original). The utopian vision in Marxism was one that Howe and Coser respected, but wished to amend. Socialism was not to be understood as a secular kingdom of heaven on earth. Rather, they argued, 'in an age of curdled realism, it is necessary

188

to assert the utopian image. But this can be done meaningfully only if it is an image of social striving, tension, conflict; an image of a problem-creating and problem-solving society.' *Dissent*'s socialist project would be to marry a utopian spirit to a non-utopian agenda of immediate and practical reform," Maurice Isserman, "Steady Work," art. cit.

10 See the forthcoming article by Michael Walzer, "Antisémitisme et Antisionisme," *Esprit*, October, 2019, translation A. von Busekist (the original text, "Antizionism and Antisemitism" is forthcoming in *Dissent*).

11 January, 1977: Mailer to Walzer, cc: Irving Howe, Meyer Schapiro, Henry Pachter, [rejected author], January 7, 1977.

Dear Mike,
[Rejected author] sent me a copy of his letter to you of December 17 and I must say I'm discomfited enough to use the word "aghast." [Rejected author] has to be one of the very few intellectuals in America with consistently new and powerful ideas, and to turn him down without even a little public soul-searching about the function of *Dissent* after the hundreds of thousands of words of wholly academic and uninspired prose-carpeting we've printed over the last decade delights no standards I know. Indeed, if the present canon, as [Rejected author] suggests, is that one's "ideas have to be verified somewhere in the formal or academic sphere before they can be considered by *Dissent*," I wonder if *Dissent* would print "The White Negro" today if it came in. I confess to not having read the piece he submitted to you, but also confess that I'd be staggered if it had nothing or very little to recommend it or, at the least, pass it to other editors.
Yours, Norman Mailer

Dear Norman, Thanks for your letter about [Rejected author]. I'm afraid that we have been rejecting his articles pretty regularly over a long period of time (so you shouldn't take the current rejection as the sign of a new, duller, more academic *Dissent*). The problem with all of [Rejected author's] pieces is roughly the same: he has a new position, which may or may not be interesting and exciting, but hasn't been argued out in any of the pieces that I have seen. He apparently feels that its full development requires technical psychological and anthropological arguments inappropriate for *Dissent*. He's probably right. Instead, he offers us sweeping surveys of world history or of the history of ideas in which position is assumed or briefly alluded to – and the result is not exciting but only eccentric. Would we print a piece like "The White Negro" today? Try us.
Yours, Michael Walzer

Quoted by Maurice Isserman, "60 Years of *Dissent*. Steady Work," art. cit.

12 Norman Mailer, "The White Negro," *Dissent*, Fall 1957. The subtitle reads "superficial reflections on the Hipster," whom Mailer defines as "the American existentialist," "a philosophical psychopath [. . .] trying to generate a new nervous system for himself." In this controversial piece about Jazz, orgasm, despair, totalitarianism, nihilism, language, and the super-ego of society, Mailer argues that the Hipsters are "a new breed of adventurers, urban adventurers who drifted out at night looking for action with a Black man's code to fit their facts. The hipster had absorbed the existentialist synapses of the Negro, and for practical purposes could be considered a White Negro." He continues his exploration of the relationship between Hipsters

189

and Negroes, the dominant culture and the place it is willing to make for equality in a very Arendtian way (see below on Little Rock): "[. . .] the most central is that the organic growth of Hip depends on whether the Negro emerges as a dominating force in American life. Since the Negro knows more about the ugliness and danger of life than the White, it is probable that if the Negro can win his equality, he will possess a potential superiority, a superiority so feared that the fear itself has become the underground drama of domestic politics. Like all conservative political fear, it is the fear of unforeseeable consequences, for the Negro's equality would tear a profound shift into the psychology, the sexuality, and the moral imagination of every White alive.

With this possible emergence of the Negro, Hip may erupt as a psychically armed rebellion whose sexual impetus may rebound against the anti-sexual foundation of every organized power in America, and bring into the air such animosities, antipathies, and new conflicts of interest that mean the empty hypocrisies of mass conformity will no longer work. A time of violence, new hysteria, confusion and rebellion will then be likely to replace the time of conformity. At that time, if the liberal should prove realistic in his belief that there is peaceful room for every tendency in American life, then Hip would end by being absorbed as a colorful figure in the tapestry. But if this is not the reality, and the economic, the social, the psychological, and finally the moral crises accompanying the rise of the Negro should prove insupportable, then a time is coming when every political guide post will be gone, and millions of liberals will be faced with political dilemmas they have so far succeeded in evading, and with a view of human nature they do not wish to accept. To take the desegregation of the schools in the South as an example, it is quite likely that the reactionary sees the reality more closely than the liberal when he argues that the deeper issue is not desegregation but miscegenation. (As a radical I am of course facing in the opposite direction from the White Citizen's Councils – obviously I believe it is the absolute human right of the Negro to mate with the White, and matings there will undoubtedly be, for there will be Negro high-school boys brave enough to chance their lives.) But for the average liberal whose mind has been dulled by the committee-ish cant of the professional liberal, miscegenation is not an issue because he has been told that the Negro does not desire it. So, when it comes, miscegenation will be a terror, comparable perhaps to the derangement of the American Communists "when the icons to Stalin came tumbling down." The article ends with a note on the "epic grandeur of Das Kapital."

13 Hannah Arendt, "Reflections on Little Rock," *Dissent*, Winter, 1959. The article had been rejected by *Commentary* in 1958. Irving Howe who had worked with Arendt at Schocken Books accepted to publish the piece with "Preliminary Remarks" by Arendt on the "controversial nature" of her reflections. Arendt comments on the Supreme Court decision in Brown v. Board of Education (with which she disagrees: "the government has no right to interfere with the prejudices and discriminatory practices of society"), and the subsequent events at Little Rock High School (the harassment of the students, Elizabeth Eckford in particular).

14 "The liberal state cannot provide a solution to the Jewish problem, for such a solution would require the legal prohibition against every kind of 'discrimination', that is, the abolition of the private sphere, the denial of any

difference between state and society, the destruction of the liberal state," Leo Strauss, "Preface to Spinoza's Critique of Religion," in Leo Strauss, *Liberalism Ancient and Modern*, Chicago, University of Chicago Press, 1995, p. 230.

15 M. Isserman, "60 Years of *Dissent*, Steady Work," art. cit.

16 M. Walzer and I. Howe, "Were we Wrong about Vietnam?", art. cit.

17 The Tet Offensive, in January and February 1968, is one of the largest military campaigns launched by the Vietcong and the North Vietnamese people's army against South Vietnam, the US, and their allies.

18 J. Toby Reiner "Toward an Overlapping Dissensus: The Search for Inclusivity in the Political Thought of '*Dissent Magazine*,'" *Political Research Quarterly*, 66/ 4, 2013: 756–767, p. 757.

19 See Irving Howe's "New Styles in 'Leftism'" from 1965.

20 Michael Walzer, "Antisémitisme et Antisionisme," art. cit.

21 Michael Walzer, "In Defense of Equality," *Dissent*, Fall 1973.

4 Thinking About War

1 West Point is the United States Military Academy at West Point, NY.

2 See ch. 4 of *Just and Unjust Wars* ("Law and Order in International Society"), ch. 5 ("Anticipations" – such as the Israeli anticipation in the Six Day War), ch. 6 ("Interventions" – such as humanitarian intervention).

3 *JUW*, "Anticipations," p. 84.

4 *JUW*, "Interventions, pp. 107–108.

5 *Jus ad vim* is the use of force short of war (see below). Daniel Brunstetter and Megan Braun provide a neat summary of Michael Walzer's conception of *jus ad vim*: "Walzer distinguishes between the level of force used: the former, being more limited in scope, lack the "unpredictable and often catastrophic consequences" of a "full-scale attack." Walzer calls the ethical framework governing these measures, *jus ad vim* (the just use of force), and he applies it to state-sponsored uses of force against both state and nonstate actors outside a state's territory that fall short of the quantum and duration associated with traditional warfare. Compared to acts of war, *jus ad vim* actions present diminished risk to one's own troops, have a destructive outcome that is more predictable and smaller in scale, severely curtail the risk of civilian casualties, and entail a lower economic and military burden. These factors make *jus ad vim* actions nominally easier for statesmen to justify compared to conventional warfare, though this does not necessarily mean these actions are morally legitimate or that they do not have potentially nefarious consequences," Daniel Brunstetter, Megan Braun "From *Jus ad Bellum* to *Jus ad Vim*: Recalibrating Our Understanding of the Moral Use of Force," *Ethics and International Affairs*, 27 (1), 2013: 87–106, p. 87.

6 Michael Walzer, *JUW*, ch. 11: "Guerrilla Warfare."

7 Michael Walzer and Avishai Margalit, "Israel: Civilians and Combatants," *New York Review of Books*, May 14, 2009. This response to Kasher and Yadlin has prompted exchanges with Kasher and Yadlin, "Israel and the Rules of War: An Exchange, *New York Review of Books*, June 11, 2009, as well as with Shlomo Avineri and Zeev Sternhell, "Israel: Civilians and Combatants. An Exchange," *New York Review of Books*, August 13, 2009.

8 Asa Kasher and Amos Yadlin "Assassination and Preventive Killings," *SAIS Revue of International Affairs*, 25 (1), 2005: 41–57.

9 "This is what each side should say to its soldiers: by wearing a uniform, you take on yourself a risk that is borne only by those who have been trained to injure others (and to protect themselves). You should not shift this risk onto those who haven't been trained, who lack the capacity to injure; whether they are brothers or others. The moral justification for this requirement lies in the idea that violence is evil, and that we should limit the scope of violence as much as is realistically possible. As a soldier, you are asked to take an extra risk for the sake of limiting the scope of the war. Combatants are the Davids and Goliaths of their communities. You are our David," Michael Walzer and Avishai Margalit, "Israel: Civilians and Combatants."

10 "Wars between states should never be total wars between nations or peoples. Whatever happens to the two armies involved, whichever one wins or loses, whatever the nature of the battles or the extent of the casualties, the two nations, the two peoples, must be functioning communities at the war's end. The war cannot be a war of extermination or ethnic cleansing. And what is true for states is also true for state-like political bodies such as Hamas and Hezbollah, whether they practice terrorism or not. The people they represent or claim to represent are a people like any other," Michael Walzer and Avishai Margalit, "Israel: Civilians and Combatants."

11 Michael Walzer, "Response to MacMahan's Paper," p. 44.

12 Michael Walzer, "War Fair. The Ethics of Battle," *New Republic*, July 31, 2006.

13 The town was Vemork. See *Just and Unjust Wars*, Noncombatant Immunity, "The Bombing of Occupied France and the Vemork Raid," pp. 158–159.

14 "Soldiers have the duty to reduce foreseeable risks to civilians to the extent that is reasonably possible, even if that means increasing risks to themselves. That amendment is a function of the duty to take 'due care' so as to limit risks to noncombatants," Michael Walzer, *Just and Unjust Wars*, p. 156.

15 "When one country imposes risks on innocent people in another country, however, it has to take positive measures to minimize those risks – and the measures it has to take are not dependent on the nationality of the innocents. That is our claim. It is demanding, but it isn't a radically absolutist demand, as our critics suggest," Reply to Shlomo Avineri and Zeev Sternhell, "Israel: Civilians and Combatants. An Exchange," *New York Review of Books*, August 13, 2009.

16 Peter Singer, "The Drowning Child and the Expanding Circle," *New Internationalist*, April 5, 1997.

17 "Supreme emergency" is the subject of ch. 16 of *Just and Unjust Wars*, p. 250f. The term refers to a prudent exemption of the rules of *jus in bello*. In exceptional situations, morality is not suspended, but the rules of behavior may be adapted to a life-threatening situation. Walzer's analysis has been heavily criticized, but he has continuously defended it. See for example Michael Walzer, "Emergency Ethics" (from 1988) which became ch. 3 in *Arguing about War*, New Haven, Yale University Press, 2004, p. 33f.

18 "I don't know whether we should acknowledge such a threshold or, if we do, whether we should regard your common-or-garden ticking bomb hypothetical as illustrating its application. But in the interest of trying to distinguish the issues that are really at stake in the debate about absolutism from those

that belong somewhere else in moral philosophy, we might want to say that
the existence or non-existence of absolute norms within the domain where
morality does or should sway, should be treated as quite a different matter
from the further and interesting question of whether there are limits to that
domain," Jeremy Waldron, "What Are Moral Absolutes Like?," Lecture presented as the Annual Lecture for the Harvard Philosophy Club Cambridge,
Massachusetts, April 2011, published in the *Harvard Philosophical Review*,
18/1, 2012: 4–30.

19 Jeremy Waldron, "What Are Moral Absolutes like?"

20 Ethics of War Conference, West Point, October 26–28, 2017.

21 "The hard left insists that the old laws should not be tampered with in the
least; the hard right insists that the old laws are entirely inapplicable to the
new threats, and that democratic governments should be entirely free to do
whatever it takes to combat terrorism, without regard to anachronistic laws.
Both extremes are dangerous. What is needed is a new set of laws, based on
the principles of the old laws of war and human rights – the protection of
civilians – but adapted to the new threats against civilian victims of terrorism."

22 A short version of Dershowitz's point "Should we fight terror with torture?"
has appeared in *The Independent*, July 3, 2006, available here: https://www.
independent.co.uk/news/world/americas/alan-Dershowitz-should-we-fight-
terror-with-torture-6096463.html.

23 I am referring to Michael Walzer's chapter on "World Government and
the Politics of Pretending," in *A Foreign Policy for the Left*, New Haven,
London, Yale University Press, 2018, pp. 116–136.

24 Michael Walzer, "The Problem of Dirty Hands," *Philosophy and Public
Affairs*, 2 (2),Winter, 1973: 160–180. See below.

25 Sir Arthur Harris (1892–1984), Marshal of the British Air Force, Commander
in Chief of Bomber Command. Responsible for bombing Dresden. In *Just
and Unjust Wars*, a subchapter of "War Crimes" ("The Dishonoring of
Arthur Harris") deals with the paradoxical situation of the obedient soldier:
morally wrong but obeying Churchill's orders. Dishonored and embittered,
Harris left Britain after the war.

26 Jean-Paul Sartre, *Les mains sales*, Paris, Gallimard, 1948.

27 "For while any one of us may stand alone, and so on, when we make this or
that decision, we are not isolated or solitary in our moral lives. Moral life is a
social phenomenon, and it is constituted at least in part by rules, the knowing
of which (and perhaps the making of which) we share with our fellows,"
Michael Walzer, "The Problem of Dirty Hands," p. 169.

28 Machiavelli's, Weber's, and Hoederer's utilitarianism.

29 Michael Walzer, "The Problem of Dirty Hands," pp. 167–168.

30 Jeff McMahan, is a "revisionist" war scholar. See "The Ethics of Killing in
War," *Philosophia*, 2006, 34 (1): 23–41.

31 McMahan challenges "three foundational tenets of the traditional theory":
"(1) that the principles of *jus in bello* are independent of those of *jus ad
bellum*, (2) that unjust combatants can abide by the principles of *jus in bello*
and do not act wrongly unless they fail to do so, and (3) that combatants are
permissible targets of attack while noncombatants are not," Jeff McMahan,
"The Ethics of Killing in War," p. 24.

32 "In the course of a bank robbery, a thief shoots a guard reaching for his gun.

The thief is guilty of murder, even if he claims that he acted in self-defense. Since he had no right to rob the bank, he also had no right to defend himself against the bank's defenders," Michael Walzer, *Just and Unjust Wars*, p. 128.

33 "[War] is a coercively collectivizing enterprise; a tyrannical enterprise; it overrides individuality, and it makes the kind of attention that we would like to pay to each person's moral standing impossible; it is universally oppressive. Just-war theory is adapted to the moral reality of war, which means that 'justice' in the theory lives, so to speak, under a cloud," Michael Walzer, "Response to MacMahan's Paper," *Philosophia*, 34 (1), 2006: 43–45, p. 43.

34 "What Jeff McMahan means to provide in this essay is a careful and precise account of individual responsibility in time of war. What he actually provides, I think, is a careful and precise account of what individual responsibility in war would be like if war were a peacetime activity," Michael Walzer, "Response to MacMahan's Paper," p. 43.

35 Comp. Michael Walzer, "The Politics of Rescue," *Dissent*, Winter 1995.

36 See ch. 2.

37 "The drone operators, however, aren't vulnerable, and so killing-by-drone is also politically easier than other forms of targeted killing: it invites us to imagine a war in which there won't be any casualties (on our side), no veterans who spend years in Veteran hospitals, no funerals. The easiness of fighting with drones should make us uneasy." Michael Walzer, "Just and Unjust Targeted Killing and Drone Warfare," *Daedalus*, 145 (4), 2016: 12–24.

38 For Jeff McMahan, "The targeted killing of a person who is in fact a terrorist is morally – though not legally – quite similar to the killing of an "unjust combatant" (that is, a combatant fighting in a war that lacks a just cause) while he is asleep, which most people regard as permissible." "Targeted Killing: Murder, Combat or Law Enforcement?," in Claire Oakes Finkelstein, Jens David Ohlin, and Andrew Altman, eds. *Targeted Killings: Law and Morality in an Asymmetrical World*, Oxford, Oxford University Press, 2012.

39 Michael Walzer, "Just and Unjust Targeted Killing and Drone Warfare," *Daedalus*, 145 (4) 2016: 12–24. Previous version published in *Dissent*, January 11, 2013. https://www.dissentmagazine.org/online_articles/targeted-killing-and-drone-warfare.

40 International Human Rights and Conflict Resolution Clinic of Stanford Law School (Stanford Clinic) and the Global Justice Clinic at New York University School of Law (NYU Clinic): *Living Under Drones. Death, Injury, and Trauma to Civilians. From US Drone Practices in Pakistan.*
The report is available here: https://www-cdn.law.stanford.edu/wp-content/uploads/2015/07/Stanford-NYU-Living-Under-Drones.pdf.
For a critical assessment, see Glenn Greenawalt, "New Stanford/NYU Study Documents the Civilian, Terror from Obama's Drones," *Guardian*, September 25, 2012, https://www.theguardian.com/commentisfree/2012/sep/25/study-obama-drone-deaths.

41 For a discussion on the justice of targeting Al Qaida members in Yemen, see Michael Walzer, "Just War and Terrorism," lecture at the Institute for Advanced Studies in Princeton, June, 2016, available here: https://www.youtube.com/watch?v=yZEprmCb5Pk&index=10&list=PL94UJTaiiod0WF QPfXhM5StY7g o93oOf-&t=3491s.

42 Michael Walzer, "Just and Unjust Targeted Killing and Drone Warfare," art. cit.

43 "Along with many others, I have argued for another rule: that the attacking forces must make positive efforts, including asking their own soldiers to take risks, in order to minimize the risks they impose on enemy civilians. How much risk has to be accepted? There is no precise answer to that question. But some risk is necessary, and if it is taken, then I think that the major responsibility for civilian deaths falls on the insurgents who are fighting from homes and schools and crowded streets. And if responsibility is understood and assigned in that way by the global public, it will be possible to fight and win an asymmetric war," Michael Walzer, *New Republic*, July 30, 2014.

44 "If you kill civilians in places like Vietnam or Afghanistan, you lose the battle for 'hearts and minds.' If you kill civilians in a place like Gaza, you lose the battle for global support. The two losses are different: America was defeated in Vietnam, while Israel in Gaza (in 2006) was merely forced to accept a cease-fire, and so prevented from winning. Indeed, the cost of winning would probably have been unbearable," Michael Walzer, *New Republic*, July 30, 2014.

45 The debate on the terminology is at once legal, moral, and ideological. A targeted killing is in principle only "extrajudicial" if domestic legislations rule against targeted killings. The US and Israel have adopted legal dispositions that allow targeted killings under given circumstances.

46 Michael Walzer, "Responsibility and Proportionality in State and Nonstate Wars," *Parameters* (The US Army War College Quarterly), Spring 2009: 40–52. The article is available here: https://ssi.armywarcollege.edu/pubs/parameters/articles/09spring/walzer.pdf.

47 Born in 1954, General Stanley A. McChrystal has been commander of the Joint Special Operations Command in Iraq and Afghanistan from 2003 to 2008, and commander of the ISAF (International Security Assistance Force) in Afghanistan from 2009 to 2010.

48 There has been a controversial exchange of arguments about the Lebanon and the Gaza War, which Michael Walzer supported. See "War Fair. The Ethics of Battle," *New Republic*, July 31, 2006; and an interview on the Americans for Peace Now (APN) website http://archive.peacenow.org/entries/archive2851. See the response by Jerome Slater "On Michael Walzer, Gaza, and the Lebanon War," *Dissent*, Winter 2007.

49 Michael Walzer, "Regime Change and Just War," *Dissent*, Summer, 2006: "So Iraq was not similar to the German or Japanese or the (hypothetical) Rwandan case: the war was not a response to aggression or a humanitarian intervention. Its cause was not (as in 1991) an actual Iraqi attack on a neighboring state or even an imminent threat of attack; nor was it an actual, ongoing massacre. The cause was regime change, directly – which means that the US government was arguing for a significant expansion of the doctrine of *jus ad bellum*. The existence of an aggressive and murderous regime, it claimed, was a legitimate occasion for war, even if the regime was not actually engaged in aggression or mass murder. In more familiar terms, this was an argument for preventive war, but the reason for the preventive attack wasn't the standard perception of a dangerous shift in the balance of power that would soon leave 'us' helpless against 'them.' It was a radically new perception of an evil regime."

50 "The French, said John Weston, had invaded first" [. . .] "Hence it has never been necessary to correct the argument of John Weston or of the members of the German Social Democratic Worker's Party who declared in July 1870 that it was Napoleon who had 'frivolously' destroyed the peace of Europe: 'The German nation . . . is the victim of aggression. Therefore . . . with great regret, [we] must accept the defensive war as a necessary evil.'" Michael Walzer, *Just and Unjust Wars*, p. 65.

51 Michael Walzer, "Just and Unjust Occupations," *Dissent*, Winter, 2004, offers an analysis of the post-war situation in Iraq ("having fought the war, we are now responsible for the well-being of the Iraqi people; we have to provide the resources – soldiers and dollars – necessary to guarantee their security and begin the political and economic reconstruction of their country."). The article ends on a somber note: "It sometimes turns out that occupying is harder than fighting."

52 Kanan Makiya, *The Republic of Fear. The Politics of Modern Iraq*, Stanford, University of California Press, 1989, 2nd edn., 1998. Kanan Makiya (born in 1949), is an Iraqi intellectual, Professor of Islamic and Middle Eastern studies at Brandeis. He was a proponent of the 2003 war and has been heavily criticized for his idealized prediction of a short and "victorious" war. He also published *Cruelty and Silence: War, Tyranny, Uprising, and the Arab World*, New York, W. W. Norton and Co., 1994.

53 This is how the *New York Times Magazine* (George Packer) recounts the discussion at NYU: "Then the last panelist spoke. He was an Iraqi dissident named Kanan Makiya, and he said, 'I'm afraid I'm going to strike a discordant note.' He pointed out that Iraqis, who will pay the highest price in the event of an invasion, 'overwhelmingly want this war.' He outlined a vision of post-war Iraq as a secular democracy with equal rights for all of its citizens. This vision would be new to the Arab world. 'It can be encouraged, or it can be crushed just like that. But think about what you're doing if you crush it.' Makiya's voice rose as he came to an end. 'I rest my moral case on the following: if there's a sliver of a chance of it happening, a 5 to 10 percent chance, you have a moral obligation, I say, to do it.'" George Packer, "The Liberal Quandary over Iraq," *New York Times Magazine*, December 8, 2002.

54 "Democratic political theory, which plays a relatively small part in our arguments about *jus ad bellum* and *in bello*, provides the central principles of this account. They include self-determination, popular legitimacy, civil rights, and the idea of a common good. We want wars to end with governments in power in the defeated states that are chosen by the people they rule – or, at least, recognized by them as legitimate– – and that are visibly committed to the welfare of those same people (all of them). We want minorities protected against persecution, neighboring states protected against aggression, the poorest of the people protected against destitution and starvation. In Iraq, we have (officially) set our sights even higher than this, on a fully democratic and federalist regime, but post-war justice is probably best understood in a minimalist way. It is not as if victors in war have been all that successful at achieving the minimum," Michael Walzer, "Just and Unjust Occupations."

55 "Intervening forces have a mandate for political, but not for cultural transformation," Michael Walzer, "Regime Change and Just War," *Dissent*, Summer 2006.

56 "Regime change, by itself, is not a just cause of war," Michael Walzer, "Regime Change and Just War."

57 "Despite all that I have said so far, I don't mean to abandon the principle of nonintervention – only to honor its exception. Yes, the norm is not to intervene in other people's countries; the norm is self-determination. But not for these people, the victims of tyranny, ideological zeal, ethnic hatred, who are not determining anything for themselves, who urgently need help from outside. And it isn't enough to wait until the tyrants, the zealots, and the bigots have done their filthy work and then rush food and medicine to the ragged survivors. Whenever the filthy work can be stopped, it should be stopped," Michael Walzer, "The Politics of Rescue," p. 41.

58 "We aim at containment but hope for regime change," Michael Walzer, "Regime Change and Just War."

59 See "World Government and the Politics of Pretending" (ch. 6), Michael Walzer, A Foreign Policy for the Left, 2018.

60 "Kurdish autonomy was not a regime imposed from the outside; though the containment system made autonomy possible, the new regime was first demanded, and then created and sustained, by the Kurds themselves. It may happen that containment anticipates rather than responds to local demands for self-determination. But this isn't an unjust anticipation, since the states organizing the containment don't themselves overthrow the old regime, and they don't establish the new one, if there is a new one. They are operating at the edge of the non-intervention principle, but not in violation of it. If preventing aggression and mass murder is justified, then so is this indirect version of regime change," Michael Walzer, "Regime Change and Just War."

5 Cooperation and Multilaterialism: Nations, States, Sovereignty

1 For example in Michael Walzer, "The Moral Standing of States: A Response to Four Critics," Philosophy and Public Affairs, 9 (3), Spring, 1980: 209–229; "The Politics of Difference: Statehood and Toleration in a Multicultural World," Ratio Juris, 10 (2) June 2, 1997: 165–176.

2 Michael Walzer, "The Politics of Difference," p. 175.

3 Michael Walzer, Arguing about War, New Haven, Yale University Press, p. 187.

4 "Begin by providing all the world's people with a decent and competent state. I know that isn't an easy thing to do, but it is possible, incrementally, here and here. What is most important is that the value of statehood be recognized. There is too much loose talk about transcending the state system, when full participation in that system is the greatest need of the poorest and most oppressed people in the world today," Michael Walzer, "World Government and the Politics of Pretending" (Conclusion).

5 Michael Walzer, "The State of Righteousness: Liberal Zionists Speak Out," Huffpost Blog, April 24, 2012, https://www.huffingtonpost.com/michael-walzer/liberal-zionists-speak-out-state-of-righteousness_b_1447261.html?guccounter=2.

6 "Palestinian leaders would be happy to accept an Israeli withdrawal from the West Bank, but they are in no way ready to end the conflict; no Palestinian leader has even hinted at a willingness to give up the right of return. None of

them are strong enough to do that, but I suspect that none of them want to do that. Their strategic goal is what I am afraid it has always been: the creation of a Palestinian state alongside a Jewish state that they don't recognize and with which they are not reconciled. But tactically they are newly inventive. They worked backward: their first resort was violence and terror; their last resort is peaceful protest. Had they reversed the order, they would have a state by now. There have been small nonviolent protests in the past, and these protests continue today in villages along the Wall, but they have been and still are marginal to the Palestinian struggle, never endorsed by Fatah or the PLO, and certainly not by Hamas. Now Israel faces the prospect of something radically new. How can it resist masses of men and women, children too, just walking across the ceasefire lines?," Michael Walzer, "What Does Netanyahu Think He Is Doing?," *Dissent*, May 26, 2011.

7 Charles Beitz, "Cosmopolitan Ideals and National Sentiment," *Journal of Philosophy*, 80 (10), 1983: 591–600; "International Liberalism and Distributive Justice," *World Politics*, 51 (2), 1999: 269–296.

8 "Beitz seems to believe that this pluralist world order has already been transcended and that communal integrity is a thing of the past. In a world of increasing interdependence, he argues, it is an 'evident falsity' to claim 'that states are relatively self-enclosed arenas of political development.'" Michael Walzer, "The Moral Standing of States," p. 227.

9 "My own argument is perhaps best understood as a defense of politics, while that of my critics reiterates what I take to be the traditional philosophical dislike for politics," Michael Walzer, "The Moral Standing of States," p. 228.

10 "The prevailing view of nationalism abroad, however, seems to be driven by and largely restricted to a kind of ideological fury at the state of Israel – followed by the demand that Israel be replaced by a post-national 'state of all its citizens', identified with none of them – and, according to recent opinion polls, desired by very few of them." Michael Walzer, "World Government and the Politics of Pretending."

11 "It [Anti-Americanism] takes the form of apology and excuse or of a simple refusal to oppose America's opponents, however awful their politics is. And in the case of America's ally, Israel, it goes much further. English leftists marching in London in 2006 with banners saying, 'We are all Hezbollah,' probably thought that they were practising a left internationalist politics. That Hezbollah is in no sense a leftist movement made no difference to them so long as it was hostile to Israel and America." Michael Walzer, *Introduction to the Democratiya Project*.

12 Michael Walzer, "A Foreign Policy for the Left," *Dissent*, Spring, 2014. See also the "The Default Position," Introduction to *A Foreign Policy for the Left*, pp. 1–10.

13 Jeremiah 7: 3–7; Isaiah 42.

14 *Democratiya*, a quarterly review of books and series of interviews, was founded by Alan Johnson in 2005. *Democratiya* and *Dissent* merged in 2009 (the Archives are available on the *Dissent* website: https://www.dissentmagazine.org/democratiya-issue). The aim, according to Michael Walzer was to "defend and promote a left politics that is liberal, democratic, egalitarian, and internationalist."

15 "Internationalism is not in fact the automatic support of any group of mili-

tants who claim to speak for the world's workers or the oppressed peoples of the old empires or the victims of American imperialism. It requires a political and moral choice; it requires what the Italian writer Ignazio Silone called 'the choice of comrades.' [. . .] The militants who act in the name of the oppressed are sometimes the agents of a new oppression – ideological or religious zealots with totalizing programs, who have a deep contempt for liberal values. And then they should be met with hostility by leftists the world over: because they don't serve the interests of the people they claim to represent and because they don't advance the cause of democracy or equality. The comrades we choose, by contrast, are the men and women who resist oppression in the name of leftist values. Left internationalism is a solidarity of leftists." Michael Walzer, Preface to *Global Politics After 9/11: The Democratiya Interviews*, The Foreign Policy Centre, 2008.

16 Michael Kazin argues along similar lines: "Let's Not Change the World After All. On the broad American left, internationalism used to be as common – and as essential – as breathing. What happened?," Michael Kazin, *Dissent*, Spring 2016.

17 Michael Walzer, *A Foreign Policy for the Left*, ch. 7, pp. 136–156.

18 Kamel Daoud is quoted on p. 142; see Michael Walzer, "The Left and Religion" in *A Foreign Policy for the Left*.

19 "Cologne, Lieu de Fantasmes," *Le Monde*, January 31, 2016, "La Misère Sexuelle d'Allah," *New York Times*, February 12, 2016; "Nuit de Cologne: Kamel Daoud recycle les clichés orientalistes les plus éculés," *Le Monde*, February 11, 2016.

20 See Michael Walzer, "The Politics of Rescue," *Dissent*, Winter 1995: "But no one really wants the United States to become the world's policeman, even of-last-resort, as we would quickly see were we to undertake the role. Morally and politically, a division of labor is better, and the best use of American power will often be to press other countries to do their share of the work [. . .]. Sometimes, the United States should take the initiative; sometimes we should help pay for and even add soldiers to an intervention initiated by somebody else. In many cases, nothing at all will be done unless we are prepared to play one or the other of these parts – either the political lead or a combination of financial backer and supporting player. Old and well-earned suspicions of American power must give way now to a wary recognition of its necessity. (A friend comments: you would stress the wariness more if there were a Republican president. Probably so.)"

21 Michael Walzer, "The Politics of Rescue," *Dissent*, Winter 1995.

22 Michael Walzer, "World Government and the Politics of Pretending," p. 130.

23 "Two forms of long-lasting intervention, both associated in the past with imperial politics, now warrant reconsideration [. . .]. Rwanda might have been a candidate for trusteeship; Bosnia for a protectorate," Michael Walzer, "The Politics of Rescue," *Dissent*, Winter 1995: 39

24 "I have a utopian solution, which is also politically incorrect. There are countries in the world today that ought to be, for a time, not-independent and not-sovereign. What the world needs, and what the UN might provide if it were the organization it was meant to be: a new trusteeship system for countries that are temporarily unable to govern themselves. The old mandate system of the League of Nations was not a great success, but it did not produce, and perhaps it prevented, disasters like the ones we are

helplessly watching today. For the last decade and a half, Kosovo has been a kind of NATO trust – again, not a glorious example, for refugees are still fleeing, but at least the killing has stopped. So perhaps it isn't crazy to suggest that Libya and Syria ought to be UN trusteeships, with some coalition of countries, different in each case, taking responsibility for maintaining law and order and providing basic services to the population – under strict UN supervision. I hesitate to suggest the countries that might serve as trustees, since I wouldn't want to vouch for any country's trustworthiness. But great virtue isn't necessary, only a readiness to stop the killing, get rid of the killers, and provide enough stability for the citizens of the war-ravaged countries to begin rebuilding. That has to be their work," Michael Walzer, "The European Crisis," *Dissent*, September 2015.

25 "Everyone knows this: the Security Council cannot prevent wars, or fight them, or end them. The usual left demand to take this or that issue (the 9/11 attack is my standard example) to the Council is really an unacknowledged demand that nothing be done. This is what I call the politics of pretending," Michael Walzer, "World Government and the Politics of Pretending."

26 Michael Walzer has written many times about 9/11 – and has argued with many people, not only about the adequate response to the 9/11 attacks, but also because he relentlessly criticized what he calls a "culture of excuse and apology" for terrorism. Walzer argues that "war" is not the right qualification to respond to the 9/11 attacks, the term is at best a metaphor: "[. . .] Instead, in this 'war' on terrorism three other things take precedence: intensive police work across national borders, an ideological campaign to engage all the arguments and excuses for terrorism and reject them, and a serious and sustained diplomatic effort. [. . .] But military action is what everybody wants to talk about – not the metaphor of war, but the real thing. So what can we do? There are two conditions that must be met before we can fight justly. We have to find legitimate targets – people actually engaged in organizing, supporting or carrying out terrorist activities. And we must be able to hit those targets without killing large numbers of innocent people. Despite the criticism of Israeli 'assassinations' by United States officials, I don't believe that it matters, from a moral point of view, if the targets are groups of people or single individuals, so long as these two criteria are met. If we fail to meet them, we will be defending our civilization by imitating the terrorists who are attacking it. It follows from these criteria that commando raids are likely to be better than attacks with missiles and bombs. [. . .] We should pursue the metaphorical war; hold back on the real thing," Michael Walzer, "First Define the Battlefield," *New York Times*, September 21, 2001. An interesting exchange with George Scialabba, can be read here: http://georgescialabba.net/mtgs/2001/09/911-an-exchange-with-michael-w.html.

Another exchange on Terrorisme.net where the interviewer (Jean-Marc Flükiger) asks whether terrorism can be explained (and legitimized) by "supreme emergency": https://www.terrorisme.net/pdf/2006_Walzer.pdf. See also: "I never felt much sympathy for the people who argued that 9/11 was a criminal incident, not an act of war, and that we should have dealt with it by going to the UN and the ICC. In a differently organized international society, it might have made sense to respond to 9/11 by dialing 911. But in 2001, nobody was there to answer the phone – and that is still true today," Michael Walzer, "Was Obama's War in Afghanistan Just?," *Dissent*,

November 2009; and Michael Walzer, "Five Questions about Terrorism," *Dissent*, Winter 2002; Michael Walzer, Alan Johnson (eds.), *Global Politics After 9/11: The Democratiya Interviews*, London, Foreign Policy Centre, 2007.

6 Israel–Palestine

1 See Michael Walzer "A Journey to Israel," *Dissent*, September–November 1970: 497–503.

2 The 1973 war, also known as the "Yom Kippur War" (October 6 to October 25, 1973), was led by a coalition of Arab states against Israel to regain the territories occupied by Israel since the 1967 Six Day War (the Sinai, the Golan Heights, and the West Bank).

3 Marty Peretz and Michael Walzer have published "Israel is not Vietnam" together in *Ramparts*, July 1967: 11–14. Marty Peretz (born 1938) was the editor of the *New Republic* for more than thirty years.

4 "In Support of Israel's Right to Security and Peace," *New York Times*, October 25, 1973.

5 Yigal Allon (1918–1980) was a commander of the Palmach (the elite force of the Haganah) and a member of the Israeli Labor Party (he co-founded the Mapam but joined Ahdut haAvoda after the split). He briefly served as interim Prime Minister after the death of Levi Eshkol in 1969. He was minister of Labor, of Education and Culture, and of Foreign Affairs. He was a Knesset member from 1955 to 1980.

6 An ulpan is a state-sponsored language training center for new immigrants.

7 Ben Gurion's *Epilogue: The Lost Interview* (Yariv Mozer, 2016). Ben Gurion is 82 years old in 1968, lives in Sde Boker (the small town in the desert he retired to) and is interviewed by Clinton Bailey. See https://www.nytimes.com/2016/08/13/world/middleeast/israel-ben-gurion-interview.html.

8 The Marches mark the Nakhba, the Palestinian "catastrophe" (the expulsion in 1948). In 2018, the Marches lasted for many weeks in a climate of unprecedented violence: more than a hundred victims and several thousand injured on the Palestinian side.

9 See Peter Berkowitz's well informed paper here: https://www.realclearpolitics.com/articles/2018/06/08/israel_can_ease_gaza_tensions_but_so_must_the_un_137221.html.

10 The evolution of the respective positions can be read in the following articles: https://www.haaretz.com/israel-news/.premium-after-three-hour-meeting-cabinet-makes-no-decisions-on-gaza-economy-1.6163334.
https://www.haaretz.com/middle-east-news/palestinians/eu-raises-half-billion-dollars-to-improve-gaza-s-drinking-water-1.5931630.
https://www.haaretz.com/israel-news/.premium-israel-will-present-plan-to-rebuild-gaza-to-be-funded-by-int-l-donors-1.5782230.

11 Michael Walzer, "What Does Netanyahu Think He Is Doing?," *Dissent*, May 26, 2011; "The Paradox and Tragedy of Israeli-Palestinian Politics," *Dissent*, November 23, 2012; and "Israel Must Defeat Hamas, But Also Must Do More to Limit Civilian Deaths," *New Republic*, July 30, 2014: "We should choose Israel – because Israel is a democracy where it is possible to imagine the political defeat of the right-wing nationalists who are now

in charge; it is possible to imagine a government that would work toward Palestinian statehood – Israel has had governments of that sort in the past, under the leadership of Yitzhak Rabin and Ehud Olmert."

12 "It is our hope that targeted boycotts and changes in American policy, limited to the Israeli settlements in the Occupied Territories, will encourage all parties to negotiate a two-state solution to this long-standing conflict." "For an Economic Boycott and Political Nonrecognition of the Israeli Settlements in the Occupied Territories," *New York Review of Books*, October 13, 2016.

13 Michael Walzer, "Five Questions About Terrorism," *Dissent*, Winter 2002.

14 The Haredi movement, often referred to as "ultra-orthodox" is a particularly observant branch of Judaism. The Haredim literally "fear God," "tremble at the word of God" (Isaiah 66: 2–5). See David Landau, *Piety and Power: The World of Jewish Fundamentalism*, New York, Hill, and Wang, 1993.

15 Adopted by a narrow majority of the Knesset on July 19, 2018 in the context of tensions within the right, the nation-state law is one of the fundamental laws of the state of Israel. Recalling elements of the Declaration of Independence (1948), the law declares Hebrew the sole official language and Jerusalem the capital of the state.

16 Vladimir Jabotinsky (Odessa 1880–New York 1940), was a novelist, a poet, a journalist, and one of the leaders of the right-wing Zionist movement. He was a "revisionist Zionist" as he pleaded for the inclusion of Jordan in the Zionist project. He left the World Zionist Movement in 1923 after a series of political quarrels, but has inspired the formation of the Irgun, the Zionist clandestine paramilitary organization that operated in Mandatory Palestine. See Yaakov Shavit, *Jabotinsky and the Revisionist Movement 1925–1948*, London, Routledge, 1988.

17 Yael Tamir, *Liberal Nationalism*, New Haven, Princeton University Press, 1993.

18 See Michael Walzer, "Antisionisme et antisémitisme," art. cit.

19 https://www.ynet.co.il/articles/0,7340,L-4089488,00.html.

20 See Yossi Shain, Ha Mea HaIsraelit (in Hebrew), Yedihot Sfarim, Tel Aviv, 2019.

21 Michael Walzer is board member of APN, Americans for Peace Now.

22 http://archive.peacenow.org/entries/archive295.

23 http://jeffweintraub.blogspot.com/2006/04/michael-walzer-rich-settlers-po or.html.

24 Michael Walzer, "The real challenge for Israel, which only the left can meet, is to defend the physical safety of Israel's citizens forcefully," http://archive.peacenow.org/entries/archive4889.

25 "For an Economic Boycott and Political Non-Recognition of the Israeli Settlements in the Occupied Territories," *New York Review of Books*, October 13, 2016.

26 The various BDS websites have templates of letters on how to respond negatively to invitations to go to Israel (teaching, conferences). The maxim is that academia should be at the heart of the boycott.

27 "I can assure you that it will greatly help the BDS movement, people who are critical of the government and also critical of BDS may think that the government is scared, that BDS is working. There will be people moving toward BDS, and I have already received emails from people who have been critical of the Israeli government but also of BDS, writing that at this point,

we might as well join BDS," Michael Walzer to *Haaretz* reporter Talia Krupkin: https://www.haaretz.com/us-news/.premium-100-jewish-studies-scholars-threaten-to-not-visit-israel-over-travel-ban-1.5447119.

7 Political Theory

1 Michael Walzer, *A Foreign Policy for the Left*, New Haven, Yale University Press, 2018.
2 Michael Walzer, *The Paradox of Liberation: Secular Revolutions and Religious Counterrevolutions*, New Haven, Yale University Press, 2015.
3 See below.
4 *ISC*, pp. 13–15: "But why should we bow to universal correction? What exactly is the critical force of the philosopher's invention – assuming, still, that it is the only possible invention? I will try to answer these questions by telling a story of my own, a story meant to parallel and heighten certain features of the Rawlsian account of what happens in the original position: a caricature, I'm afraid, for which I apologize in advance; but caricature has its uses.

Imagine, then, that a group of travelers from different countries and different moral cultures, speaking different languages, meet in some neutral place (like outer space). They have to cooperate, at least temporarily, and, if they are to cooperate, each of them must refrain from insisting upon his own values and practices. Hence we deny them knowledge of their own values and practices; and since that knowledge isn't only personal but also social knowledge, embodied in language itself, we obliterate their linguistic memories and require them to think and talk (temporarily) in some pidgin-language that is equally parasitic on all their natural languages – a more perfect Esperanto. Now, what principles of cooperation would they adopt? I shall assume that there is a single answer to this question and that the principles given in that answer properly govern their life together in the space they now occupy. That seems plausible enough; the design procedure is genuinely useful for the purposes at hand. What is less plausible is that the travelers should be required to carry those same principles with them when they go home. Why should newly invented principles govern the lives of people who already share a moral culture and speak a natural language?

Men and women standing behind the veil of ignorance, deprived of all knowledge of their own way of life, forced to live with other men and women similarly deprived, will perhaps, with whatever difficulties, find a *modus vivendi* – not a way of life but a way of living. But even if this is the only possible *modus vivendi* for these people in these conditions, it doesn't follow that it is a universally valuable arrangement. (It might, of course, have a kind of heuristic value – many things have heuristic value – but I won't pursue that possibility now.) There seems to be a confusion here: it is as if we were to take a hotel room or an accommodation apartment or a safe house as the ideal model of a human home. Away from home, one is grateful for the shelter and convenience of a hotel room. Deprived of all knowledge of what my own home was like, talking with people similarly deprived, required to design rooms that any one of us might live in, we would probably come up with something like (but not quite so culturally specific as) the Hilton Hotel.

With this difference: we would not allow luxury suites; all the rooms would be exactly the same; or, if there were luxury suites, their only purpose would be to bring more business to the hotel and enable us to improve all the other rooms, starting with those most in need of improvement. But even if the improvements went pretty far, we might still long for the homes we knew we once had but could no longer remember. We would not be morally bound to live in the hotel we had designed."

5 "We need strong moral commitments and small theories of how things work – with these two we are OK."

6 "The piecemeal engineer will, accordingly, adopt the method of searching for, and fighting against, the greatest and most urgent evils of society, rather than searching for, and fighting for, its greatest ultimate good," Karl Popper, *The Open Society and its Enemies*, vol. 1, Princeton University Press, 1971, p. 158.

"[. . .] We make progress if, and only if, we are prepared to learn from our mistakes: to recognize our errors and to utilize them critically instead of persevering in them dogmatically," Karl Popper, *The Poverty of Historicism (1957)*, London, Routledge, 1997, p. 87.

7 Michael Walzer, "World Government and the Politics of Pretending," in *A Foreign Policy for the Left*, 2018.

8 "There are some useful, and to my mind justified, contemporary examples: India in East Pakistan, Tanzania in Uganda, Vietnam in Cambodia. Interventions of this sort are probably best carried out by neighbors, as in these three cases, since neighbors will have some understanding of the local culture," Michael Walzer, "Politics of Rescue," *Dissent*, Winter 1995.

See also Michael Walzer, "Responsibility and Proportionality in State and Nonstate Wars," *Parameters*, Spring 2009.

9 Robert Nozick (1938–2002), was an American libertarian philosopher, Professor of Philosophy at Harvard (1969–2002), best known for his *Anarchy, State and Utopia*, London and New York, Blackwell, 1974, a response to John Rawls' *Theory of Justice*. "It is no exaggeration to say that Nozick, more than anyone else, embodied the new libertarian zeitgeist, which, after generations of statist welfarism from Roosevelt's *New Deal to Kennedy, Johnson and Carter*, ushered in the era of Reagan and Bush, père et fils" (*The Telegraph*, January 28, 2002). His later books were quite different from *Anarchy* (*Philosophical Explanations*, Cambridge MA, Harvard University Press 1981; *The Examined Life: Philosophical Meditations*, New York, Simon & Schuster, 1989; *Invariances: The Structure of the Objective World*, Cambridge MA, Harvard University Press, 2001), as he didn't want to "spend [his] life writing 'The Son of Anarchy, State and Utopia'" (*The Harvard Gazette*, January 24, 2002).

He was a great teacher according to Michael Walzer, his colleagues and his students: "Nozick's teaching followed the same lively, unorthodox, heterogeneous pattern as his writing. With one exception, he never taught the same course twice. The exception was 'The Best Things in Life', which he presented in 1982 and 1983, attempting to derive from the class discussion a general theory of values. The course description called it an exploration of 'the nature and value of those things deemed best, such as friendship, love, intellectual understanding, sexual pleasure, achievement, adventure, play, luxury, fame, power, enlightenment, and ice cream'. Speaking without notes,

Nozick would pace restlessly back and forth, an ever-present can of Tab in his hand, drawing his students into a free-ranging discussion of the topic at hand. He once defended his 'thinking out loud' approach by comparing it with the more traditional method of giving students finished views of the great philosophical ideas. 'Presenting a completely polished and worked-out view doesn't give students a feel for what it's like to do original work in philosophy and to see it happen, to catch on to doing it',," *The Harvard Gazette*, January 24, 2002. See David Schmidtz's biography: *Robert Nozick*, Cambridge, UK, Cambridge University Press, 2002.

10 Thomas Nagel (born 1937 in Belgrade to German Jewish refugees), is an American Professor of Law and Philosophy. He taught at New York University from 1980 to 2016. A Kantian rationalist, he studied with John Rawls and specialized in ethics and moral philosophy. His book *Equality and Partiality* (New York, Oxford University Press, 1991) is a close reading and a critique of Rawls in which Nagel argues that Rawls' difference principle is not demanding enough. His books include *The Possibility of Altruism*, Princeton NJ; Oxford University Press, 1970; *The View from Nowhere*, New York, Oxford University Press, 1989; *Secular Philosophy and the Religious Temperament: Essays 2002–2008*, New York, Oxford University Press, 2010, and many essays.

11 Stuart Hampshire (1914–2004), whom Michael Walzer often quotes in his work, was a Professor of Philosophy at UCL, Oxford, Princeton, and Stanford. Expert on Spinoza (*Spinoza and the Idea of Freedom*, London, Oxford University Press, 1960), influenced by Merleau Ponty, his major books include *Thought and Action*, London, Chatto and Windus, 1959; *Freedom of Mind, and other Essays*, Oxford, Clarendon Press, 1972; *Morality and Conflict*, Cambridge, MA, Harvard University Press, 1983; *Justice is Conflict*, Princeton NJ, Princeton University Press, 2000. See his Obituary in the *Guardian* on his wartime activities and how they influenced his thinking: https://www.theguardian.com/news/2004/jun/16/guardianobit uaries.obituaries.

12 Michael Walzer, *Obligations. Essays on Disobedience, War and Citizenship*, Cambridge University Press, 1970.

13 John Rawls, A *Theory of Justice*, Cambridge MA, Harvard University Press, 1971.

14 Michael Walzer wrote "WW II. Why Was This War Different?" for the first issue (Autumn 1972, pp. 3–21), which has become a classic. In the same issue, Judith Jarvis Thomson published her famous piece on abortion, "In Defense of Abortion," pp. 47–66, and Shlomo Avineri contributed with "Labor, Alienation, and Social Classes in Hegel's Realphilosophie," pp. 96–119. The second issue (Winter 1973) has papers by Tom Nagel on "War and Massacre," Scanlon's piece on "Freedom of Expression," and G. A. Cohen's article on "Marx and the Withering Away of Social Science."

15 See my Introduction.

16 Robert Nozick, *Anarchy, State and Utopia*, London and New York, Blackwell, 1974. See above.

17 Sydney Morgenbesser (1921–2004), became Professor of Philosophy at Columbia after he was ordained as a rabbi. Known for his witty quotes ("He was the quintessential New York Jewish intellectual: Isaiah Berlin, Woody Allen, and Isaac Bashevis Singer rolled into one," *The Independent*, August

6, 2004; he "prompted comparisons to Socrates – minus the Yiddish accent," *New York Times*, August 4, 2004). A site is dedicated to his quotes: https://en.wikiquote.org/wiki/Sidney_Morgenbesser. He co-edited *Philosophy of Science Today*, New York, Basic Books, 1967.

18 Bob Nozick is supposed to have said "I graduated in Morgenbesser." He indeed wrote his BA senior thesis with Morgenbesser at Columbia in 1959.

19 The Shalom Harman Institute conference cycle takes place in Jerusalem every year. Invited philosophers from Europe, the US, and Israel debate during an intensive one-week program. https://hartman.org.il/. See ch. 9.

20 Morgenbesser was an anti-war activist during the Vietnam period.

21 Here is the story Sartre tells about his attempt to reconcile Camus and Merleau Ponty: "One night, at Boris Vian's house, Camus challenged Merleau and blamed him for justifying the trial. It was terrible: I can still picture them, Camus appalled, Merleau-Ponty polite and firm, slightly pale, the former indulging in, the latter refraining from violence. All of a sudden, Camus turns around and walks away. I ran after him [. . .] in the empty road; I tried my best to explain Merleau's thinking, Merleau himself hadn't done that much. With the sole result that we left each other on bad terms; it took six months and a chance encounter to make up. This is not a fond memory: what a silly idea to offer my help. It is true that I was on the right of Merleau, on the left of Camus; what kind of Black humor to try to play mediators between my two friends who resented me later for my friendship with the Communists and who are both dead irreconciled?," J. P. Sartre, "Merleau-Ponty Vivant," *Les Temps Modernes*, 1961 (nos. 184 and 185), p. 61.

22 Michael Walzer and Michael Rustin, "Les Travaillistes au pouvoir" (trans. Paul Thibaud), *Esprit*, Janvier 1965. From 1991 to 2010, Michael Walzer has published 13 articles in *Esprit*, most of which have appeared in *Dissent*. The last one (2010) is co-authored with Avishai Margalit ("Israel et le statut des civils dans la guerre antiterroriste"), a translation of "Israel. Civilians and Combatants," *New York Review of Books*, May 14, 2009.

23 Michael Walzer, "The Lonely Politics of Michel Foucault," in CC, p. 192.

24 Leo Strauss (1899–1973) was an influential German-born American philosopher, who taught classical philosophy and Jewish thought at the University of Chicago. He inspired (and still does) generations of (conservative) philosophers – the Straussians – and political thinkers – the neoconservatives. He famously wrote on Machiavelli (*Thoughts on Machiavelli (1958)*, Chicago, University of Chicago Press, 1995); Spinoza (*Spinoza's Critique of Religion (1930)*, University of Chicago Press, 1997); Maimonides (*Philosophy and Law: Contributions to the Understanding of Maimonides and His Predecessors (1935)*, Suny Series); *Jewish Writings of Strauss*, New York State University Press, 1995; *Leo Strauss on Maimonides: The Complete Writings*, Kenneth Hart Green (ed.), Chicago, University of Chicago Press, 2013); Mendelssohn: On Natural Right and History (*The City and Man*, Chicago, R & McNally, 1964; *Natural Right and History (1949)*, Chicago, University of Chicago Press, 1953); the art of writing, tyranny, historicism (against Max Weber), nihilism, relativism, Athens and Jerusalem (*Liberalism Ancient and Modern*. New York, Basic Books, 1968). For a comprehensive account of his philosophy and politics see Robert Howse, *Leo Strauss, Man of Peace*, Cambridge University Press, 2014.

25 Harvey C. Mansfield (born 1932) is Professor of Political Theory at Harvard.

Known as a conservative, Straussian scholar, close to Allan Bloom and Irving Kristol, he wrote on Machiavelli, Tocqueville (whom he translated), and Burke. His books include *The Spirit of Liberalism*, Cambridge MA, Harvard University Press, 1979; *Taming the Prince*, New York, Free Press, 1989; *Manliness*, New Haven, Yale University Press, 2007.

26 Clifford Orwin (born 1947) is a Canadian Professor of Ancient Greek and Jewish thought. Identified as a Straussian, but resisting Strauss' identification with neoconservatism (a harsh review to that effect is available here: https:// web.archive.org/web/20070610012332/http://www.claremont.org/publications/crb/id.982/ article_detail.asp). He published several books and translations: *The Humanity of Thucydides*, New Haven, Princeton University Press, 1994; and, with Nathan Tarcov, *The Legacy of Rousseau*, University of Chicago Press, 1997.

27 Stephen B. Smith (born 1951) is Professor of Political Science at Yale. Expert on modern philosophy (Spinoza) and Strauss, he has published several books: *Spinoza, Liberalism and the Question of Jewish Identity*, New Haven, Yale University Press, 1998; *Spinoza's Book of Life: Freedom and Redemption in the Ethics*, New Haven, Yale University Press, 2003; *Reading Leo Strauss. Politics, Philosophy, Judaism*, University of Chicago Press, 2007; *Modernity and Its Discontents. Making and Unmaking the Bourgeois from Machiavelli to Bellow*, New Haven, Yale University Press, 2016.

28 Joseph Cropsey (1919–2012) was Professor of Philosophy at the University of Chicago where he was a student of Leo Strauss, with whom he published *History of Political Philosophy* (1963), Chicago and London, University of Chicago Press, 1987. He published essays in honor of Strauss one year later: *Ancients and Moderns: Essays on the Tradition of Political Philosophy in Honor of Leo Strauss*, New York, Basic Books, 1964. He is known for his work on Plato: *Plato's World: Man's Place in the Cosmos*, Chicago and London, University of Chicago Press, 1997.

29 "Michael Harrington's 1973 article, 'The Welfare State and its Neoconservative Critics', represented a spirited defense of the increasingly beleaguered War on Poverty." (The question of whether or not Harrington actually coined the phrase "neoconservative" in the pages of *Dissent* is a vexed one, but it is certainly the case that he popularized its usage.) M. Isserman, "Steady Work," art. cit.; See also M. Isserman, "Starting out in the 1950s," *Dissent*, Winter 2014.

30 Immanuel Kant, *Critique of Pure Reason (1781)*, G. W. F. Hegel, *The Phenomenology of Spirit (1807)*.

31 Habermas, J, 1989, *The Structural Transformation of the Public Sphere (1961)*, trans. from German by T. Burger and F. Lawrence, Cambridge, Polity Press, 1989.

32 Michael Walzer, "A Critique of Philosophical Conversations," *Philosophical Forum*, 21 (1–2), 1989: 182–196. The article is a critique of "ideal speech situations" in which the final agreement is built into the design of the situation itself (typical examples are J. Habermas, J. Rawls, and B. Ackerman). "Real talk," democratic real-life conversations on the other hand, are "indeterminate, unpredictable and inconclusive." "[. . .] Conversation is only one among many features of the complex social process that produces consensus and shared understandings. That process includes political struggle, negotiation and compromise, law making and law enforcement, socialization

in families and schools, economic transformations, cultural creativity of all sorts [. . .]. No conclusion is imaginable without authority, conflict and coercion (socialization, for example, is always coercive)."

33 Avishai Margalit (born in 1939), is an Israeli Professor of Philosophy, Emeritus at the Hebrew University in Jerusalem. Peace activist, member of B'Tselem, author of many books in the field of ethics, political philosophy, language, and logic. He co-authored "Israel. Citizens and Combatants," art. cit., with Michael Walzer and wrote a witty piece on Michael Walzer, "Liberal or Social Democrat" (*Dissent*, Spring, 2013): "Michael Walzer is a social democrat; it is an honorary badge. For a long time, he wore his badge while driving an antique Volvo – the second-hand car for mature social democrats." His books include *The Decent Society*, Cambridge MA, Harvard University Press, 1996; *Views in Review: Politics and Culture in the State of the Jews*, New York, Farrar Straus & Giroux, 1998; *On Compromise and Rotten Compromises*, New Haven, Princeton University Press, 2010; *On Betrayal*, Cambridge MA, Harvard University Press, 2017.

34 Jacques Derrida, *Monolingualism of the Other, or, the Prosthesis of Origin*, trans. Patrick Mensah, Stanford, Stanford University Press, 1998 (*Le Monolinguisme de l'autre*, Paris, Galilée, 1995).

35 David Rodin, *War and Self Defense*, Oxford, Oxford University Press, 2002. David Rodin is co-director of the Oxford Institute for *Ethics, Law, and Armed Conflict*. He is one of the founders of "revisionist" just-war theory and has widely published on ethics of warfare. His books include (with Henry Shue), *Preemption: Military Action and Moral Justification*, Oxford, Oxford University Press, 2007; *Just and Unjust Warriors: The Moral and Legal Status of Soldiers*, Oxford, Oxford University Press, 2010; *War, Torture and Terrorism*, London, Wiley Blackwell, 2008.

36 See for example Judith Shklar, "The Liberalism of Fear," in Nancy Rosenblum, *Liberalism and the Moral Life*, Harvard University Press, 1989.

37 CC, p. xvii.

38 "The trolley problem" is a well known and widely discussed thought experiment in moral philosophy with its dedicated websites. See https://en.wikipedia.org/wiki/Trolley_problem.

39 Judith J. Thomson, "A Defense of Abortion," *Philosophy and Public Affairs*, 1 (1), Fall 1971.

40 Kwame Anthony Appiah, *Experiments in Ethics*, Cambridge MA, Harvard University Press, 2009.

41 Jeremy Waldron, "Right and Wrong. Psychologists v. Philosophers," *New York Review of Books*, October 8, 2009.

42 Michael Kazin, "A Decent Leftist," *Dissent*, Spring, 2013.

43 Michael Walzer, "Can There Be a Decent Left?," *Dissent*, Spring, 2002.

8 *Spheres of Justice*

1 The different spheres are: Membership, Security and Welfare, Money and Commodities, Office, Hard Work, Free Time, Education, Kinship and Love, Divine Grace, Recognition, Political Power.

2 "That one is successful in the economic realm shouldn't allow them to be

successful in the political realm through their economic success. Inequality in one sphere shouldn't be able to dominate other spheres – dignity, family, life, health, education, etc." "No social good x should be distributed to men and women who possess some other good y merely because they possess y and without regard to the meaning of x," *SOJ*, p. 20.

3 "My purpose in this book is to describe a society where no social good serves or can serve as a means for domination," *SOJ*, p. xiv.

4 Charles Taylor, *Sources of the Self. The Making of the Modern Identity*, Cambridge, Cambridge University Press, 1989, p. 26.

5 Michael Walzer, *SOJ*, p. 35; "Liberalism and the Art of Separation," *Political Theory*, 12 (3), August 1984: 315–330.

6 Michael Walzer, *SOJ*, p. 312.

7 Ronald Dworkin, "To Each his Own" (Review of *Spheres of Justice*), *New York Review of Books*, April 14, 1983; "*Spheres of Justice*: An Exchange," Reply by Michael Walzer followed by an answer by R. Dworkin, *New York Review of Books* July 21, 1983.

8 Michael Sandel, *What Money Can't Buy. The Moral Limits of Markets*, New York, Farrar, Straus & Giroux, 2013; Joseph Carens, *The Ethics of Immigration*, USA, Oxford University Press, 2013; David Miller, "Justice in Immigration," *European Journal of Political Theory*, 14 (4), 2015.

9 David Miller, "Justice in Immigration": "If state officials are not willing to admit such a person to the territory, they must ensure that he is escorted to a place of physical safety: they cannot simply turn his boat around if it is likely to sink. The duties that apply at land borders and airports follow the same logic. They arise merely from the fact of physical proximity coupled with the capacity to assist, in the same way as does my duty to find help for someone who collapses on my doorstep; I need not take her into my house but I may have an obligation to take her to hospital or to a shelter. It goes without saying that state officials also have duties of civility toward the immigrant. In refusing entry they should explain why admission cannot be granted, they must not be abusive etc. These are general duties of respect for another human being that are triggered by the fact of physical presence."

10 Michael Walzer, *SOJ*, p.58.

11 Joseph Carens, "Aliens and Citizens: The Case for Open Borders," *Review of Politics*, 49 (2), 1987: 258; Charles Beitz, "Cosmopolitan Ideals and National Sentiment," *Journal of Philosophy*, 80 (10), 1983: 591–600.

12 David Miller, "Justice in Immigration," art. cit.

13 Michael Walzer and Nicolaus Mills, *Getting Out. Historical Perspectives on Leaving Iraq*, Philadelphia, PA, University of Pennsylvania Press, 2009.

14 The Reparations Agreement between Israel and West Germany, signed on September 10, 1952.

15 Ronald Dworkin, "To Each his Own," art. cit.; "Spheres of Justice: An Exchange," art. cit.

16 Michael Walzer, *Thick and Thin: Moral Argument at Home and Abroad*, Notre Dame Press, 1994.

17 Susan Moller Okin, *Justice, Gender and the Family*, New York, Basic Books, 1989.

18 Michael Walzer, "Feminism and Me," *Dissent*, Winter 2013. "Okin argued that a theory of this sort could not be helpful to women, because the social meanings of education, professional work, political office, and much else, in

our society and in every other, excluded women in radical ways or pushed them into marginal positions. [. . .]"

19 "The practical critique of gender inequality is only just begun. I would still try to make it a 'spherical' critique, worked through our understanding of the different social goods and bads, the different distributive criteria, and the different agents of distribution. But exactly how to realize complex equality in the family is less clear to me now than it was in 1980, and that is perhaps a small advance. The family has to be what Christopher Lasch called a 'haven in a heartless world.' But it can't continue to be a source of the inequalities that make the world heartless. The defense of intimacy and justice at the same time – that is the task of the next generation of political theorists," Michael Walzer, "Feminism and Me."

20 Michael Walzer, "Objectivity and Social Meaning," in A. Sen and M. Nussabum (eds.), *The Quality of Life*, Oxford, Clarendon Press, 1993, pp. 165–175.

21 See the introduction to ch. 12 "Political Power," *SOJ*, p. 281.

22 In *Liberalism and the Limits of Justice*, Michael Sandel discusses the Lincoln–Douglas debates in the 1850s and asks how liberalism can oppose slavery without endorsing a comprehensive moral doctrine, in this case the religious conviction that slavery is morally wrong. One should not put morality between brackets for the sake of political agreement: comprehensive (religious) doctrines are not only morally necessary in the political debate, but also impossible to eschew in such important matters. See *Liberalism and the Limits of Justice*, Cambridge University Press, 2nd edn., 1998, p. 198f.

23 Michael Walzer, *What it Means to be an American. Essays on the American Experience*, New York, Marsilio Publishers, 1996. "What it means . . ." is also the title of an article published in *Social Research*, 71 (3), Fall 2004: 633–654.

24 The Passover Haggadah telling the Exodus story is recited during the Seder and commemorates the liberation of the Israelites from slavery in Egypt.

25 Pascal and Marx are present in the "draft version" of *SOJ* already ("In Defense of Equality," *Dissent*, Fall 1973: 402).

26 See *SOJ*, p. 18: "The nature of tyranny is to desire power over the whole world and outside its own sphere. There are different companies – the strong, the handsome, the intelligent, the devout – and each man reigns in his own, not elsewhere. But sometimes they meet, and the strong and the handsome fight for mastery – foolishly, for their mastery is of different kinds. They misunderstand one another and make the mistake of each aiming at universal dominion. Nothing can win this, not even strength, for it is powerless in the kingdom of the wise [. . .]. Tyranny. The following statements, therefore, are false and tyrannical: 'Because I am handsome, so I should command respect'. 'I am strong, therefore men should love me' . . . 'I am . . .', etc. Tyranny is the wish to obtain by one means what can only be had by another. We owe different duties to different qualities: love is the proper response to charm, fear to strength, and belief to learning." Pascal, *Pensées*, London and Baltimore, Penguin Classics, 1961, p. 244.

"Let us assume man to be man, and his relation to the world to be a human one. Then love can only be exchanged for love, trust for trust, etc. If you wish to enjoy art you must be an artistically cultivated person; if you wish to influence other people, you must be a person who really has a stimulating and encouraging effect upon others . . . If you love without evoking love in return, i.e., if you are not able, by the manifestation of yourself as a loving person, to make yourself a beloved person, then your love is impotent and a misfortune," Marx, *Early Writings*, London, Watts, 1963, pp. 193–194.

27 See my introduction.

9 *In God's Shadow* and *The Jewish Political Tradition*

1 "These and these are the words" refer to the words spoken by God to settle the controversy between the two major representatives of schools of thought (liberal and conservative roughly speaking), Hillel and Shammai, to show that two different and non-converging opinions can both reflect righteousness, virtue, and justice. See Eruvin, 13b.

2 The openness also prevents "exegetical chaos" by admitting instead of ignoring contradictory arguments: "knowledge increases" and "the diversity itself [of interpretations], and the debates it produces, serve significantly to enhance our understanding," *JPT*, vol. 1, p. 354.

3 See *CC*, *ISC*, and my Introduction.

4 Michael Walzer, Menachem Lorberbaum, Noam J. Zohar, and Yair Lorberbaum, *The Jewish Political Tradition*, vol. 1 *Authority*, New Haven, Yale University Press; Michael Walzer, Menachem Lorberbaum, Noam J. Zohar, and Ari Ackerman, *The Jewish Political Tradition*, vol. 2 *Membership*, 2006; Michael Walzer, Menachem Lorberbaum, Noam J. Zohar, and Madeline Kochen, *The Jewish Political Tradition*, vol. 3 *Community*, New Haven, Yale University Press, 2018.

5 Michael Walzer, *Exodus and Revolution*, New York, Basic Books, 1985.

6 Michael Walzer, *In God's Shadow*, p. 199.

7 Michael Walzer, *In God's Shadow*, p. 207.

8 Moshe Halberthal and Stephen Holmes, *The Beginning of Politics. Power in the Biblical Book of Samuel*, New Haven, Princeton University Press, 2017.

9 See the passage on Nahshon in our conversation, ch. 6.

10 "*Galut*" is the Hebrew word for exile.

11 "We must think in terms of a state, in terms of independence, in terms of full responsibility for ourselves – and for others. In our state there will be non-Jews as well, and all of them will be equal citizens, equal in everything without any exception, that is, the state will be their state as well. The attitude of the Jewish state to its Arab citizens will be an important factor – though not the only one – in building good neighborly relations with the Arab states. The striving for a Jewish–Arab alliance requires us to fulfill several obligations which we are obliged to do in any event: full and real equality, de jure and de facto, of all the state's citizens, gradual equalization of the economic, social, and cultural standard of living of the Arab community with the Jewish community, recognition of the Arabic language as the language of the Arab citizens in the administration, courts of justice, and above all, in schools; municipal autonomy in villages and cities, and so on," "Michael Walzer responds" [to Jim Rule], *Dissent*, Fall 2012.

12 https://www.youtube.com/watch?v=vANFcZhXtBM&index=2&list=PL94 UJTaiiod0WFQPfXhM 5StY7go93oOf-&t=1s. And https://www.youtube. com/watch?v=axcQbPe8cYc&t=1960s.

13 Y. H. Yerushalmi, *Servants of Kings, not Servants of Servants: Some Aspects of the Political History of the Jews*, Atlanta, GA, Tam Institute for Jewish Studies, Emory University, 2005, is, in part, a response to Hannah Arendt's misunderstanding of the relationship between the Jewish communities and the state. "'Serviteurs des rois et non serviteurs des serviteurs'. Sur quelques aspects de l'histoire politique des Juifs," *Raisons Politiques*, 7, 2002/3, Paris, Presses de Sciences Po, 2002: 19–52.

14 Max Weber, *Ancient Judaism (1917–1919)*, New York, The Free Press, 1967.

15 The Shalem Center in Jerusalem was founded in 1994 by Yoram Hazony. It became the Shalem College in 2013 when it got academic accreditation. Initially created to publish scholarship on Jewish philosophy and history in a period of much debate on post-Zionism, the center, founded by Hazony, also published a bilingual Quarterly called *Azure* (Ideas for the Jewish Nation) in English and Tchelet (כת) in Hebrew.

16 Yoram Hazony is a Modern Orthodox Bible scholar and currently the chairman of the Herzl Institute in Jerusalem. Founder of Shalem (see above), he has mostly published on the Scriptures and Israel (*The Philosophy of Hebrew Scripture*, Cambridge, Cambridge University Press, 2012). His latest book is called *The Virtue of Nationalism*, New York, Basic Books, 2018.

17 Michael Walzer, "Prophecy and International Politics," *Hebraic Political Studies*, 4 (4), Fall 2009: 319–328.

18 Fania Oz-Salzberger (born 1960) is Professor of History at Haifa University. She is an expert on Enlightenment and the Jewish sources of Western thought. With her father Amos Oz, she published *Jews and Words*, New Haven, Yale University Press, 2012. Among many other books, she edited one book with the Shalem Center (with Gordon Schochet and Meirav Jones), *Political Hebraism: Judaic Sources in Early Modern Political Thought*, Jerusalem, Shalem, 2008; and published "The Political Thought of John Locke and the Significance of Political Hebraism" in *Hebraic Political Studies*, Shalem, 2006: 568–592.

19 Eric Nelson, *The Hebrew Republic: Jewish Sources and the Transformation of European Political Thought*, Harvard/Belknap, 2010.

20 "Brit" is the Hebrew term for alliance or covenant.

21 See Michael Walzer, *Exodus and Revolution*, ch. 3; and the following passage in *God's Shadow*, p. 5: "Moses read aloud to the people all of the Torah, 'that they might know exactly what they were taking upon themselves'. The crucial conditions of what is today called consent theory are here recognized. Before consent is effective, there must be full knowledge and the possibility of refusal. [. . .] But is it really possible to say no to an omnipotent God? A more skeptical and ironic rabbinic story suggests the difficulty. Now God is said to have lifted up the mountain, held it over the heads of the assembled Israelites, and told them: 'If you accept the Torah, it is well; otherwise you will find your grave under this mountain.' One of the rabbis, a good consent theorist, says of the telling of this story that it is 'a great protest against the Torah'. Indeed, it makes the Torah into nonbinding law, grounded on force alone, not on commitment (BT Shabbat 88a). The book of Exodus has nothing to say about these theoretical issues. But it does insist upon the consent of the people and so provides a platform, as it were, for later speculation."

22 Michael Walzer, *In God's Shadow*, ch. 12.

23 Exodus, 32: 27 (King James): "And he said unto them, Thus saith the Lord God of Israel, Put every man his sword by his side, and go in and out from gate to gate throughout the camp, and slay every man his brother, and every man his companion, and every man his neighbor."

24 Michael Walzer, "Exodus 32 and the Theory of Holy War: The History of a Citation," *Harvard Theological Review*, 61 (1), 1968: 1–14.

25 Lincoln Steffens (1866–1936), *Moses in Red*. The revolt of Israel as a typical revolution, Philadelphia, Dorrance & Company, 1926. Peter Hartshorn published a biography in 2011, named after Steffens' text upon returning from the Soviet Union "I Have Seen the Future and it Works" (1921). Peter Hartshorn, *I Have Seen the Future. A Life of Lincoln Steffens*, Berkeley CA, Counterpoint, 2011.

26 The "Second Bar Mitzvah" is usually celebrated at age 83. Psalm 90: 10 says that 70 is the expected lifespan. Reaching age 70 is therefore considered a new start, and age 83 would be the equivalent of reaching the Bar Mitzvah age again.

27 Also called "Oracles against the Nations" in the prophetic literature. The nations are Egypt, Gaza, Nineveh, Babylon, Damascus, Moab, etc.

28 Michael Walzer, *Dans L'ombre de Dieu: la politique et la Bible*, trans. P.-E. Dauzat, Paris, Belin, 2016.

29 David Ben Gurion, *Ben Gurion looks at the Bible* (trans. Jonathan Kolatch), Middle Village, New York, Jonathan David Publishers, 2008.

30 Joshua is the successor of Moses; portrayed as the ideal leader, he renews the covenant, crosses the Jordan River, conquers Jericho, and leads the Israelites into the Promised Land.

31 Horace Kallen (1882–1974) was a founding member of the New School for Social Sciences in New York. He graduated in philosophy from Harvard, and taught briefly at Princeton and Madison, Wisconsin. Militant Zionist, member of the ZOA, author of many books, Kallen has invented the term "cultural pluralism." His books and articles include *Cultural Pluralism and the American Idea (1956)*, Philadelphia, University of Pennsylvania Press, 2016; "Democracy Versus the Melting-Pot," *The Nation*, 100, February 18–25, 1915: 190–194, 217–220; *Zionism and World Politics, A Study in History and Social Psychology*, London, William Heinemann; *'Of Them Which Say They Are Jews': And Other Essays on the Jewish Struggle for Survival*, Ohio, Bloch Pub. Co, 1954; and a wonderful "ethereal" dialogue with Socrates ("Socrates and the Street Car," *Wisconsin Quarterly*, 1 (4), 1914: 358–374). His obituary can be read here: https://www.nytimes.com/1974/02/17/archives/dr-horace-kallen-philosopher-dies.html.

32 2010 Kogod Lecture, Shalom Hartman Institute, Jerusalem June 22, 2010.

33 Rabbi Haim Herschensohn (1856–1930), was an early Zionist; he grew up in Israel, assisted Ben Yehuda in the making of Modern Hebrew. He moved to New Jersey in the early 1900s. While still in Israel (he was born in the holy city of Safed), he tried to lay out a "halakhic foundation for a democratic, theological and political regime" for the new state of Israel (quoted by Eliezer Schweid, *Democracy and Halakha*, Lanham MD, London and New York, University Press of America and Jerusalem Center for Public Affairs, 1994). A very modern and open rabbi and scholar, he was convinced that the halakha is not an obstacle to democratic government. His biographer, David Zohar writes of his "efforts to combine the commitment to Halakha and adoption

213

of modern values with respect to a free, egalitarian, democratic country, governed and ruled by the people. Under the assumption that the Jewish nation has a national and ethnic infrastructure, rather than only a religious one, Rabbi Hayyim Hirschensohn grants a common identity to religious and secular Jews." David Zohar, *Jewish Commitment in a Modern World: Rabbi Hayyim Hirschenson and His Attitude to Modernity* (in Hebrew), Jerusalem, Shalom Hartman Institute, 2003.

34 The Bar Kokhba revolt, led by Simon Bar Kokhba, is the last war between the Judean Jews and the Romans (132–136).

35 Michael Walzer et al., *The Jewish Political Tradition*, vols. 1–3. To volume 1, Michael Walzer contributed (aside from the introduction): "A Monarchic Constitution," "Prophetic Criticism and its Targets," "Pluralism and Singularity"; to volume 2 "The Pit," "Exiles and Citizens"; to volume 3 "Distributing the Burdens of Taxation," "Autonomy and Cultural Reproduction," "Positive Freedom."

36 Pirke Avot (c.190–c.230 CE) are the "Teachings" or the "Ethics" of the Fathers.

37 "Gadol" means big or great in Hebrew.

38 *The Jewish Political Tradition*, vol. 1, pp. xiv–xv.

39 Michael Fishbane, *The Jewish Political Tradition*, vol. 1, p. lv.

40 "The biblical texts are in constant need of exegesis and refinement [. . .] as a home might be of refurnishing and repair" (my italics).

41 "Reiterated political and intellectual challenges"; "a common regime with a common legal system, reiterated across a wide range of countries, in very different circumstances"; "the tradition is an ongoing argument"; "aspects of one truth are reflected in diverse interpretations." See also Michael Walzer's commentary "Pluralism and Singularity" in vol. 2: "The actual history of each *kahal* took shape as a compromise between a universally binding law and a set of particularist arrangements and decisions"; see also the Introduction to vol. 3.

42 "Writing a commentary is an act of engagement, and this commonly is, and should be, a critical engagement, an effort to get things right."

43 "*Stam,*" in the biblical tradition is the abbreviation of *sifrei tora, t'filin um'zuzot*. In *JPT*, *stam* refers to the final Talmudic editor, the one who knits together traditions and opinions from different times and different corpuses in order to reconstruct intertextual reasoning on theoretical and practical topics, legal disputes for example. "If there is a 'mind' in the Talmud, it is the mind of the *stam*, who thinks through the traditions, citing and criticizing them through other voices and deliberating their implications with respect to religious action," Fishbane, *JPT*, vol. I, p. xlv.

44 The Great Sanhedrin (the Jewish High Court in ancient Israel composed of 71 members) was re-created in 1806 after the reestablishment of the Israelite cult by Napoleon, and convened by the Emperor in 1807. The Sanhedrin was asked to give its imprimatur to the responses drafted by an "Assembly of Notables" composed by Jewish representatives from France and Italy. The latter had been convened by Napoleon to answer twelve questions on the rules governing the Jewish communities. Three questions in particular pertain to the relationship between French and Jewish citizens: "In the eyes of Jews are Frenchmen not of the Jewish religion considered as brethren or as strangers?" (Question 4); "What conduct does Jewish law prescribe toward

Frenchmen not of the Jewish religion?" (Question 5); "Do the Jews born in France, and treated by the law as French citizens, acknowledge France as their country? Are they bound to defend it? Are they bound to obey the laws and follow the directions of the civil code?" (Question 6)

The answers of the Sanhedrin have been published in French in the *Moniteur Universel* (April 11, 1807, pp. 398–400). "That marriages contracted between Israelites and Christians are binding, although they cannot be celebrated with religious forms (Question 4); "That every Israelite is religiously bound to consider his non-Jewish fellow citizens as brothers, and to aid, protect, and love them as though they were coreligionists" (Question 5); "That the Israelite is required to consider the land of his birth or adoption as his fatherland, and shall love and defend it when called upon" (Question 6). See René Gutman, *Le Document fondateur du judaïsme français: les décisions doctrinaires du Grand Sanhédrin 1806–1807, suivi de Joseph David Sintzheim et le Grand Sanhédrin de Napoléon*, Strasbourg, Presses Universitaires de Strasbourg, 2000.

45 In his commentary on Shimon (*JPT*, vol. 3), Michael Walzer writes about the importance of communal education, and comments on Simon Dubnow's Zionism and nationalism. Dubnov was convinced that an elaborate network of diaspora institutions was a better answer than the creation of a state. "Today many Zionists, looking at the Jewish world from their own sovereign state, have learned the value of a vibrant Jewish life abroad. Some might even describe themselves as Dubnovians for the diaspora." (*JPT*, vol. 3, p. 447).

46 "Liberal pluralism not only made place for Jews in the gentile world; it also made a place for many different kinds of Jews in the Jewish world," *JPT*, vol. 1, p. 7.

47 Michael Walzer mentions the Reform proposal to recognize patrilinear descent for example, and Ruth Adler goes as far as suggesting that the in-between category of *pilagshut* (concubinage), neither *kiddushin* nor *z'nut*, could in fact fill this semi-void in the halacha and become a *placeholder* (her italics) for egalitarian relationships including gay, lesbian, and transsexual couples (*JPT*, vol. 3, p. 146–154).

48 "Coping with physical need, social conflict, natural disaster [...] the scribes are often deeply involved in local political struggles," *JPT*, vol. 1, Introduction.

49 "The *kahal* is historically and symbolically important; it is the polis of the exilic Jewry," Ibid.

50 "[...] perseverance in the law and a structure of authority that was as much political as religious"; "The miracle of Jewish politics is the persistence of this formation [the self-governed *kahal* system] over many centuries – a common regime with a common legal system, reiterated across a wide range of countries, in very different circumstances, without the benefit of (and sometimes in opposition to) state power," *JPT*, vol. 1, Introduction, p. xxix. See also, vol. 3, Introduction: "So the role of 'the good men of the town' was doubly limited: by gentile rulers and by Jewish sages."

51 M. Fishbane, *JPT*, vol. 1, p. xxxii.

Coda

1 Avishai Margalit, *On Compromise and Rotten Compromises*, Princeton University Press, 2013.
2 Bertold Brecht, "To Posterity," 1938.
3 עם לא עכשיו אז מתי, *Pirke avot* 1, 14.

Index